GW00501997

THE PHILOSOPHY
OF THE BIBLE
AS FOUNDATION OF JEWISH CULTURE

The Reference Library of Jewish Intellectual History

THE PHILOSOPHY OF THE BIBLE

AS FOUNDATION OF JEWISH CULTURE
PHILOSOPHY OF BIBLICAL NARRATIVE

Eliezer Schweid

Translated from Hebrew
by Leonard Levin

Academic Studies Press
Boston
2008

Library of Congress Cataloging-in-Publication Data

Schweid, Eliezer.
[Filosofyah shel ha-Tanakh ki-yesod tarbut Yisra'el (Biblical narrative). English]
The philosophy of the Bible as foundation of Jewish culture. Philosophy of biblical
narrative / Eliezer Schweid ; translated from Hebrew by Leonard Levin.
p. cm. — (The reference library of Jewish intellectual history)
Includes bibliographical references and index.

ISBN 978-1-934843-00-0 (alk. paper)

1. Bible. O.T. — Philosophy. 2. Bible. O.T. — Criticism, interpretation, etc.
3. Bible. O.T. Pentateuch — Criticism, Narrative. 4. Bible. O.T. — Influence.
5. Narration in the Bible. 6. Jews — Civilization. I. Title.

BS645.S39313 2008
221.6 — dc22
2007051562

ISBN 978-1-934843-00-0

Book design by Yuri Alexandrov

Published by Academic Studies Press in 2008
145 Lake Shore Road
Brighton, MA 02135, USA
press@academicstudiespress.com
www.academicstudiespress.com

Contents

Preface

Schweid's Crossroads and our Own

In 1948, the young Eliezer Schweid stood at a crossroads. In 2007, the world stands at a crossroads.

The common denominator of those two crossroads is the theme of the current book.

In 1948, Eliezer Schweid, a soldier in the new Israeli Defense Forces, had to confront his responsibilities as an Israeli and as a Jew. As an Israeli, he had to act in the interests of his country, to defend its interests and stand firm against any adversaries who might pose a threat to him and his loved ones. As a Jew, he had to examine the moral dimensions of his actions, to consider their ramifications in the light of their impact to all parties affected, to all humanity, to God (if there was a God). The tension between these two perspectives led Schweid to digress from his chosen path as Zionist pioneer and kibbutz-member and to research the history of Jewish philosophical and moral thought, in order to obtain guidance for how he and his comrades ought to act in such cases as their fragile history repeatedly forced them to face. This led ultimately to his embarking on a career as philosopher, scholar, educator and public intellectual, in the course of which he has written extensively on the history of Jewish thought in all periods and taught thousands of students the legacy of Jewish traditional wisdom and its application to our time.

Schweid's dilemma in 1948 may be summarized: Is national interest enough for the members of a nation to decide a common course of action? Or must their deliberation be rooted in something deeper, "long-term memory," the wisdom of the ages, rooted ultimately in an attitude toward the transcendent?

In 2007, the world faces a three-way crisis. One way points to economic optimization on a globalized model: calculate what will achieve the highest standard of living for the most people in the most efficient way. A second way points to religious-political fundamentalism: adopt some ancient scriptural tradition and clothe yourself in it, using it as armor to block out the monster of modernity and hopefully re-establish your tradition's hegemony along medieval lines — find God's will in your scripture and impose it on the world, whatever the cost. The third way is what Schweid calls "creative mediating interpretation": affirm your cultural tradition as an ever-evolving, ever-adapting complex entity, rooted in ancient narratives and folkways, but open to assimilating the experience of the present and dialogue with other cultural traditions, forming syntheses of past and present that can address new challenges based on the best available wisdom, rooted in patterns of value that have stood the test of time.

The Uses of "Culture"

"Culture" is a central notion for Schweid throughout most of his thought and writings. The various uses of this term that he developed elsewhere are important background for the current work.

In *The Idea of Jewish Culture: Its Origins and Development in Modern Times*, Schweid spoke of "culture" in at least three senses:

1. In the period of Emancipation, "culture" (actually, modern European culture) confronted ghettoized Jewry as the challenging Other. "Acquire culture" meant: leave the ghetto; shed your medieval, too-Jewish garb; become modern, European, "enlightened," "man-in-general"! In the moderate version, this meant: become a *maskil*, an Enlightened Jew, after the example of Moses Mendelssohn and his followers. In the extreme version, this meant: assimilate; drop your Jewishness altogether!

2. In the next generation (the period of *Jüdische Wissenschaft*, i.e. historical Jewish scholarship), "culture" was used in a different sense: Are not Jews a culture? By studying Judaism as a culture, one defended Jews' right-to-exist against the challenge of the extreme modernizers, but at a price. Judaism had to give up its traditional pretense of being the exclusively God-ordained correct way of thinking and living, and had to view itself as a human creation — in dialogue with God, but of human authorship — like any other national-historical tradition.

This historical-cultural view of Jewish existence was linked to a prescription for Judaism's continual existence, which found expression in the modern liberal Jewish religious movements: Jews could constitute themselves as a religious minority in the context of Western national societies, cultivating their own tradition in dialogue with the more dominant religious and cultural traditions of their host countries.

3. But already almost at the same moment in history, another sense was coined: Is not Hebrew the authentic Jewish cultural language? Is not Israel its historical homeland? For Judaism to truly exist as a culture in the modern world, it had to achieve national rebirth and reconstitute itself on its homeland, reviving at the same time a secular-national Jewish culture that would be as fully autonomous as ancient Hebrew culture. This was the ethos of cultural Zionism, which together with political Zionism was dominant in the founding of the modern state of Israel.

In his Introduction to the current volume, Schweid speaks of "culture" in a fourth sense.

4. In our post-modern age, we are confronted with the fragmentation and collapse of cultural tradition altogether, and with it a challenge to moral education as the formation of purposive personalities rooted in a consciousness of group-belonging and historical continuity. Culture, rooted in long-term group historical memory, is the matrix of society as an ongoing project which can give a sense of purpose and meaning to the individuals nurtured in it. As such, it cannot be taken for granted but must be consciously cultivated if we are to remain truly human.

The Bible and Culture — Word of God and Word of Man

The Bible is central in the formation of Jewish culture, and also of Western culture, in the senses specified. In speaking of "philosophy of the Bible as foundation of Jewish culture," Schweid explicitly addresses the second and third senses of "culture" just enunciated, but implicitly the fourth as well. Jews living in post-modern societies, both in Israel and in the communities of the Diaspora, are challenged to preserve cultural continuity as Jews, and to share in the general human challenge to preserve a basis of meaningful existence as human beings. Schweid proposes his "creative mediating" reading of the Bible's message as a central resource in addressing all these challenges.

Neither Jewish existence nor general meaningful human life is possible on the basis of throwing away the historical past, which after all has shaped our societies and ourselves as cultural beings. Both will survive but only in a narrow, stunted way — at the cost of escalating intolerance and violence — if the past is adopted as a straitjacket, in a literalist sense. It is only by adopting the past as a treasurehouse of archetypes and models for creative elaboration that it can both guide our efforts at self-definition and allow us the freedom to develop our unique identities as variations on these time-honored themes.

The thinkers whom Schweid cites as models in his interpretation are keys for understanding its objectives. Hermann Cohen was among the most rationalistic and universalistic of modern Jewish religious thinkers. Martin Buber and Abraham Joshua Heschel were among the most personalistic ("existentialist") and committed to Jewish particular survival (though in neither case contradicting their equal commitment to universal human causes). This signals to us that this interpretation will feature a mediation between rational and personalistic perspectives, between universal and particularistic concerns.

Heschel spoke of the Bible as "the word of God and the word of man." Franz Rosenzweig similarly expressed that though the address of God to humanity is at the root of the Biblical outlook, it is the human interpretation of that encounter that finds expression in the Bible's words. Both were influenced by the 19th-century German philosopher Schelling, who considered early myth (including both the Bible and Greek myth under this rubric) as reflecting to us the dialogue between early mankind with divinity, filtered by the cultural consciousness of the peoples at the inception of their cultural traditions. Schweid echoes this idea here, saying that "the narrative of Genesis is thus a dialogical confluence of divine thought relating to humanity and human thought relating to God, taking into account the boundaries that limit the human being's ability to see."

Divine Action Frames Human Action

Schweid probes the rhythms of the Genesis narrative to reveal the continuity and subtle transition from the mythic preamble of creation to the quasi-historical narratives of the patriarchal and subsequent periods. "History" in Hebrew is *divrei ha-yamim* — "the accounts of the days," and the enumeration of days starts at the beginning, with the "days" of creation, which gradually accumulate into weeks, months, years and generations. This continuity points to a deeper continuity between the acts of God and the acts of human beings. Human endeavors — whether on the personal, familial, or historical level — thus derive their significance from being framed by God's cosmic drama. When they succeed, they aspire to sanctity; when they fail, they fall into the wretchedness of evil. Yet there are always "second beginnings," and even "dreams" (the most famous being Jacob's Ladder) in which heaven and earth imaginatively touch each other for a fleeting moment to light the way for the hard journey ahead.

In this context, a new people — Israel — arises, to help initiate a "second beginning" on behalf of all humanity. Their mission is fraught with ambiguity. On the one hand, they have the potential to be "different" in a positive way, discovering how to live in accord with God's will and to be an example to all. On the other hand, they are subject to the same rules — and the same temptations — as everyone else, as well as the additional temptation of spiritual pride. Schweid shows how the narratives of Abraham and Sarah, Rebekah and Isaac, Jacob, Rachel and Leah are emblematic of the historical dilemmas which the nation of Israel has faced throughout its history, and still must cope with today.

Every generation must read the Bible afresh. By offering his own reading, Schweid challenges us to come up with our own. What kind of God does the Bible portray? What is the world's origin and purpose? What is our task in it as human beings — in relation to ourselves, our families, our compatriots, the human race, and the world itself? How do the days of creation unfold into the days, years and generations of human history? What is special about Israel, and what are the limits of that specialness? What can we learn about the achievements and failings of the Biblical heroes and heroines to guide our own lives? The author addresses all these issues and more with originality, insight, warmth and humor.

Leonard Levin,
November 2007, New York

THE PHILOSOPHY OF THE BIBLE

AS FOUNDATION OF JEWISH CULTURE
PHILOSOPHY OF BIBLICAL NARRATIVE

Introduction
Modern Jewish Culture's Relation to the Bible: Creative Mediating Interpretation

Jewish Scholarship as a Factor in Jewish Modernization

From its beginnings in the Jewish Enlightenment, modern Jewish culture developed as a spectrum of religious, national, and religious-national movements in several languages and especially in Hebrew, German, Yiddish, and English, and in several lands, especially Germany, Eastern Europe (Poland, Russia, and Lithuania), Israel and the United States.[1] This was a many-faceted phenomenon, variegated and complex, replete with polarities and contradictions. The sources that nourished this culture were also many and varied, and it is possible to categorize them generally into two groups:

1. Internal sources — the canonical legacy of written and oral Torah in its various strata, in the domains of halakhah (law), aggadah (lore and interpretation), liturgy and poetry, philosophy and kabbalah. There was the tradition of customary religious practice that was united across communities by a common legal-theoretical structure but differentiated locally by cultural influences. There was the popular artistic culture in its various branches (poetry, narrative, music, dance, synagogue architecture, decorative art, illumination, and ritual crafts) that received its Jewish character from the tradition but absorbed important elements from the cultures of the neighboring peoples.

---

[1] For a full account of the development of modern Jewish culture — the motivating factors in its development, its sources and characteristics, see Eliezer Schweid, *The Idea of Modern Jewish Culture*, published in Hebrew by Am Oved, Tel Aviv 1995, English translation: Academic Studies Press, 2008, especially the Introduction and the first five chapters.

1

2. External sources — in this context we refer especially to the high culture of the nations among whom Jews lived, developing their own culture in a network of reciprocal influences. They absorbed its influences while also making their own independent contributions in such areas as religious thought, patterns of religious behavior (Christian and Moslem), science, philosophy, law and jurisprudence, literature (especially poetry), social and political institutions, industry, technology, and patterns of economic activity. As these external cultural influences were internalized holistically, so that the Jews perceived them as the secular component of their own culture, affecting them internally — so the sources that Jews regarded as autochthonous and distinctively Jewish nevertheless carried external influences that had been absorbed through dialogue with the environment. This resulted in a multifaceted complexity even in the canonical sources, from the Bible through all the strata of the oral tradition, including the halakhah.

Modern Jewish scholarship with its critical philological-historical method, itself a creature of the Jewish Enlightenment, was the first to see Judaism as a holistic national culture.[2] This definition, that reevaluated the legacy of the past in order to develop it in a new way, marks the difference between the old religious-traditional Jewish culture and modern Jewish culture. It was the purpose of the Jewish Enlightenment to create this new entity through a process of rebirth — "renaissance" — a process that fostered continuity inasmuch as it was nourished from the people's own sources, but was nevertheless revolutionary inasmuch as it also borrowed from the external sources of Western culture, which itself had passed through a similar process from a religious to a secular-national identity.[3] Modern Jewish scholarship played a major role in fostering this process of change. It served as a conservative-yet-innovative replacement for traditional Torah-

[2]   For the role played by the *Jüdische Wissenschaft* movement in shaping the vision of modern Jewish culture, see Paul Mendes-Flohr (ed.) *Ḥokhmat Yisrael (Jewish Science: A Source Reader)*, Merkaz Shazar, Jerusalem 1980; Nathan Rotenstreich, "The Characteristics of Jewish Science" in the same volume; *Jewish Philosophy in Modern Times* (Hebrew), I, Am Oved, Tel Aviv 1945; and Ben-Zion Dinur's article *Ḥokhmat Yisrael* in *Encyclopedia Ha-Ivrit* XVII 405–417.
[3]   On the development of modern Jewish culture as a renaissance movement, see Schweid, "The Idea of Modern Jewish Culture," Chapter 13.

study, and its scholarly and philosophical output provided a basis for transition and continuity between the old and the new forms.

In its research method and assumptions, the new Jewish scholarship represented the general secular outlook that was absorbed from the outside environment, while in its topics of research it continued the autonomous Jewish legacy. Indeed, the new Jewish scholarship reflected the external viewpoint that embodied a critical attitude toward Judaism, the standpoint of a Christian society whose own secularization highlighted its ambivalent feelings towards Jews and Judaism. Since the modern movements in Jewry developed out of the yearning for emancipation — i. e., out of the desire to become like their secular cultural environment, together with the desire to perpetuate and preserve aspects of Jewish identity — modern Judaism fulfilled a double role: it defined and clarified what was distinctive in the sources, and thus revealed their many facets, which originated in the dialogue that the Jewish people conducted with the cultures of the nations among whom it dwelt for all these generations. In this way, the new Jewish scholarship formulated the criteria for enlightened discrimination between those elements of the tradition that were worth perpetuating as vital, and those that ought to be discarded or neglected; and also between those outside influences that were worthy of adoption, and those that ought to be rejected in self-defense. As we said, Jewish scholarship effected a revolution in its critical stance not only with respect to the conception of present-day culture but also with respect to the attitude toward the past. From the critical viewpoint, the religious heritage appeared differently than its traditional students had represented it. Whoever considers the matter in depth will find that this procedure validated the transfer of contents that had been stored in traditional religious vessels to the newer vessels of secular culture.

The proponents of Jewish enlightenment were aware that the process of cultural rebirth was not the first of its kind in Jewish history, and in order to validate their enterprise they held up for example similar efforts from the past.

The most important were the creative productions of the Golden Age of Spain in the 11th and 12th centuries of Islamic influence, and those of Italian Jewry during the Renaissance. In both of these periods, there were obvious evidences of secularization. Nevertheless, it was already apparent in the first stages of the Enlightenment that the external challenges with which they needed to grapple were greater and much more problematic than those confronting traditional Jewish culture in previous times, for several reasons:

1. The unequivocally worldly character of modern culture.
2. Its all-encompassing scope and its scientific and technological advancement, which could only be mastered by sustained immersion.
3. Its public character, by which it must become the property of the whole people, not just a social elite.

The whole process of rebirth was associated with an identity crisis. There were also crises in the past that had divided the Jewish people and cast off sub-groups that assimilated to their surroundings. But the crisis that broke out with the Enlightenment was the greatest and most serious in comparison with all the preceding, so that the rifts that were generated 250 years ago have still not healed. If we examine the history of the people in this period, we can identify a cyclical alternation of outward-directed movements that seek to attain the developments that are being advanced in the general culture, and inward-directed movements that seek to return to the roots that are formative of Jewish identity, and to bridge the gaps and fissures that threaten to divide and fragment the people. But even the movements of return to the roots were accompanied by a deepening awareness of crisis, for the very roots to which they sought to return were being defined and interpreted differently by each successive movement in modern Judaism. It was hard to define them as common roots, as a foundation of unity.

In view of the frustrating dynamic of managing the crisis of modernity, the Bible became the only major independent source of Jewish culture, the source on which all the movements of the people agreed, the master-source of Jewish culture in all ages. We should emphasize that even in those movements that strove for cultural assimilation to the point of self-effacement, the Bible was accorded the status of a source that every Jew ought to study and hold precious as a formative influence. The Bible thus filled the same role in modern as in traditional Jewish culture: it was the "book of books," the canonical book whose authority emanated to the succeeding books, anchored in it as its commentaries and its successor-works in its values, its laws, its beliefs, its symbols and its visions of the future for the Jewish people and for humanity.

The special status of the Bible in traditional and modern Jewish culture has its source in two of its qualities. First, it is considered the first source in which are comprised the permanent, timeless elements that identify the culture of the Jewish people in its total extent and for all ages. Second, it is considered the primary fount from which flow the unique creative powers of the people, and from which they are renewed in every generation. They turned to the Bible to draw from it fundamental ideas, formative of identity. They turned to it to draw inspiration, language and exemplars for contemporary literary creation; they turned to it to validate the Jewish authenticity of contemporary literary efforts confronted with outside cultural influences and the challenges they presented. But it is important to articulate the difference between the traditional and the modern approaches. In the traditional and orthodox Jewish movements, the source of the Bible's authority and its message in all its details were attributed to divine revelation: "Torah from Heaven" or "Torah from Sinai," whereas the modern religious and secular national movements attributed it to the people itself, to its historical memory and the educational institutions that transmitted its legacy. The former saw in the power that created the national culture the overflow of a trans-temporal source, while the latter saw in it a flow that derives from the spiritual potencies embodied in the people. This does not mean that the conception that sees cultural creativity — including religion — as a human creation must necessarily deny the possibility of a divine revelation obligating man. Belief in a present and commanding God continued to strike a chord in the modern religious movements and even in the secular national movements. Modern religiosity differs from the traditional or orthodox variety in the view that the details of divine revelation are a human creation, i.e. they are a creation whose source is in the human response to a commanding divine presence, which the person experiences in nature or in the depths of one's soul.

In order to delve into the profound meaning of the transformation implied in turning to the Bible as a canonical text that obligates by virtue of the human creativity invested in it, one should pay attention to the implications of the relation to the Oral Torah, and especially to its late rabbinic layers that are the product of exile. According to the traditional religious outlook, the Bible as "written Torah" has a fundamental importance as the absolute revelation of God, whereas in the "oral Torah" there come to expression the creative insights of people who learned Torah and also learned about the real world in which its commandments must be realized. The written Torah is considered to be the absolute source of divine revelation, but when we ask what is the authority that determines the norms of thought and religious behavior in every generation, we can be sure that this is the oral Torah, especially its most recent stages. The guides for practical observance were always the latest authorities, and so the work that embodies the authority of practical halakhah is the Shulhan Arukh, along with the works that continued to interpret it and apply it. But according to the outlook that aspires to a Jewish renaissance, the literature of Oral Torah has lost its preeminence. On the contrary, the more we approach its present layers, the more opposition there is to its authority. The primacy of the Bible is accorded direct and present significance. Moreover, whereas the traditional and orthodox religious perspectives interpret the Bible from the perspective of the Oral Torah through the ages, the modern movements interpret the Bible within its own context, though with modern tools of research and interpretation.

These differences between the traditional-orthodox approach and the modern have implications for the place of the Bible and the rabbinic literature in various kinds of Jewish schools up to our own day, as well as for the methods of instruction for these subjects. In orthodox schools preference was given to instruction in the Oral Torah — legal codes and Talmud — while instruction in Bible was limited and subject to the traditional interpretation. In so-called "secular" schools, preference was given to studying the Bible, and it was interpreted in the light of its own literary and historical context using the tools of scientific scholarship and modern interpretations.

We must qualify these assertions. The Enlightenment rebellion against the dominance of rabbinic tradition over the Bible did not lead to rejecting it entirely. From the standpoint of developing the national culture, and all the more so from the standpoint of developing religious life and thought, every stage of development that expressed the life of the people was important in its own right. Moreover, when one passes from study to establishing a way of life it is impossible to dispense with the layers of oral Torah, tradition and popular culture that have accumulated over the generations. Sabbath and festivals, norms of ethics and justice, literary creation, science and philosophy that dealt with the changing realities in every age — all these are bound up with the development of the oral Torah in its many layers.

The traditional-religious and modern-cultural outlooks differ, though, in how they relate to these layers of the Jewish legacy as sources whose contribution must be evaluated independently as re-workings and creative interpretations of the biblical legacy. This must of course be done with the same scholarly and hermeneutic tools that are applied to the study of the Bible.

Spinoza's and Mendelssohn's Contributions to the Modern Approach to the Bible

What were the results of the Enlightenment's stance toward the Bible? How did it contribute in practice to the development of Jewish culture? A full answer to these questions would require an investigation that would exceed in depth and scope the requirements of the present discussion. However, for the sake of example we shall discuss two works germane to the Bible that were created at the beginning of the Enlightenment period. Both of these had a formative influence on the scholarship, education, and literary and artistic creativity of modern Jewish culture, and so we can learn from them the ways in which the values of the Bible were incorporated into modern Jewish culture. I am referring to the *Theological-Political Treatise* of Baruch Spinoza (Netherlands, 1632–1677) and the interpretive-translating enterprise of Moses Mendelssohn (Germany, 1729–1786).

Spinoza's work presented first of all a critical challenge.[4] He was the rebel who came to rattle the walls of the rabbinic edifice and to protest against them. His personal path led him outside the Jewish camp, into the public square of Christendom and into that universal modern culture that started to develop in the spirit of the Enlightenment. In the long run, his personal rebellion and the cultural transformation to which he contributed had a lasting influence on his own people.

---

[4]   Spinoza's direct contribution to the development of modern Hebrew culture in connection with the Bible is focused in his *Theological-Political Treatise*. Concerning Spinoza's influence on the secular national Jewish Enlightenment and on Zionism, see Eliezer Schweid, " 'In Amsterdam I Conceived the Jewish National State' — Spinoza and Jewish National Identity," in *Jewish Political Studies Review*, Volume 13 (2001), No. 1–2.

The first assimilator who left the Jewish ghetto but did not adopt another religion was also the first Jewish philosopher who countered the traditional designation of the Mosaic Torah as "religion" with a new national-secular definition of it as a political constitution whose objectives were all worldly: prosperity and happiness in their material, social, political and cultural senses in this world. He did this by way of criticism of rabbinic Judaism, which in his view had perverted the original nature of the Mosaic legislation, as well as of the moral, social and political teachings of the Biblical prophets. But Spinoza made a positive contribution as well. He proposed an alternative to the theocratic rabbinic Judaism that had developed in exile. Spinoza contributed to the Hebrew enlightenment (that was nationalist from its inception), and subsequently to Zionism, the idea of a return to Nature as the source of creativity in life, ethics and knowledge of truth; the idea of return of the nation to its natural state, striving for independent political existence; and the idea of finding God in Nature as an alternative to supernatural religion; the idea of return to Hebrew as a national language, and the idea of return to the Bible as a positive source from which it is possible to develop a worldly Hebrew culture, positive in its moral and political aspects.

In Spinoza's thought, the return to nature is expressed first of all in the development of the natural and social sciences (social ethics and politics) that should have useful application for establishing human civilization and its orderly functioning to advance human happiness. It is expressed further in proposing the identification with nature in its unity as the supreme vocation of the person, the vocation in which one achieves self-fulfillment. Of course Spinoza leveled devastating criticism against all religions that believed in a supernatural, supra-rational God. The pantheism (equating God and Nature) that he developed in his *Ethics* is a kind of alternative natural religion that culminates in the "intellectual love of God" (love through knowledge) that brings one to identification with God (= Nature). It follows from this that intellectual love of God includes love of all humanity and of all existence. As a scientist and philosopher, Spinoza strove to achieve this objective in an intellectual way. But in the secular Romantic nationalist movements that developed from Enlightenment rationalism, a popular-experiential dimension was added to the aristocratic-intellectual dimension. Through it, the natural-religious alternative could be developed further. It is instructive that Spinoza's

followers in the movement for Jewish-natural enlightenment discovered the similarity between Spinoza's intellectualist pantheism and the
pantheism of the Hasidim of the schools of the Baal Shem Tov and
the Maggid of Mezritch, who saw in nature the unmediated presence
of God Himself.[5] Thus they endorsed Hasidism as a world-affirming
religious movement parallel to the scientific-intellectual Enlightenment,
and approved drawing on its creative popular teachings for the sake of
the Jewish national cultural renaissance. In this connection we should
mention particularly the teachings of Solomon Maimon, Moses Hess,
Micah Joseph Berdichevsky, Hayyim Nachman Bialik, A.D. Gordon
and Mordecai Kaplan, whose contributions to modern Hebrew culture
in eastern Europe, Israel and the United States were decisive.

There is a parallel between Spinoza's commonalty with Hasidism and
his connection with political Zionism, the Bible and the Hebrew
language, which are his special contribution to his people's culture.
As we said, Spinoza was the first Jewish thinker who saw Judaism as
a nationality in the political sense, and on that basis he was a prophet
of political Zionism. He foresaw that the rise of the secular-democratic
state would force the Jewish people to choose between assimilation
into the surrounding peoples and returning to its land to renew its
national-political life as a nation among nations. Spinoza himself chose
to assimilate, but he knew that his people persisted in surviving out
of their loyalty to the Torah, and he therefore foresaw that many of
his fellow Jews would organize to return to their land. (We should
recall the historical experience to which he was witness: Spinoza lived
through the apogee of the Sabbatean movement which encompassed
the entire people, and which demonstrated to what extent the Jewish
people remained wedded to its homeland and still believed in the
fulfillment of the dream of a return to Zion.) On what foundations,
then, should they build their state? Obviously on the basis of their

---

[5]   The first who paid attention to the similarity of Spinoza's pantheism and
that of the Baal Shem Tov was the philosopher Solomon Maimon. See the
appendix on Hasidism to his *Autobiography* (Hebrew edition, Mossad Bialik,
Tel Aviv 1942, and Chapter 16 of the English translation *Solomon Maimon:
An Autobiography*, Schocken, 1947/1967). The writer M. Y. Berdichevsky and
the philosopher Martin Buber broadened the comparison and influenced the
acceptance of Hasidism as a source of folk Jewish culture from which values
can be derived for shaping modern secular Jewish culture. See Schweid, *The
Idea of Modern Jewish Culture*, Chapter 17.

Torah. These are the natural foundations of Jewish nationalism, but in order to return to a landed national existence the Jews would have to return to the source of their worldly culture in accordance with the law of the Mosaic Torah and the ethics of the prophets, in which Spinoza likewise saw a natural-worldly ethic. It was out of this recognition that Spinoza foresaw a rebirth of a national Jewish culture, not as a vague general vision. In this way Spinoza made an important scholarly and philosophical contribution to the enterprise of the Hebrew Enlightenment that is relevant to its connection to the Bible.

This contribution reveals the depths of Spinoza's ambivalent relation to his Jewish heritage. He was estranged from it, but his education in its heritage shaped his life-work. Despite his devastating criticism of rabbinic Judaism, he sought in its ancient source — the Bible — the paradigm of the democratic-national polity that he sought to present to all the nations of Europe. In this way he became the first political philosopher who discovered in the constitution of the Mosaic Torah and in the teachings of the prophets the fundamental principles of the ideal democratic charter, based on the social, law-abiding character of human nature and on the notion of the "contract" (the "covenant" in Biblical language). In the same *Theological-Political Treatise* where Spinoza criticized rabbinical Judaism, he also developed his political philosophy with the Bible as his source. This work had a critical viewpoint, but in the main it was a philological-historical and political-philosophical inquiry from which immediate positive lessons were derived. We can establish unequivocally that Spinoza's theory of national democracy was drawn from the laws of the Mosaic Torah with corrective additions whose purpose was to give consistent application to the principles that Moses developed from his confrontation with the Pharaonic regime of slavery.

Spinoza placed the Bible at the center of the Western national-cultural renaissance, as well as at the center of the culture of the Jewish people, should it be renewed on its land. His great creative contribution was to develop and implement a Biblical political theory that was transferred from a religious-halakhic to a secular-judicial framework, and to develop the necessary scholarly-hermeneutic method to transform the legal, ethical and political ideas of Moses and the prophets — such as the "kingdom of God" (which for Spinoza was equivalent to the kingdom of natural law) — into the ideas of democratic social contract, which was basically an expression of the will of the people.

The scholarly-hermeneutic tool that he used for this purpose was the scientific criticism of the Bible. It was Spinoza, and not Wellhausen (the 19th-century German Protestant credited with establishing the "higher criticism" of the Bible), who laid the foundations for modern criticism of the Bible, both with respect to its overarching theory and forging its specific analytical tools.[6] In the process, Spinoza was the first to demonstrate the relevance of the Bible to the establishment of modern political life in the Western nations and thus in his own people as well. His influence bore fruit in the Jewish Enlightenment and in Zionism, especially social Zionism.

We should add finally that for the purpose of his critical research on the Bible Spinoza composed a book of Hebrew grammar that may be regarded as the first modern scientific work in that genre. It is not known to have had any great influence in linguistic studies, but his disciples in the Hebrew Enlightenment viewed it and his purpose in writing it as having instructive significance: it demonstrated the need to develop the study of the Hebrew language using modern methods. From Spinoza's standpoint, this was in order to study the Bible scientifically; from his Jewish followers' standpoint, it was in order to develop Hebrew as a national cultural language.

Moses Mendelssohn was regarded as the father of the Jewish Enlightenment.[7] A cadre of *"maskilim"* (proponents of Jewish Enlightenment) worked alongside him, and in discussing the place of the Bible as a source of the Jewish cultural revival we should mention especially the scholar, thinker and poet Naphtali Herz Wessely (Germany, 1725–1805).[8]

---

[6] In his *Theological-Political Treatise* mentioned above, Spinoza devoted Chapters 7–13 to criticism of the Hebrew Bible and the New Testament.

[7] Mendelssohn's principal book on Judaism was *Jerusalem* (for most recent English translation, see Allan Arkush, translator, Moses Mendelssohn — *Jerusalem: or On Religious Power and Judaism*, Brandeis University Press, Waltham, Massachusetts, 1983. On Mendelssohn's thought, see Eliezer Schweid, *The History of Modern Jewish Thought: the 19th Century*, Keter Press, Jerusalem 1978, Chapter 3. On the project of translation and commentary (the "Be'ur") and its influence, see P. Sandler, *The Be'ur on the Torah of Moses Mendelssohn and His Circle*, Magnes, Jerusalem 1941.

[8] Naphtali Herz Wessely, *Selected Writings* (Hebrew), Avar, Jerusalem 1952. On his educational activities, see M. Eliav, *Jewish Education in Germany During the Enlightenment and Emancipation* (Hebrew), Jewish Agency Publications, Jerusalem 1961.

Mendelssohn himself, as the outstanding philosopher of the Jewish Enlightenment, was at the same time Spinoza's disciple and his first Jewish critic. There pulsated in him Spinoza's yearning to return to nature, both in the relation to natural science and in striving for a life that would be an expression of human nature, living in immediate contact with nature. For Mendelssohn this was a double task: to return to nature as the source of civilization, and also to rediscover it in the sensory experiences and esthetic feelings that had been suppressed by the Judaism of the Exile. Mendelssohn accepted Spinoza's critique of rabbinic Judaism and charged it especially with the sin of being cut off from nature in all the above senses. In this respect it is possible to find in Mendelssohn the motifs of "negation of Diaspora" that developed later in secular Zionism: accusing Jewish culture of detachment from real life; of disorientation and loss of direction with respect to the surrounding civilization; of an unproductive economy based on the "middle-man" role as opposed to producing directly from natural resources; of a tendency to abstract ideals incapable of realization; of repression of the instincts and natural feelings, especially esthetic and erotic feelings; hence, of the one-dimensionality of literary creativity and estrangement from art.

Unlike Spinoza, Mendelssohn did not blame the failures, deficiencies and perversions that he found in the ghetto Judaism of his day on the theocratic character of Jewish religion or on the teachings of its prophets, but rather on the circumstances of life in exile, and especially the oppression that was initiated by the Christian Church and carried out in evil measure by the gentile governments. These, in his view, were the factors that cut Jews off from a productive work life and from a natural morality that relates on a basis of equality to all human beings as such. In Mendelssohn's view the Jews had generally not been given the opportunity to develop their natural talents. They had been forced into a cruel struggle for survival that corrupted their moral qualities, especially towards the gentiles who persecuted them, and who did not permit them the leisure for cultural and esthetic cultivation that is nourished by the encounter with natural beauty.

However, Mendelssohn did not rebel against rabbinic law, and his people's threatened situation in exile was not sufficient ground to dissociate oneself from it — on the contrary! It motivated him to fight on behalf of his people for civil liberties, while at the same time advancing its socio-economic, cultural and moral situation through the propagation of modern enlightenment. This should not be instead of sacred studies, but side by side with them in living complementarity that would serve them as well. The same applied in his attitude to divine revelation. Like Halevi and Maimonides, Mendelssohn showed that there is no contradiction between revelation and reason, and that there was no basis for questioning the tradition's testimony about the Sinai revelation. Therefore the return to nature, in all the aspects we have mentioned, should be perfectly compatible with a way of life regulated by Torah and the commandments. Indeed, he recognized that the Jewish people's return to its original nature would require a religious restorative effort as well, in other words a return to the prophetic spirit of the Bible with its social, traditional and this-worldly aspects, and a return to the literary esthetic and natural eroticism that pulsate in its poetic creations, especially in the Psalms and the Song of Songs.

Mendelssohn's literary enterprise represented the crossroads between the Hebrew national enlightenment that developed in eastern Europe and the assimilationist German enlightenment. His first work was the Hebrew periodical *Kohelet Musar* ("*Tribune of Morals,*" published in 1750)[9] in which he preached the ideology of the Enlightenment: a humanistic ethic, return to a life of nature, a renaissance of literary creativity drawing on nature. His Hebrew style drew on the Bible, and he thus offered — in contrast to the undisciplined rabbinic style — a model of classical Hebrew style, superior for esthetic literary creativity. After two issues which he apparently wrote entirely on his own, he encountered opposition from the leaders of the Jewish community and the project came to a halt. From that point on Mendelssohn wrote and published mainly in German, and not just for a Jewish readership. However, his major project for spreading enlightenment among his coreligionists was bilingual, consisting of a translation of the Torah and Psalms into German (in Hebrew characters) together with a commentary in Hebrew. He prepared the translation entirely himself, but for the commentary he enlisted a group of fellow *maskilim* including Naphatli Herz Wessely, a disciple of the Enlightenment who was a thinker in ethics and education, a scholar of the Hebrew

---

[9] Because of its limited press run, *Kohelet Musar* is hard to find, however H. Bar-Dayyan included it in his edition of Mendelssohn's complete writings (Berlin 1929).

language and a Hebrew poet, a pioneer of the Enlightenment poets in central Europe.[10]

The translation of the Torah into German, published in Hebrew letters (resembling Yiddish) was of course addressed only to Jewish readers. In Mendelssohn's time most of the Jewish public neither spoke nor read German, but they read Hebrew and spoke Yiddish. This audience did not require a German translation for the purpose of learning the Torah. They also were not demanding a new commentary in the spirit of the Enlightenment, for most of them were quite satisfied with the traditional commentaries. Why, then, did Mendelssohn take the trouble to translate the Bible into German? First of all, to enable Jews who spoke Yiddish — a kind of "jargon," intermixed German with Hebrew — to purify their language, which was perceived by their enlightened German neighbors as ignorant, crude and lacking in cultural refinement. They should learn to speak proper German, the language of enlightened, cultured people. The enlightened Mendelssohn attached great importance to the esthetic aspect of language, and its ability to make Jews more acceptable and pleasing to their neighbors. He also hoped that mastery of correct and elegant German would enable the younger Jews enamored of general enlightenment to proceed to read the necessary German books required for that enterprise.

So far we see here an instrument designed for the spread of general enlightenment. But an authorized Jewish translation of the Bible into German — different from the already existing and famous Christian German translation of Martin Luther — had another far-reaching purpose, namely to equip the modern Jew, once he had learned German and acquired a general education, with tools that would enable him to grapple with a culture permeated with Christianity, suffused with fixed ideas hostile to Judaism. Thus Mendelssohn wished that the enlightened Jew who availed himself of a German translation of the Bible would see in it the canonical work that identified his own

---

[10] The publication of Mendelssohn's German translation of the Torah with Hebrew commentary is a fascinating episode of history that should be treated in its own right as a chapter in the history of the development of modern Jewish culture. The publication was done in installments from 1780 to 1783. Mendelssohn intended to translate and comment on the entire Bible. The translation of the Psalms was published in his lifetime, and the translation of Song of Songs after his death. This emphasizes the importance that Mendelssohn ascribed to Biblical poetry as a source of inspiration for the revival of modern Hebrew poetry.

people among the other peoples who were influenced by it. This could be accomplished only by a translation that was faithful to the Jewish conception, not by a translation, however impressive, that turned the Bible into a Christian work suffused with prejudicial ideas about Jews and Judaism. In this respect, Mendelssohn's translation is distinguished by its fidelity to the biblical commentary of the rabbis, especially in the areas of law, jurisprudence and ethics. Thus he prepared a vital basis for the development of the modern Jewish religious movements, especially Reform, which based the distinction of Judaism from Christianity on the Hebrew Bible and defined Judaism as "Mosaism."

So much for the translation component of this dual work. What was the purpose of the commentary in Hebrew? First of all, to present a model of correct Hebrew, in place of the medieval rabbinic Hebrew which Jewish scholars continued to employ in their religious-halakhic works. This would be grammatical, literary and fine, lucid, exact and esthetically pleasing, in the spirit of the Biblical original that it was explicating. Second, to present the plain meaning of the text — faithful, of course, to the rabbis' understanding in matters of Jewish law, but purified of fanciful homiletical twists and in harmony with common sense. Third, and the crowning touch: to point out the literary-esthetic qualities of the Bible for which the traditional commentaries had no use, and thus to develop literary taste and sensitivity to the formal aspects of Biblical composition. For this purpose Mendelssohn added to the translation and commentary on the Torah a translation and commentary of the Psalms which he wrote himself. Thus he took the opportunity to impart to his readers knowledge of Biblical poetics, which he had learned from the great German humanist Herder and enriched by his own observations. In other words, if the German translation paved the way to immerse oneself in German culture without neglecting one's distinct Jewish identity, the Hebrew commentary paved the way for reviving the Hebrew language as an esthetic literary language in which literature of Hebrew enlightenment could be developed, paralleling all the genres of the literature of the German enlightenment. Mendelssohn's contribution in this area was modest, and it was his student-colleague Wessely who developed it systematically, both in his researches on the qualities and style of the Hebrew language, and in his poetic works, especially the "Songs of Splendor" — a broadly-conceived Biblical epic that revolved around the story of the Exodus and the wandering of the Israelite tribes in the wilderness until they settled in their land.

Wessely's first publication as Enlightenment trail-blazer were the two "letters" (publicity articles) entitled "Words of Peace and Truth."[11] They aroused a storm of controversy in the rabbinic camp. In these letters, which one may see as introducing a new genre to Hebrew literature, he recommended a positive response to the proposal of the Austrian Emperor, who had extended a generous offer to the Jews, offering them equal civil rights on condition that they send their children to state schools in addition to continuing their Jewish education under their own private auspices. This was in effect the first educational program in the spirit of "Torah with *derekh eretz*."[12] Wessely used the phrase *Torat ha-Adam* — "the law of man" — to denote humanistic learning, that would be taught in German alongside *Torat ha-Elohim* — "the law of God" — i.e., religious studies, that would be studied in Hebrew. This was in effect an adaptation of Mendelssohn's own bilingual practice. But alongside this, his "Songs of Splendor" indicated an alternative way: a national Hebrew renaissance. One may regard Wessely's epic as a manifesto of a rebirth of modern Hebrew literature in the spirit of the Bible, with respect to the topic, language, and style, while adapting the forms of modern literature to its purpose.

In summary, the efforts of Spinoza, Mendelssohn and Wessely presented three different conceptions, each of which took the Bible as the source of the rebirth of Judaism in modern, this-worldly terms and served as examples of its implementation:

1. The secular-political conception, whose goal was to create a modern Jewish national civilization. According to this conception, the Bible is the source of a this-worldly national outlook which strives for worldly happiness through creating an economically productive and just society, a democratic polity, and artistic creations in a pantheistic vein as an alternative for religion as the basis of a cultural way of life. With respect to the creation of modern Hebrew culture, this conception expresses itself in developing modern Jewish critical study of the Bible as one of the central areas of Jewish historical scholarship, and in developing

---

[11] See Note 8 above.

[12] *Derekh eretz* ("the way of the world") is a time-honored Hebrew phrase with a variety of meanings ranging from "worldly occupation," "good manners," and "common usage." Here it means "worldly knowledge." The slogan "Torah with *derekh eretz*" would be used to justify the dual-curriculum private Jewish schools pioneered by the modern Orthodox leader Samson Raphael Hirsch in the mid–19th century. (LL)

a national and social ideology that has absorbed general principles of European nationalism and socialism but has interpreted them with respect to those special problems and ideals specific to the Jewish people. This conception was implemented by establishing Biblical studies in the regular Hebrew curriculum in Israeli schools, as well as in the manner it was taught, presenting it as a foundational source of the national renaissance in its political and social aspects. It embodied a way of life incorporating social ethics, national social and political objectives, and a fabric of daily living comprising workdays, holidays and special occasions. Its centrality was given official expression in the Israeli Declaration of Independence.[13]

2. The religious-humanistic conception, that strove for straightforward integration of the Jewish people in those national cultures conceived in a spirit of liberal humanism and devoted to pluralism in the Western countries. This conception latched on to the idea of the Jewish people's mission as a "chosen people" among the nations. The thinkers who adopted this idea developed it along the universal lines of "ethical monotheism" whose source is the Bible. From the prophetic stratum in the Bible these thinkers and educators derived the elements of "Jewish ethics" and the aspiration to unity as the supreme goal of life: unity of the personality, of the family, of the community, unity of the Jewish people and of humanity as a whole. All these unities would complement each other in a harmony that would form a bridge between individual existence and the universal whole.

3. The national-cultural conception (with culture conceived spiritually), according to which the Bible was the source of the cultural language of the Jewish people, of common values, of identifying symbols, of historical memories that tie the people to its land, its language and its national sovereignty as well as to the literary-artistic forms of expression of its unique culture. This conception was expressed especially in setting up the structure of the Jewish-humanistic school in the land of Israel, while at the same time establishing the shape of a society striving for social justice as the foundation of Jewish nationalism, as well as the inspiration that nourished Jewish literature and art. The Bible was the primary source of inspiration for the culture of the land of Israel in respect both to topics and style.

[13] On the place of the Hebrew Bible in Israeli education and the different approaches to teaching it, see J. Schoneveld, *The Bible in Israeli Education*, Amsterdam 1976.

A detailed survey of the creations of modern Jewish culture in all its areas of endeavor and in all its strata, from the beginnings of the Enlightenment era to the present – in its values, its topics and its experiences – confirms that these three conceptions were implemented in impressive breadth and depth. The Bible has truly been the first and primary resource for concretizing the unique and characteristic identity of modern Jewish culture. If one intends to perpetuate this enterprise, one must therefore reexamine how Jewish culture in our time grapples with its problems in continuity with the same sources and creations.

Vicissitudes of Jewish Culture in the Modern and Post-Modern Eras

Spinoza and Mendelssohn laid the foundations for modern Judaism, which for the first time viewed religion within the philosophy of culture. Belief and theology were discussed from the standpoint of a human society's structuring a life-world to satisfy its members' needs and objectives, and for this purpose establishing moral and political norms that are formative of the personality of the individual. From this standpoint, religion – rooted in original and continuing divine revelation – is conceived as a constituent of culture, indeed its primary spiritual constituting factor, providing it with unity as a totality with meaning and purpose.[14] We should emphasize that viewing religion as a human enterprise does not necessarily entail denial of divine revelation or of the belief that the power revealed in the creation of culture is a divine power embodied within the human being or endowed on him from above. These two alternatives are presented by Spinoza and Mendelssohn. Spinoza identified God with nature and therefore saw the human culture-creating power as a divine power. Mendelssohn saw human beings as distinguished from animals through their innate intellect, which itself constituted that universal divine revelation from which derived that "natural religion" common to all humanity.

---

[14] On the development of Jewish religion in the first half of the 19th century from these sources, see Max Wiener, *Jüdische Religion in Zeitalter der Emanzipation,* translated by Leah Zagagi as *Jewish Religion in the Time of the Emancipation* (Hebrew, Mossad Bialik, Jerusalem 1974).

Spinoza's conception entailed denial of any religion based on supernatural revelation. But that denial established philosophy as a revelation of the rationality of nature through human understanding, which would inevitably serve a role similar to that of religion. Mendelssohn's approach, on the other hand, required a rational interpretation of divine revelation and of the Torah based on it. These two conceptions generated two opposing philosophies of modern Jewish culture, and consequently (from a common source) two varieties of contemporary Jewish culture. The one conceives Jewish culture in terms of a national-political civilization, the other in terms of a spiritual-religious culture that can find its place in other national entities and is therefore not wedded to its own national civilization. The secular-national movements grew out of Spinoza's theory, and from Mendelssohn's developed the religious movements of modern Judaism — Reform, neo-Orthodoxy, and positive-historical (Conservative) Judaism. There also developed mediating positions that sought to unify these two conceptions as two complementary aspects of the same cultural enterprise.

The cultural complex depicted thus far attests to the depth of the crisis that Spinoza's and Mendelssohn's followers sought to solve for two centuries. This was a period characterized by the continual pressure of powerful revolutionary currents and wars of unprecedented violence. Looking at the Jewish people's situation in that time from the vantage point of the present, it appears as a period in which destructive forces from the outside combined with disintegration from within, both unusual in scope and impact; yet they were offset by material and spiritual creative processes that were also exceptional in scope, richness and quality. The destructive processes eventually resulted in the devastation of all the great centuries-old communities of the Jewish people in central and eastern Europe, as well as the displacement of the major Jewish communities of the Moslem world. The creative processes brought about the establishment of new Jewish communities created from the ground up, both in Israel and in the United States.

We should emphasize that the need of Jews to act collectively, not individually, if they were to keep their cultural identity while building a civilization, was common to all the new centers, though the circumstances were different in each. In Israel they established an independent national Jewish civilization, while in the new Diaspora communities, particularly in the United States, they established the necessary social, economic and cultural infrastructures within a multicultural civilization comprising diverse ethnic groups that had immigrated there to find a new homeland. The need to guide both of these methods of establishing Jewish culture brought about a spectrum of practical ideologies that may be viewed as continuous with the two basic directions we have described. In Israel there developed especially the direction which had its start in the national-political philosophy of Spinoza, while in the Diaspora there developed the direction which had its start in the spiritual-religious philosophy of Mendelssohn. In the one we have secular Zionism; in the other, the modern religious movements — Reform, Conservatism, and modern Orthodoxy. But because it was necessary to build from the ground up (literally recreating the land and its nature as well as recreating human nature), a closeness was established that enabled these differences to be transcended. For most of the twentieth century, Zionism was the most popular movement embracing Jewry both in Israel and in the United States. These were two varieties of Zionism, with conflict and disagreement between them, but they achieved their objectives through cooperation and mutual support. The major philosophers of Jewish culture whose theories guided the development of Jewish culture in Israel were Ahad Ha-Am, Micah Joseph Berdichevsky, Chaim Nachman Bialik, A.D. Gordon, Yehezkel Kaufman, and Rabbi Abraham Kook. In the United States the leading influences were Ahad Ha-Am, Simon Dubnov, Solomon Schechter, and especially the most systematic, comprehensive and practically-oriented theoretician of Jewish culture of all — Mordecai Kaplan.[15]

These thinkers guided the creation of Jewish culture in Israel and the United States through World War II and the next two decades. From the implementation of the ideologies formulated before the war arose the challenges that followed from the great transformations: the trauma of the Holocaust, the establishment of the State of Israel, the full acceptance of American Jewry into American culture, and the development of American culture itself from modernism to the post-modern stage moving toward globalization. These transformations dealt a crippling blow to the creative processes nurtured by the preceding philosophies, those that boasted the name of "modern" but now

---

[15]   On the thought of these personalities on the issue of the substance and qualities of modern Jewish culture, see Schweid, *The Idea of Modern Jewish Culture,* Chapters 17–22.

appeared antiquated, for the modern solutions of the 19th century had perished in the war. The crisis arose anew, and its severity in respect of the foundation that had established the continuity and identity of Jewish culture finds expression in the changed relation to the Bible.[16] Its status as a common source, forming a connection between the secular and religious conceptions of Jewish culture, had been disrupted. Like the rabbinic legacy, the Bible was now relegated to the movements of religious orthodoxy, for in the framework of the secular curriculum it now appeared antiquated and irrelevant to contemporary culture. This had far-reaching implications. If the Bible is irrelevant to contemporary culture, then so are most of the cultural products of modern Judaism, whether religious or national, for these are all based on the Bible and on other sources that have absorbed its influence. This is manifested as a problem of linguistic accessibility: Diaspora Jews do not know Hebrew, while in Israel spoken Hebrew has become emptied of its traditional cultural content and filled with resonances of the contemporary life-flow, bearing linguistic influences of the countries of origin of immigrants and especially American English, for Israel grows culturally closer to the United States with every passing generation. The result is the inability to understand the creations of modern Hebrew culture, whose language is steeped in cultural memory.

This is the result of another value-change that together with the difficulty of understanding has brought about a change in the place of the Bible as a source of the formation of modern culture. In light of today's rampant individualism, together with the globalization of mass-media culture, the Bible appears not only antiquated but closed off behind a wall of religious particularism and national chauvinism, and an obstacle to identification with the individualistic-universal values on which contemporary culture is based. Estrangement from the Bible thus receives ideological sanction, blocking any remaining motivation to struggle with the difficulties of linguistic accessibility. The curriculum of general education in Israel still assumes that the Bible is a required subject of study. This still reflects the educational philosophy that saw the Bible as a source of cultural identity, precisely because it combines

---

[16]   On analysis of the nature of the post-modern crisis after World War II in greater breadth, see Eliezer Schweid, *Zionism After Zionism* (Hebrew), Zionist Library, Jerusalem, 1996, the first two essays.

national identity with universal values that provide a meeting-ground
between Jewish culture and the cultures of the Christian and Moslem
worlds. Because of political considerations pertaining to the relations
between religious and secular groups, it is impossible to rid oneself of
the baggage of this educational philosophy, at any rate not all at once.
Nevertheless, the effort invested in this area of instruction is on the
decrease, and the educational philosophy that required this instruction
in the first place has little influence on the way it is carried out now.
There is no creative absorption of the spirit of the material, but only
rote memorization, to be regurgitated at the matriculation exams and
almost certainly forgotten shortly thereafter.

The advocates and purveyors of global culture see it as a kind of progress
whose principal expression is based on the economic abundance
based on competitive individualism that it serves. It is presented as
necessary, as a condition for perpetual growth. But the ideological,
interest-serving nature of this outlook is evident from the heavy
prices of a psychological, existential, ethical, social and cultural kind
that it exacts from the family and community. These are paid in the
form of loss of identity, of solidarity, of the fragmentation of ways of
life, of the sense of responsibility to the other and to the community.
Everyone pays these prices, but especially those whom this economy
of abundance exploits more than it satisfies their needs. The rifts in
society portending upheaval are all too recognizable. It is therefore
imperative to address the factors of post-modernism for the sake of a
corrective reorientation.

Post-modernism has a positive aspect. It has its source in the lessons
learned from the destruction that World War II visited on the Western
nations. The extreme collectivist ideologies — Marxist socialism and
Fascist-Nazi nationalism — brought the great mass movements into
confrontation on two fronts — between the Communist and Fascist
states, and between these and the states who held by liberal social-
national values. For the sake of recovery and the promise of the
future of humanity, it was necessary to break from the legacy of
the totalitarian movements. From this developed the thrust toward
individualism — enthroning the sovereignty of the individual, whose
rights take priority over obligations to his fellow-person or to the
community. But in over-emphasizing this principle, individualistic
post-modernism has cut itself off from the liberal-national legacy and
has pushed the legitimate affirmation of the individual personality

into principled egotism. The states that stood for liberal nationalism won the war, but the price of their victory was heavy and led them to the threshold of cultural collapse. Therefore the social elites of the liberal and social-democratic states engaged in searching self-criticism. In their careful analysis of the causes of the two world wars of the 20th century, it was not possible to ignore the responsibility of these states for the wars and revolutions. They had failed to implement their constitutional principles internally in their social relations, or externally in their international relations, and their failure allowed the ascendancy of the totalitarian movements that pursued their anti-liberal path to apocalyptic solutions. Acknowledging responsibility for failure led them to break completely with the legacy of values, of social ethics, and of ethical nationalism of the modern period, and only the achievements that had proved their usefulness in those cruel wars stood the test: the sciences, technology, and efficient administration. It was natural to conclude that one must develop these aggressively in order to maximize their utility in order to satisfy universal human needs. The principle of unfettered competition among individuals within a group and between groups within each nation seemed the most practical principle for economic prosperity: it was in keeping with human beings' egoistic nature and would maximize the incentive that motivated them to greater achievement in their standard of living and social status. All society would benefit from the unleashed achievement-drive of its members. Thus egoistic-individualistic liberalism displaced that older personal-national liberalism that had felt the responsibility of the community for the just distribution of resources to its members. The recovery of the liberal nations from the destruction of the war was based, then, on these two elements: aggressive development of the sciences and technology, and the free-market economy based on an ethos of private achievement. Those individuals who managed to base their achievement on direct contributions to science, technology, economic and political management became the winners. Their achievements were held up as an example of "self-actualization," individualism and success. In the developed nations, the wealth created from competitive pressure enabled a rise in the standard of living of a broader range of social classes than in the past. Still, the price was a continual widening of social gaps as well as the exploitation of the cheap labor power of undeveloped countries. Reliance on these factors points up the true ethical meaning of the cutting off from the past and from the visions of a utopian future that were a part of that legacy. Moreover, the very gesture of looking to the past for moral authority, or the readiness to sacrifice something in the present for the sake of a utopian future, were disqualified. The effort necessary for learning, for creation, for successful endeavor was focused only on the present: to locate resources at the disposal of the developed nations, to define their capabilities and to set attainable objectives based on current possibilities according to criteria of maximizing utility in terms of measurable achievements, especially the raising of the standard of living and security of those citizens able to fend for themselves, each to the extent that he can prove his ability to compete. This utilitarian egoism was regulated only by the rules of the free marketplace and by the law forbidding one to infringe on the *rights* of the fellow-person and the community, but not by any imposing of *responsibility* twards the fellow-person and the community on the members of society. Even mutual aid was conceived only as part of utilitarian tit-for-tat considerations.

A culture that operates on the basis of such values and norms as these will see its energies focused on developing scientific-technological civilization, but not culture for its own sake, and utilitarian achievement will determine the definition of success and happiness. Such a society will not do away with the cultural dimension for two reasons: first, because a certain cultural level is a precondition for scientific and technological development; and second, because culture is a vital ingredient in people's happiness and well-being — providing them with social communication on the interpersonal and collective levels; articulating their emotions, outlooks and the like; and expressing the spiritual-creative dimension of their personalities. The religious and humanistic outlooks of modernity regarded culture as the end-goal of human life, striving for ethical uplift. But for the post-modern outlook, it is only an instrument serving a technological society. This outlook is expressed in the postmodern craze for competitive achievement. Like its technical achievements, the culture of post-modernity is focused on celebrating the present existence of successful individuals, and it is interested neither in the past, nor in the dreams of the future that our predecessors dreamed of, nor in the collective well-being expressed through identification with one's family, community and people.

Even the cultural achievements of the past are now used only to the extent that they satisfy the needs of the present. Any sense of responsibility to the values and norms embodied in past traditions has disappeared, and the sense of obligation to preserve continuity and a fixed sense of identity and cultural momentum has also disappeared. Just the opposite: fidelity to the past is considered a vice. Being wedded to the present requires not reviewing it more than once. The present as such must always be new and self-sufficient. As developing technology brings about an accelerated pace of revolutionary changes, a culture that expresses identification with these changes must be novelty-seeking in the same sense and to the same extent: traditional values and eternal verities are identified with conservatism, with ossification and boredom, whereas interest is found in the surprising and astonishing in every brand-new present. The frenzy of change becomes the only constant. To be interesting, every present moment must be different — surprising and astonishing in its difference from what preceded it, because the value of every present must be embodied in itself, and in order to experience it as such one must have absolute satisfaction that is expressed in astonishment and surprise. The products of traditional culture serve as raw materials that may be used however one wishes to satisfy present-day tastes, but on no condition to strike root in them and plumb their depths. On the contrary! To be wedded to the set patterns that flow from the rhythmic cycle of human life is regarded as conservatism in the negative sense, tedious and boring.

This approach has certain advantages. To a creative personality that has absorbed a broad cultural background, it offers a feeling of limitless freedom for creation expression of one's inner spirit. But from the standpoint of ordinary people dependent on a culture, or of collective humanity, it is defective and harmful. It offers a kind of entertainment that is stimulating and arousing but superficial and lacking depth. Mass entertainment depends on the creative activity of the artists and the hypnotic passivity of the spectators. The relation between artist and audience turns into that of seller and consumer: both stand to gain from the sale of goods at market price in accord with the laws of supply and demand. The consumer responds as he wishes, but he is not called on to participate in the creative process but only to enjoy it. The artists are allowed to reveal through their creation the depths of their experience and their broad knowledge. The spectator-masses have no demands placed on them and are not invited into the process of reflection that might reveal to them the depths of their own lives.

In order to create an experience of this kind that submerges the entire personality, one must exchange the depth that penetrates into the existential constancy of a person's life with an unreflective power of the spectacular that has the ability to excite and overwhelm us. It is clearly counterproductive to the surprise element of this experience to undergo it a second time. But this poses a problem. When an experience like this is past, the spiritual hunger remains. The person did not internalize any value of the kind that builds a personality and provides guidance for life. A person may experience surprise after surprise, but they do not offer anything new of substance, and apart from a superficial interest, there is generated a feeling of alienation, emptiness and desolation. The individuals who hope for "self-actualization" as their salvation are disappointed in the depths of their souls without acknowledging it to themselves, and on the conscious level they express feelings of loneliness and alienation. These unpleasant feelings lead the disappointed ones, those who are unsuccessful by the standards of the post-modern ethic, to strong venting. They end up preaching against the violence that is increasing in the family and the community; but with a hypocrisy that characterizes the mass-media culture, they incite the violence that is nourished by the commercial, forced-competitive, egoistic, libidinally-driven mass culture in the very act of preaching piously against it. Post-modern philosophy has no convincing remedy for such problems as these, and their appearance is a sign of an approaching ethical, social and philosophical bankruptcy, the same bankruptcy that the totalitarian philosophies arrived at in an earlier generation.

Diaspora Jewry was attracted to the post-modern global cultural syndrome, which offered the advantage of its characteristic openness to pluralism and difference, as well as its readiness to include everyone. Whereas the classic national culture, which strove for unity and tended to uniformity, posed obstacles to Jews who wanted to belong to their environment, post-modern culture removed these obstacles and welcomed sweeping pluralism of all elements into its midst, which melted together into one gooey mass of many colors. The result was necessarily a process of rapid absorption. The legacy of distinctively Jewish ethnic life-experience was given up as a contribution to the rainbow of global culture. Jewish leadership, worried about the disappearance of the Jewish people in the diaspora, was required to change its previous position and to swim with the flow. In the prior modern experience they had tried to impart long-term memory selectively, based on the Bible. Now the long-term memory was entrusted to the

Orthodox movements, who indeed had succeeded in showing relative firmness in the face of the post-modern temptation. The modern movements, for their part, neglected long-term memory or minimized it; it was imparted in small doses so as not to put an undue burden on the limited tolerance of the contemporary student. In compensation they increased the emphasis on short-term Jewish memory, whose spectacular impact is fit competition for anything that post-modern culture can come up with — the Holocaust, and the establishment of the State of Israel!!! — and with them, the message of the obligation of the survivors to restore the Jewish people, to bring it back to life and a healthy existence among the nations of the world.

In Israel the process was different but it arrived at a similar result.[17] Zionism became a success after the Second World War. Its success, at the same time that most other national and social ideologies failed, prolonged the influence of its own national and socialist ideologies as a vital intellectual resource for strengthening the State of Israel in the two decades after its establishment. However, the transformation regarding long-term memory began immediately, principally for practical reasons: focusing on strengthening the infrastructure of the Jewish homeland, especially building its strength in the economic, technological and military areas, along with the rapid developments in science and technology, where Israel could not afford to lag behind for the sake of its survival — all these had a direct impact on the school curriculum and its educational messages, as well as on the relation between the development of material civilization and higher culture in Israel's national life. The share of attention given to Jewish studies and humanistic learning declined continually, while the share given to sciences and technology rose proportionately. In order not to sacrifice the consciousness of Jewish identity and the obligation bound up with it, they were forced to adopt a similar solution to that of diaspora Jewry: to impart the mystique of the Holocaust and the establishment of the State as short-term memory that would inform Jewish identity in respect of belonging to a people and being devoted to its welfare. The winds of global culture had their effect on this picture when the maturation of the Israeli State reached the point that the competitive

---

17   On the crisis of humanistic-Jewish education in Israel, see Eliezer Schweid, *Humanistic-Jewish Education in Israel* (Hebrew), Ha-Kibbutz ha-Meuḥad, Tel Aviv 2000.

benefits of participating in the advances of material civilization took priority over the national need to unite against the dangers of a second Holocaust.

In the process of absorbing waves of immigration and strengthening Israel's economic and military posture, profound socio-economic and intellectual-cultural gaps developed in the strata of Israeli society. There were old-timers and new immigrants, communities of different ethnic origin, religious and secular, Jews and Arabs. As long as the collective effort to strengthen the homeland was strongly felt, the interests of unity prevailed, and the forces of division were repressed or deferred. But in the 1960s Israel arrived at a position of economic and military power sufficient to overwhelm its enemies. At that point, all these divisions rose to the surface. Along with them, there arose to public awareness also the difficulties in many vital areas of Israeli life: the cultural divisions; the place of religion in a secular Jewish state; the connection between Jewish national identity and democracy, especially in relation to Israeli Arabs; and of course the ongoing conflict between Israel and the Palestinians, as well as the neighboring Arab countries. In view of these difficulties, the sense of success in Israel was overshadowed by a sense of failure and shame, and criticism of Zionism and socialism as failed modern ideologies broke out in full force. "Post-modernism" arrived in Israel in the form of several varieties of "post-Zionism," and it became an existential challenge to the Jewish identity of Israel both politically and on a social-cultural level.[18]

Israeli leadership, fearful of the destructive impact of the post-Zionist tendencies, has tried to counter the threat by enhancing the message of short-term memory. We should remember not only the Holocaust and 1948, but also the legacy of the Jewish world that perished in the Holocaust, which must be rescued from oblivion. It appears that the memory of the Holocaust still has a formative influence on the sense of Jewish identity, perhaps because of the renewed specter of catastrophe in the wake of the crisis of the Oslo accords, which had generated an illusion of imminent peace. It now becomes clear that the struggle for survival continues. In order to succeed in it we need perseverance, unity and national dedication. In the diaspora, it appears that the faith that the Jewish people were finally released from the cycle of hatred that had engulfed them in the period of the Holocaust has also been

[18] See Schweid, *Zionism After Zionism*, first two essays.

disappointed. In the face of the threats of assimilation on the one hand and anti-Semitism on the other, the question arises: Is the short-term memory of events such as the Holocaust and 1948 sufficient to sustain a deep sense of Jewish identity? Does it generate motivation for continuity of everything connected to the struggle for a people's existence and its destiny? Does it answer the spiritual and moral needs of a contemporary Jew, whether in respect of belonging to his people or his spiritual, social, ethical and cultural life as a human being?

There Is No Substitute for Long-Term Cultural Memory

The foregoing analysis demonstrates that the answer to these searching questions is negative. From all the aspects that we have examined, it follows that a reorientation is called for in education and in the creation of the culture, proceeding from the realization that there is no substitute for long-term memory, for it alone carries those constant perceptions that serve as the foundation for the sense of group identity of a culture, as well as the sense of individual identity of a person who internalizes the values of that culture as a basis for new creativity. Reorientation is required first of all in education, and the questions that arise relate to the function of education in the broadest sense: preparation for life in all aspects through which individuals are integrated into the life of their society and their people. Professional training is a central component of education as preparation for life, but it is not the only one. When it is provided in isolation and presented as the sole objective, it fails to achieve the goal of integrating the professional worker into the general fabric of the life of his society — his family, his community, his country. For the sake of these it is important to inculcate values that develop a person who has an ethical world-outlook, belief in God or in a humanity faithful to its destiny, and a sense of responsibility to one's fellow-person and to the community. These are rooted in the language of a culture and in the cultural memory that a person receives and transmits to his posterity through a way of life. The memory and the way of life maintain those fundamental ethical and spiritual constant perceptions that form the personality of the individual out of a connection to the hierarchy of values of his people's identity.

Education in the sense defined here is a process of cultural socialization through imparting a heritage. In order to reconstitute it, one must renew the common "core" that all educators in a given community accept as a repository of memory and as a language that functions on all levels of the collective life. Through this common core, the group is transformed from a random collection of individuals into a society, and the school becomes a miniature community integrated with the society around it. This connecting core provides a bridging continuity across the generations, and it transmits the moral code by which solidarity between members of a society and a people is preserved. The moral code is embodied in a tradition that this core represents, and through it the lessons of the sources of the heritage are implanted in the way of life — in the holidays and in social existence. This is the educational conception in whose framework the Bible can find its place again as the work that stands at the foundation of the culture of the Jewish people.

Of course, the core that is designated for imparting this heritage must be representative of all the layers of the sources of Judaism, and it must also represent the dialogue that was carried on between Jewish culture and general culture over the generations. Moreover, the core curriculum must emphasize alongside the ancient Bible the sources of modern Jewish culture as well. Only the voices of the recent past can properly be the channel through which the heritage is passed to the next generation and finds its renewed application. Nevertheless, both as the foundational layer for transmitting the Jewish heritage, and as necessary background for understanding the recent Jewish cultural past in all its depth — for both these reasons, the Bible must be restored to the place of honor that it had in Jewish education in recent generations.

What Makes the Bible Unique?

In one of his famous essays, Franz Rosenzweig (Germany, 1886–1929) asserted that the Bible is the most important book not only for Judaism but for world literature.[19] He presented this judgment not as a matter

[19] For Franz Rosenzweig's essays on the Bible as a foundational source of Jewish and general culture, see above: *Naharayim — Selected Writings*, Mossad Bialik, Jerusalem 1961, First Series: "In the Gate of the Bible."

of personal taste but as a scientific, objective fact. The Bible is the only book that was translated into all world languages, and its translations in each language are updated periodically. It was propagated in the past and continues to be propagated in the present in an unequalled number of copies and continually without a break. It is continually studied and serves as a source for the inspiration of literature and higher thought among many nations. There is no educated person in the world who has not read it. It follows that its influence is the broadest of any book, and in several cultures — not only Judaism — its influence is fundamental.

What explains the unique importance attributed to the Bible? Rosenzweig answers that the Bible's foundational role in the three monotheistic religions is a partial explanation but is not the whole story. There is something exceptional in its literary character that stands at the basis of its acceptance as a canonical work and its propagation beyond the circle of authority of the religions that institutionalized it. What is that exceptional characteristic? Rosenzweig replies that although the Bible is a collection of books that were written and edited in certain definite periods in the history of one nation, and although it bears in its pages the characteristics of the periods in which those books were written, the personal characteristics of its authors and the cultural characteristics of the people, still the Bible as a sacred work deals directly with the fundamental timeless questions of human existence. It takes positions with respect to these questions that are arrived at from a lofty perspective that embraces all times, but not in the generalizing way of philosophy, rather out of an empathic entering into the inner being of flesh-and-blood human beings, enabling us to see their here-and-now existence. Therefore the questions that the Bible raises and the positions that it takes are always here-and-now for us in a way that the people of every period understand it and interpret it from their own unique here-and-now vantage point. They discover in it something precious that relates to them directly, and therefore it imparts to them a new dimension of depth. In every time and place, to the amazement of every individual, the Bible is reinterpreted anew in yet another way without contradicting the infinity of its previous interpretations, and it reveals depths that were not revealed to other interpreters. It does not follow from this that the readers of the Bible always receive its positions as given, certainly not all of them. The Bible is a challenge that raises questions and doubts, riddles and contradictions even for one who believes that it is the divine word. Indeed, it is impossible to react to its teachings with indifference or to ignore the challenging truth reflected in them. Therefore even one who takes a stand against the positions of the Bible feels it is a matter of supreme eternal importance to grapple with them and to forge his own views in response to them, and he sometimes internalizes the Bible's spirit more profoundly than dogmatic believers.

Such an extravagant appreciation may seem an exaggeration, but here too we are dealing with facts, not mere opinions. The Bible is not only the most widely-read book, but it is also the most oft-interpreted book in world literature. No other book was interpreted so much in both past and present, and the need to do this attests to the interpreter's sense that he has discovered something essential and important that was not expressed previously by the other interpreters with whom he is familiar.

The present book is offered as a part of that infinite chain of interpretation. My goal in it is to renew the philosophical task with which the philosophers of Jewish culture grappled from the beginning of the Enlightenment, each one addressing the challenges of his own time. It is to examine how the books of the Bible raise the timeless questions and how they respond to them addressing our contemporary reality: Are these answers acceptable? Is it possible to update them and apply them? How are they to be evaluated in the light of other solutions offered by contemporary thought? What can we learn from all this in order to advance Jewish culture in our day? The interpretation that will be presented here is a creative interpretation in the sense that it is offered in awareness of its subjective point of origin. Its goal is to facilitate a meeting-place between the concerns of contemporary Jews and those of the legislators, prophets, poets, and sages of the Bible, by relating to them as presenting a timeless viewpoint that has the ability to address every reader in his own present.

Towards a Contemporary Plain-Sense Interpretation / Is the Bible One Book?

Defining the theoretical-interpretive task in these terms connects this book with the tradition of Biblical interpretation that has been perpetuated in the Jewish people over the generations. This continuity is expressed first of all in study of the accumulated wisdom and secondly in the form of the methodology of interpretation. In this respect, this book has a significant connection to two modern traditions of interpretation. The first is the philosophical tradition whose prominent representatives are Hermann Cohen, Franz Rosenzweig and Martin Buber. The second is that of creative literary interpretation, whose prominent representatives are Ahad Ha-Am, Micah Joseph Berdichevsky, and Chaim Nachman Bialik. These two traditions shared the traditional assumption that the Bible should be treated as a unity in its capacity as canonical source. Though they were not unaware of the conclusions of historical-literary criticism concerning the origins and composition of the Bible, this was not sufficient reason in their eyes to abrogate the authority of the traditional canon.

This critical adherence to the traditional position was based on the fact that the rabbis and their successors did not avoid the fact that the Bible was a library composed over many generations. It is fair to emphasize that the traditional outlook did not infer from the unity of the Bible that it was uniform. The rabbis and later commentators were as aware as modern scholars of the many-faceted nature of the Bible, of the different traditions within it, the contrary outlooks, the contradictions and difficulties that arose from attending to the plain sense of the scriptural text, but they viewed these difficulties as challenges to creative interpretation, not a contradiction to the established faith that the Bible derived from a single source of inspiration. Given this background, not only did the modern thinkers find no difficulty in accepting the conclusions of critical scholarship, but it may have provided them with an advantage. The conclusions of critical scholarship draw the reader away from the traditional forced casuistic interpretations and enable a responsible, exact appraisal of the literal, plain sense of the text as it can be understood with the background of everything known to us from the Bible and other sources concerning the time and circumstances of the writing and editing of these books.

This brings us to the second aspect of the two modern traditions that we mentioned in their attitude to traditional Biblical interpretation. This is found in their making common cause with the traditional commentators who specialized in studying the plain sense of the Biblical text, but who even went further and pursued "the hidden [or profound] plain sense of the text." This expression (*omek peshuto shel ha-mikra*) is a milestone in the history of biblical exegesis. It was coined in the Middle Ages by Rashbam (R. Samuel ben Meir, grandson of Rashi), and it implies a distinction between the original understanding of the scriptures and the deeper insight that can be derived from it by studious reflection that delves into the deeper implications of what the text says. It is possible to discover this deeper meaning by examining the complex interconnections between a text under discussion and the totality of the Biblical world of ideas, as well as by examining the connections suggested by contemporary fields of culture in the minds of present-day interpreters.

In what sense can the Bible be viewed as a unified book in a contemporary interpretation that does not ignore the findings of critical scholarship? First of all, it can adopt the traditional outlook that all the books of the Bible had a common source in the same fountain of religious inspiration, despite their varied periods and other differences. Even if one does not accept the principle of revealed Torah in a fundamentalistic sense, one can maintain that the books of the Bible embody a single tradition of faith based on the same religious truth that modern Jewish philosophy of religion defines as "ethical monotheism." Not only does modern historical research not undermine this view, but it proves its validity by historical evidence and by showing the intertextual connections among all the component parts of the Bible. They are based one on another; they reflect, comment on, interpret and even quote each other. Certain differences, disagreements and contradictions come to light from comparing the strands. But this phenomenon is natural in any living tradition that has many streams, and that combines the contribution of many tributaries throughout its journey. The many and varied aspects and disagreements within it do not disrupt the unity of the tradition. On the contrary! The many and varied aspects and disagreements are the source of the creative adaptive energy that pulsates in it and sustains it.

One must add to this the influence of the institutional authority that unified the books of the Hebrew Bible as a single canon. This canon was created by a formative institution whose instruction was recognized by the people as authoritative. We are speaking of the "Great Synagogue" which was founded under the aegis of Ezra the Scribe during the return after the first Babylonian exile. This constellation of events was crucial in the transformation of the "Israelite" nation into the "Jewish" people. Thus it may truly be said that the canonization of the Hebrew Bible marks the beginning of Judaism, drawing on the authority of the Oral

Law. Thanks to the authority of the Great Synagogue, the Jewish people received the gift of the Bible as a single book, and so it was passed on and studied, though they were not unaware of the multifaceted nature of the work and the problems of interpretation that resulted from it. The Bible would be interpreted in many different ways, but they all thrived on the variegated character of the integrated work. In this way was developed an interpretative tradition of oral Torah which was also single in its origin but multifaceted in its development. The sense of unity was rooted in the complementarity of many interpretations, each of which expressed a truth deriving from the source, though none of them possessed the whole truth. That truth was to be found only in the Torah as God understands it, whereas human beings can only strive towards it, each according to his ability and from his point of view. When one arrives at this level of awareness, every interpretation that aims at the truth of Torah presents an aspect of the complete truth even when it disagrees with other interpretations. The rabbinic dictum, "These and those are the words of the living God" is based on the faith that the divine perfection reconciles in itself contradictions that are not subject to reconciliation by human understanding, which is necessarily finite and incomplete.

Still, we may question the way that the official tradition understood the unity of the Bible — it set all the books together on a trans-temporal plane as if they stood in relation to each other as the chapters of a book written by an author according to a pre-arranged plan. Is it permitted to a modern interpreter, aware of the historical criticism of the Bible, to follow the traditional maxim of "there is no earlier or later in the Torah"? In other words, is it permissible to interpret the Bible in its unity as a book that expresses a consistent outlook despite everything known to us from critical scholarship about the authorship, redaction, and canonization of its books?

The positive answer given by modern philosophers of religion rests on the fact that through the ages the Bible was interpreted on the one hand as "God's Torah" and on the other hand as "the people's Torah." In other words, it functioned in effect as a single book, and therefore from the standpoint of its receivers through the tradition of the generations it became one even if it was not so originally. But even beyond the historical perspective that was produced by canonization, from the philological-historical viewpoint the positive answer is based on the assumption that the institutional act of canonization was not merely technical and perfunctory, but was a synthetic creation that treated all the books as the raw material for carrying out its plan. This creative synthesis was expressed in several ways: (1) By sorting out those books that were included in the canon from those that remained outside. (2) By means of the redaction that combined these books with each other. (3) By the interpretation that accompanied the redaction as a tradition that preserved it.

It is this creative achievement that sanctified the "twenty-four" books as the Hebrew Bible and invested them with their authority as components of a holy canon. This is what Rosenzweig meant when he argued that for those who read the Bible as a canonical work, the supreme author whom they heed is the anonymous "redactor," "Rabbenu," who is identified primarily with the college of sages whose authority was recognized by the people. That is why it was obligatory to attend to the many facets of the text, to the difficulties and contradictions that surely did not escape the attention of "Rabbenu." If he had wanted, he could have eliminated them. The fact that he refrained from doing so implies that in his view the truth is disclosed only in this manner. If people strive for knowledge of the complete truth, they must engage continually in the enterprise of harmonizing interpretation.

We thus return to the issue of the "hidden plain sense." From Rashbam's traditional viewpoint, the "plain sense" and its "hidden depth" are objective insights in which the intention of the author is identical to the understanding of the reader. From the modern hermeneutic standpoint, the "plain sense" is arrived at by the interpreter in his attempt to arrive at the objective meaning of the text, but we do not ask "what did the author really intend?" because there is no way to determine it unless we attain empathy with his own subjective self-understanding. The experienced interpreter knows that no interpretation can be wholly insulated from the subjectivity of the interpreter. In this respect, scientific interpretation that strives for objectivity is just another of the modes[20] of the subject's relation to himself and his environment. If one can speak objectively of the "hidden plain sense," it is rooted in the recognition that the way that the subject relates to himself and to his world expresses a conception that

[20] Appropriate to our theme, in Spinoza's thought the "modes" were also the plural manifestations of being that were embraced by a higher unity, namely God!

proceeds from objective contemplation of the manner in which he —
as a subject aware of the uniqueness of his situation, his aspirations
and the totality of his experiences as a human individual or member of
a collective (family community or nation) — perceives a message that
he received from a given source to whom he is responsible. Indeed,
an objective regard for one's own subjectivity can make its own
insights objective even from the standpoint of other subjects, for it
illuminates their own subjectivity to themselves. Thus every objective
judgment has a subjective aspect, and every subjective apperception
has an objective component. These distinctions open the door to a
many-sided hermeneutic that does not force its subjective insights
onto the plain-sense of the text and does not read foreign ideas into
it, but seeks to realize the full potential of the objective plain-sense to
generate subjective understandings.

The dimension of the "plain sense" is one in which the value of philological-
historical research is expressed, and in which the advantages of its
more developed tools over traditional plain-sense exegesis is apparent.
Modern scholarship developed consistent, fundamental and exact
methods for philological-historical study. It thoroughly researched
issues of linguistics and grammar, literary consistency, reconstruction
of traditions and redaction, description of the historical circumstances
in whose context the biblical books were written and edited, as well
as the cultural-historical realia, to the extent that historical evidence
of them remains. In response to this approach, modern philosophical
hermeneutics developed precise tools for empathically regarding the
subjective aspects of creative interpretation. In the coming chapters
we shall make an effort to utilize both these kinds of tools in order to
glean instruction from the Bible that will relate to the moral, social,
political and spiritual problems — concerning the destiny of humanity
and the destiny of the Jewish people — with which Jewish culture is
struggling in the difficult crisis in which the world and our people find
themselves.

It is important to remark: It is not my purpose to offer solutions that will
lead to a Messianic fulfillment. The last Jewish prophets yearned
for it so much that they saw it as if realized before their eyes, and in
every succeeding age, when calamities became overwhelming, similar
Messianic visions were renewed. They were in plentiful supply just
before and during the Holocaust. But we must content ourselves with
what ordinary people with determined will and devotion can achieve

in real history, which after every impressive moral achievement relapses into the abyss of crises. As these transformations are especially rapid in our time, the experience of our personal lives teaches us how dangerous it is to be enthralled by delusions of realization of Messianic utopias, but also how vital is the hope that by the merit of our deeds the world of tomorrow — in our children's and grandchildren's days — will be more perfect than it is today. Without that hope, and without the readiness to devote ourselves to its realization, will we and our children still have the motivation to continue the history of the human race and the history of the Jewish people in their midst?

Philosophy of the Biblical Narrative

Is There Philosophy in the Bible?

In Chapter 1 of *Religion of Reason out of the Sources of Judaism* (Berlin, 1919), Hermann Cohen asserts that even if the critics of Maimonides are right in their claim that the Bible contains no philosophical thought in the strict methodological sense, nevertheless it is replete with insights of a philosophical character that do not fall short in profundity, complexity and consistency from those of the great philosophers. The example that he cites as evidence there is God's revelation to Moses at the burning bush of the divine Name that is key to understanding the concept of divinity: "I Am that I Am." Cohen sees in this name, offered in the dialogical encounter that is a kind of first introduction of God to Moses, an element of philosophical reflection. This forms the basis of what Cohen calls the "correlative" connection between God and Moses: YHWH[1] (= Being), who is absolute Being beyond all conception, prepares the connection with His emissary through reflection on the meaning of what it is to be God to Moses and to His people. Through reflection on His name, that is revealed now for the first time, YHWH provokes Moses to reflect on the meaning of his being an emissary of that mysterious Being who reveals in Himself the mission that He lays on Moses to redeem His people in His name. Through the futuristic overtone of the name (which can also be translated "I will be what I will be"), Moses is informed that by carrying out this mission and

[1]   YHWH (unpronounceable; the reader may substitute "Yah" or "Hashem" or "Adonai" when reading orally). Translator's note: I have exercised discretion in translating the Hebrew 'ה alternately as "God" where reference is to God in the universal or colloquial sense, and as "YHWH" where emphasis is on the etymological meaning of God as "source of being" (related to *havayah*) or to God's personal identity as the covenantal God of Israel. (LL)

bending himself to the demands of the future, he will know his Sender now and for all time to come. According to Cohen, this is indeed the proper philosophical sense of the notion of "God" in its exact nuance.

Cohen acknowledges that this passage which is nearly philosophical in its conceptual level is unusual in the Bible. Still, throughout all the chapters of his magnum opus he grounds all of his philosophical insights — developed on the foundations of Kantian philosophy in an effort to overcome its shortcomings — on the Bible and the rest of the "sources of Judaism" that grow out of it. He does this not in the spirit of one who finds inchoate notions and raises them to philosophical clarity, but rather as one who finds them in all their reflective clarity and evidential ground in the texts. Moreover, in tracing these ideas from the earlier to the later books of the Bible (according to their modern philological-historical dating), he shows a growth of philosophical thought attested by the course of historical experience of the Israelite people from one stage to the next. In other words, the Bible's "love of wisdom" may not be philosophy in the strict methodological sense. It is lacking in natural science, mathematics, and formal logic. But in the realm of human understanding — according to Cohen, this is the science of volition, as opposed to the science of pure reason — in the human being's understanding of himself as an ethical personality with a mission to perfect the world — here the Bible's "love of wisdom" does not fall short of that of formal philosophy, and it may very well surpass it in standing the test of implementation.

Cohen differed, however, with the view of the "Higher Critics" — tainted by Christian anti-Jewish bias — that the Hebrew Bible represented a primitive stage of religious thought, only slightly more advanced than crude idolatry. Against this view, Cohen sought to show that the Hebrew Bible was the product of a high culture, rich in ideas, striving for a universal view of the world and of humanity's place in it, permeated with reflection and self-critical insight. The cultural level of ancient Israel was not less than that of Greece, which saw the first appearance of philosophy as a methodical discipline. No doubt the culture that produced the Bible had arrived at that intellectual stage where it could have produced philosophy; and if it refrained from doing so, it may have been inhibited by compelling ethical-religious considerations. The first stage of philosophy saw an integral connection between a philosophy based on natural science and an idolatry subservient to the forces of nature. Cohen saw evidence for the Bible's philosophical stature of thought in the accomplishment, complexity, profundity and nuance in the art of biblical writing in all its genres — historical mythos and epic, the expression of national themes in prophetic poetry and personal themes in lyric, judicial legislation and wisdom literature. Each of these artistic literary genres embodies a philosophical vision although it does not express it in abstract conceptual terms. (Aristotle already remarked on this distinction.) Literary art does not give a factual report of events, experiences, institutions and patterns of life, but it offers a fictive account that reflects reality through reconstructing and interpreting it. It is impossible to achieve this without first having a comprehensive view of reality. In the case of the Bible, it was clearly created in order to impart the prophetic world-view as an interpretation of reality from which a way of life necessarily follows, for the Hebrew Bible in its all-embracing unity is synonymous with Torah in the larger sense.

Cohen expressed these ideas on a general theoretical level. He did not develop them by way of detailed literary analysis, but he preferred to hold up his neo-Kantian philosophy as a mirror to the sources, to show that the Bible is rational, and that it expresses its philosophical ideas in a way that ordinary unphilosophical people can absorb them in depth and internalize them. Cohen was drawn to this course by the methodological constraints of his philosophy, which tended toward conceptual abstractions and avoided concrete examples. But he did so also because he lacked the tools of literary analysis that are now available to literary scholars of the Bible. In our day, literary-comparative study has become one of the central branches of biblical scholarship. In the second half of the twentieth century, educators have had recourse to such methods in teaching the Bible to students who regard it not as divine revelation, but as a product of human culture.

The promising development of studying the Bible as literature is rooted in a hermeneutic philosophy of education. This philosophy developed tools for personal interpretation in a variety of types, including philosophical interpretation, by relying on the notion that a literary text stands to the interpreter as the clay to a potter. But clearly this approach tends to obscure and even to contradict Cohen's insight that the literary text of the Bible contains a philosophy that seeks to be uncovered. Indeed, this fact points to prior assumptions relating to the unique status of the biblical text and thus also to its unique quality. Cohen, as a believing philosopher, related to the text as an expression of God's word. From his assumption, a text expressing God's word is a rational text, even if it is not of a philosophical genre. On the other hand, the biblical scholars who see it as a cultural expression assume that the biblical text is no different from literary texts written in the same genres. Thus these scholars assume that the claim of divine revelation advanced by those prophets and scribes who created the Bible was simply a dogmatic belief that gave them an institutionalized role as authoritative teachers, and that the same institutionalized status gave the religious interpreters who came after them the authority to interpret these texts in the light of their own outlook, on the assumption that all truth was embodied in these texts, including even science and philosophy. The believers will continue to interpret the biblical texts as they wish even in our own times because they regard them as comprising all truth. But to scholars and readers who do not accept this religious dogma, there is no difference between what prophets say in the name of their God and what poets inspired by genius say in their own name.

By this assumption, it would be possible to talk of the "philosophy" of the prophets only if the Bible contained philosophical works or fragments. But since the component parts of the Bible are written in the genres of poetry, narrative, law and ethical instruction, but not science or philosophy, it would be an arbitrary abuse of interpretive license to ascribe to the biblical text an independent philosophical meaning. For this reason, only religious philosophers who emulated Hermann Cohen in their relation to the biblical text (by regarding it as a divine text embodying philosophical content that should be uncovered) but who exchanged his neo-Kantian methodology for an existentialist methodology that is sensitive to the philosophical meaning of symbolism — only those philosophers developed tools of literary analysis to understand the deeper thought-dimensions of the biblical text on the assumption that the experience of divine revelation throbs within it and consciously determines the vision of reality depicted in it. We mention the two most prominent of these thinkers: Martin Buber and Abraham Joshua Heschel.

The present work is based on their insights, but also on those who have studied the biblical narrative in its literary aspects. It was their special objective to discover, in addition to its purely literary values, the substance of prophetic testimony, the ethical teaching, the social teaching, the judicial teaching and the political teaching of the Bible, as well as the sources of knowledge and forms of thought through which the Bible documents the life-destinies of its heroes — the human individuals, families, tribes and peoples — as the story of the relations between them and their God.

Prophecy: Speaking and Hearing, Seeing, Fear and Knowledge

Some modern Jewish philosophers of religion of a mystical tendency (the most prominent of them being Rabbi David Ha-Nazir, the student of Rabbi Abraham Kook, who wrote a whole book about this) suggested that one should make a distinction between pagan Greek culture, whose highest achievements were in the plastic arts, drama, and philosophy, and Israelite culture, whose highest achievements were found in its Torah based on revelation, on the basis of each culture's relation to seeing or hearing as a source of knowledge. According to their suggestion, Greek culture is based on what a person apprehends by himself, through his senses and intellect. Israelite culture, by contrast, is based on what one apprehends from divine revelation and from tradition, and therefore it derives its knowledge primarily from the sense of hearing. This distinction has implications, according to those philosophers of religion who propose it, for one's view of the world and similarly for one's way of life. A culture that derives from seeing strives for the knowledge of a truth that a person apprehends independently (without the mediation of others), for freedom in the sense of a life lived by the law of human nature (conceived fatalistically), out of striving for happiness, which is the fullest possible satisfaction of all the natural needs of existence, from the material-libidinal to the psychological-emotional and the spiritual-intellectual. A culture that derives from hearing strives, in contrast, to know the truth that is beyond the natural, independent ability of the human being, in other words a truth that is given to a person by grace, just as his natural life is given to him by grace. This culture also strives for freedom, but in the sense of a life lived according to the commandment of God, out of discipline that requires voluntary choice, out of a striving to fulfill one's appointed destiny that imparts eternal meaning to one's transitory earthly life.

This suggestion seems at first sight convincing from the force of its inner logic. Yet familiarity with several expressions in the written and oral Torah that relate to hearing in a visual way must convince us that even if this view has a kernel of truth (especially in the emphasis on knowledge for its own sake in Greek philosophy in contrast to the emphasis on commandedness and ethical action in the Israelite Torah), for us to present it as the priority of hearing over seeing or vice versa as regarding the source of knowledge informing human

43

existence would be simplistic and guilty of over-generalization. In the narrative of the revelation at Mount Sinai in Exodus we read: "All the people were seeing the thunder and lightning, the blare of the horn and the mountain smoking; and when the people saw it, they fell back and stood at a distance." (Ex. 20:15) Apprehension of the word of God in prophecy is given through symbolic visions and glimpses of the future more typically than through hearing verbal utterances. The rabbinic literature commonly uses an expression indicating that one sage accedes to another's views: "I see your words" (i.e., I see the logic of your argument). Such expressions indicate that it is impossible to establish a priority of seeing over hearing or of hearing over seeing, either in Jewish culture or in Greek culture or in any other culture. The two senses are required in interaction in order to know or understand (for there is no knowledge without understanding, just as there is no understanding without knowledge). It is possible, however, to distinguish between different relationships of seeing and hearing that are manifested in the preference for one or another kind of knowledge. In response to the question, "What's happening?" we are likely to privilege seeing over hearing, whereas in response to the question, "What's the right thing to do?" hearing takes precedence over seeing. It is true that the Torah of Israel places the primary importance on correct action, to which knowledge is a means, whereas Greek philosophy emphasizes knowledge as an end-goal and action as a means to it. But without eyes, action is blind; and without ears, the truth is deaf. Indeed, blindness is a kind of deafness, and deafness is a kind of blindness.

We have testimony on the general interdependence of seeing and hearing as sources of knowledge from the philosopher who introduced the notion of "oral authority" into Jewish philosophy — R. Saadia Gaon.[2] In the introduction to his work *Book of Doctrines and Beliefs* Saadia listed four sources of knowledge on which all people are dependent: (1) the five senses that perceive the forms and qualities of objects; (2) the independent insights of the intellect, based on its innate axioms; (3) knowledge that can be derived from sensory data by rational deduction; and finally (4) "reliable report" — knowledge that one learns from other people who can be trusted. Saadia points out that the more that our knowledge increases, the more the proportion of knowledge

---

[2] When Saadia divided the commandments into two categories — rational and non-rational — he called the latter *shim'iyot*, i.e. those that have authority because they are "heard."

that we learn from "reliable report" increases in comparison with the knowledge that we obtain from the other sources mentioned. There are three complementary reasons for this. First, if we took the trouble to verify through sensory experience and rational deduction all the knowledge that we learned in school, we could not advance rapidly enough to master entire areas of knowledge. Second, there is knowledge that is vital for the foundation of a culture that can be directly verified a single time and then retained in the memory of the individual or the group, and known later only through report — namely, historical knowledge. Third, there is knowledge that no human being can know unless God, who created the world and humankind, reveals it to them — and this, too, falls under "reliable report."

It seems to follow from this that R. Saadia Gaon also prefers "auditory" knowledge that is transmitted by reliable tradition. But if that is the case, why did he mention the first three sources before "reliable report"? And why did he mention the senses as a source that precedes the intellectual sources, and mention seeing before the other senses? The reason is simple. Without knowledge of the first kind, especially without knowledge obtained by seeing, it would impossible to impart other knowledge through words with an established meaning, and it would be impossible to understand the meaning of the words that pass from the speaker to the listener. When we absorb knowledge transmitted orally, the voice of the speaker (or the printed letters that stand in for the voice, which the reader hears in his mind) is only a medium for transmitting the words, which enable the speaker to encode his visual representation into spoken words, and for the listener to decode those words into a pictorial representation or a mental image. But by the same token, learning to speak in words, which is identified with the capability of intellectual thought, is also based on "reliable report": words are learned through hearing them spoken. Without learning speech from others, a person would not discern the essences and qualities of objects or know how to define them. Without language that one acquires from tradition, a person could not process the input of his senses to distinguish their relevant characteristics from which he can define the concepts of external objects. This deductive process is not performed by the senses themselves, but by the perceiving intellect, that distinguishes and processes sensory input.

Saadia's views, presented on the plane of sustained epistemological analysis, are confirmed by study of the biblical text. From the vantage point of this analysis we can pay attention to the considered, distinct and nuanced use that the biblical text makes in specifying the sources from which the content of the story is derived: speech that is heard or visions that are seen, both taken together to know that this is what the narrator wishes to tell his listeners-readers so that they in turn may see and desire to act. The considered, distinct and nuanced use of these words is evidence that we have here a central, consciously intended component not just of the art of biblical narrative but also of its intrinsic message. Aristotle has said that in the art of rhetoric form and content are combined. In order to illustrate this principle with respect to the art of biblical narrative, we cite the text which in Hermann Cohen's view was "nearly philosophical" in its mode of expression. It is the text that describes God's revelation to Moses in the burning bush:

An angel of the Lord *appeared* [= was seen] to him in a blazing fire out of a bush. He *saw,* and there was a bush all aflame, yet the bush was not consumed. Moses said, "I must turn aside and *see* this marvelous sight; why doesn't the bush burn up?" When the Lord *saw* that he had turned aside to *look,* God *called* to him out of the bush: "Moses! Moses!" [Moses] *said,* "Here I am." And He *said,* "Do not come closer. Remove your sandals from your feet, for the place on which you stand is holy ground. I am," He said, "the God of your father, the God of Abraham, the God of Isaac, and the God of Jacob." And Moses hid his face, for he was *afraid*[3] to *look* at God. And the Lord continued: "I have *seen* well the plight of My people in Egypt and have *heard* their outcry because of their taskmasters; yes, I *know* their sufferings. (Exodus 3:2–7)

In the continuation God commissions Moses to redeem the people. Moses originally demurs with various excuses, but in the end he accepts. In the course of this dialogue between God and His emissary Moses seeks to learn the name of his Sender, the name which reveals Him in His essence, to prove to the people the proof of his mission. God responds, "I Am that I Am." (verse 14) This name, which is given as an explanation of the proper name YHWH, is offered as an utterance for Moses and the people to hear. But in order that they will believe his words, Moses requests a "demonstration" that can be seen by others, and he is answered by way of several "signs" such as the rod that turns into a snake, and the hand that when placed in his bosom is taken out

---

[3]   In Hebrew, *yarei'* ("he was afraid") is phoneticically close to *va-yar'* ("and he saw"), suggesting a further connection to the ideas behind these words: fear is a natural reaction to seeing a frightening spectacle.

leprous, then is put back in his bosom and restored to its healthy state. We thus learn that the demonstrative sign — a visual phenomenon that can show something to observers and thus provide grounds for knowledge — such an exhibit can serve as testimony or evidence[4] for an established factual truth that forces itself on our awareness irrefutably, which is not the case with a verbal report unaccompanied by visual support.

If we examine the above passage as a literary text, we find that the words connected to appearing, seeing, fearing, speaking, vocalizing, hearing and knowledge occupy a central place in the discourse. We soon discover that this stylistic feature is not decorative but intrinsic to the meaning of the text. Through these words the narrative text presents to its readers two kinds of knowledge whose source is in seeing sights and hearing utterances, and to which the readers have recourse in absorbing the meaning of the text: to see and hear; to hear and see; to fear and know and respond to what is described/said in the narrative. This is the method of the art of biblical narrative: to show the readers, to make them hear, and thus to impart to them knowledge of supreme importance from their standpoint — concerning their relation to their God — in a way that they can internalize it and make it a part of their life experience.

Let us reconstruct the thematic line of the narrative. It is the story of Moses, the man of God, who fled Egypt and was pasturing his flock in the wilderness. His role as a shepherd preoccupies him to the exclusion of all other concerns. Thus his coming upon the foothills of what will someday be called "the mountain of God" appears to him and to the reader a chance occurrence. Moses and the reader know nothing about this place or its destiny. The prophetic revelation occurs suddenly through a spectacle that deviates from the course of his life and from the normal course of the surrounding wilderness landscape. Moses is startled and awakened to see this spectacle and wants to know what it portends. Does it have any significance from his standpoint? This awakening transforms what he first saw as chance into destiny, a pre-ordained encounter. God initiates, and Moses responds. This response brings Moses into touch with another responsibility from which he was running away, although he does not know what it is, for he does not remember what that responsibility was. The recognition of God who has revealed Himself in the bush starts to awaken in him — together

---

[4]   The Hebrew *ra'ayah* (evidence) is a homograph of *re'iyah* (seeing).

with the curiosity to see — the memory that he sought to repress. This is the purpose of the encounter that will turn Moses into a prophet.

The recognition that comes immediately after seeing the awe-inspiring vision is expressed in the speech that Moses now hears, telling him that the God who revealed Himself in the bush is "the God of Moses' ancestors." Moses had known this appellation and forgotten it. The speech that he hears is thus a double recollection: first, that he is the child of his people, and second, that he is consequently responsible before God to his people, whom he has not so far been moved to help. Moses remembers this well despite his imagined forgetfulness. Indeed it is because of the failure that he experienced that Moses ran away to the wilderness after he had attempted to redeem his people through his initiative that was based on his standing in Pharaoh's court. The reader knows this as well. He remembers what Moses is called on to remember by this spectacle. But the recollection through re-encounter reverses the picture: it is now Moses' life as a shepherd that appears incidental from the standpoint of his mission, and not the encounter, which comes to restore his life to its preordained course. The first step of return to memory and destiny is the true marvel. In addition to awakening Moses' curiosity — the eagerness to approach and see — the extraordinary vision arouses fear. This turns the seeing on its head literally as well as figuratively: what Moses was shown is too frightful to see.[5] The implied moral is to be inferred from the trembling that takes the place of the preceding curiosity. Moses had taken the place on which he trod for granted, perhaps because of the habit of life in the open wilderness, in which there are no domains of authority or boundaries of permitted and forbidden, nor is there apparently anyone who sees a person's behavior there and judges him. Nevertheless, that place is holy ground. The reader learns with Moses what is sanctity: a power that relates to a person from beyond the boundary that determines what is permitted for him to approach and see; nevertheless, one must encounter it, because his life depends on it. Therefore, only if he tries to approach to see, he will learn that sanctity involves more than seeing; it is forbidden to see it, and therefore it lays on whoever sees it and fears the same absolute responsibility.

---

[5] Both the Exodus text and Schweid play on the verbal homonymity of *ra'ah* (see) and *yir'ah* (fear) that was pointed out above. (If the Bible were originally composed in English, maybe the author would have played on the similarity of "fear" and "hear"! — LL)

The memory that is awakened in Moses in the presence of this sanctity is expressed in the words of the angel whom he sees in the bush (for God Himself is not seen). Therefore the text here uses the name *elohim* (the generic "God") associated with "God of Abraham, Isaac and Jacob," who is already familiar to Moses. We note that *elohim* ("God") is a functional-descriptive term, not a proper name. "God" is the supreme ruler, judge, guide and commander. The angel, as emissary of God to do His will as guide, is permitted to use only this descriptive epithet, and this is the evidence that the first words that Moses heard at the burning bush were spoken by the angel. Moses is reminded of the God of his ancestors, and then appears the divine "I" whose proper (not merely functional-descriptive) name is YHWH. It reveals the omnipresent Power that has created the world and has guided it by its sovereign will. The proper name which reveals the divine "I" is "YHWH," and it is the "I" Himself, not an angel, who utters this name, and who interprets the meaning of the name as "I Am that I Am" (or "I will be that I will be"). This expresses both the presence of the divinity and also the promise implicit in the present mission that Moses will fulfill on behalf of the people just as the angel fulfilled his own mission to Moses. The "I" will be with Moses; He Himself will bring the people out of Egypt and will bring them to the mountain where they will be privileged with a revelation similar to that which Moses experiences now.

The speech and the hearing, the seeing and the knowledge that are bound up with this process as objects of the story of revelation, come to tell us not only about the meaning of the name of the God who is revealed as Redeemer, and not only about the characteristic of Moses who becomes His prophet, but also of the substance of prophecy as a form of relationship between God and humanity who are destined for it, as well as about the function of speech and hearing, seeing and knowledge in prophecy. We learn what prophecy is from the description of its root-experience, but the story later also leads us to a more precise definition, which may be inferred from comparing God's utterance of "I am that I am" to Moses to the relationship that is formed between the tongue-tied Moses and his brother Aaron when they meet and become reacquainted on the border of Egypt. The parallel is instructive in all its details. The "I" that was revealed to Moses cannot reveal itself to a people that is submerged in the oppressive, degrading depths of slavery. It needs Moses. But even Moses — the man who ascended to a state of intimacy with the God who revealed Himself with such a name — does he suffer from a communication limitation, and a physical one at that? Or a spiritual limitation? Moses has difficulty communicating with ordinary people, and all the more so with his people suffering under slavery. Moses needs Aaron, who lives with his people in slavery, for Aaron has the facility to speak with Moses on the one hand and with his people on the other hand.

According to the story that defines the concept of prophecy, Moses will be a "god" to Aaron[6] and Aaron will be Moses' "prophet." (Exodus 4:16) In other words, a prophet is a person who is appointed to bring the word "I am that I am" to the people and to guide it. "I am that I am" thus proceeds from the mysterious source that cloaks Him and becomes "God" to Moses, and through the mediation of Moses, his emissary-angel, YHWH becomes leader to His people. But Moses himself is not the leader. He has no independent authority to speak or to lead. By virtue of the revelation that establishes his mission, he is obligated to be absolutely faithful to his Sender, and he is tested for fidelity the whole length of the journey. He must deliver the utterance "I am that I am" to his people as it was spoken to him, and he must operate in the midst of his people as he is commanded without injecting his own opinion and his own desire. In the language of contemporary philosophy we can say: The prophet is responsible to recognize and to deliver with absolute objectivity the truth and the commandment that was given to him by his God, who is the true Being, Creator, and Ruler of the world, and therefore the source of all truth and the source of all "ought." In all these matters, it is incumbent on Moses not to inject his personal subjective thinking.

From this we learn that the encounter that establishes Moses' mission is also his first test that seeks to examine whether he is worthy of it. It is probably for that reason that the revelation of the bush starts with the vision that tests the ability of the designated emissary to see and respond as he ought to this phenomenon. Only afterwards comes the utterance through which "I am that I am" encounters Moses, first as the "God of his ancestors" and subsequently through that name that expresses what He is in Himself and to the totality of existence of which He is the Creator.

Let us start with the substance of seeing. Two sentences of the story enable the reader to judge the exact sense and complexity of the concept of seeing in the Bible. First, we have what is told about Moses after the

---

[6] This confirms incidentally that the term "god" is a functional-descriptive term connoting leadership in all its aspects.

angel who was revealed in the bush told him that he was standing on holy ground: "Moses hid his face, for he was afraid to look at God." (3:6) From his hiding his face we learn that a holy sight (which is revealed by its marvelous aspect) awakens fear, and we have spoken of the substance of fear earlier. For our purpose, it is significant that we are told that Moses refrained from "looking" at the sight. How is "looking" different from "seeing"? From the context it seems that "looking" is directing the seeing eyes in the direction of the thing seen. The physical-sensory result of looking is that the object is reflected in the eye. This is a condition of seeing, but is not yet seeing itself, which requires the intention of the seer to pay attention to the object reflected in his eyes.

Looking does not always or necessarily turn into seeing in the active sense. Just the opposite: a person looks with his eyes at many phenomena without focusing on them to see them as they are. He turns his attention away from them; he does not know them or remember them. The objects were reflected in his eyes, but he himself has to decide in that blinking of an eye if he will turn looking into seeing. This is the first test of Moses in the encounter of the bush: he is shown a marvel that stands out from the appearance of the surrounding landscape, and he is tested — is he the kind of person who sees what is present to his eyes? Is he captured by the sight and does he feel responsibility to see what he sees? Does he feel responsible to know it and to act correctly in accordance with what he sees? Moses' fear is an indication that indeed he saw what was shown him and felt the obligation to know and act accordingly.

The confirmation of these things is found in the second testimony. It says there of Moses at the time that he looked and saw: "He saw, and there was a bush all aflame, yet the bush was not consumed. Moses said, 'I must turn aside to see this marvelous sight; why doesn't the bush burn up?' When the Lord saw that he had turned aside to look, God called to him…" (3:2–4) Two words express the same meaning in this passage. The one is "[Moses] *said.*" This denotes thought expressed in action, not an utterance directed at another. Moses says, "I must turn aside to see," to himself, not to another. This reveals an ability that is a precondition for thought — to be able to turn inward to a deeper depth within oneself to examine what one has absorbed from what one has seen or heard in the external environment. The second word — "[he] *saw*" — denotes seeing as an activity that does not stop with the stimulation of the eyes by the phenomenon, but involves the person's directing his thought purposely towards it. Seeing is thus a mode of perception in which one marks a distinction between this sight and other sights; one determines what one sees in this sight as compared with other sights; one wonders what is found at the bottom of this phenomenon that is not reflected directly in the looking eye, but is implicit in what he saw as its cause or its purpose.

This cognitive dimension of seeing highlights the volitional aspect that coordinates looking with seeing. When Moses turns aside to see the unusual spectacle out of curiosity to know its marvelous nature, he is not yet ready to take on responsibility for what he will see, but the responsibility to see leads to the responsibility to act in accord with what he will see. This is the next stage of Moses' test. When he responded in fear to what he saw, this demonstrated his responsibility to act in accord with what he saw. The continuation of the story about Moses' struggles reveals to us the process of his decision: Moses' desire for personal happiness tempts him to turn his back on the truth that he saw, but his fear of looking — perhaps the first expression of his dread of his mission that will uproot him from his private life and will dedicate him entirely to his Sender and to his people — this fear reveals to him that he will not be able to refuse the mission. The obligating power of truth is already familiar to him from what he has seen, and we thus learn what is the knowledge that is acquired from seeing: internalizing the reality that was seen externally, and impressing it in the personality of the seer, until he experiences it in the manner that this reality is in itself (in the case of objects) or in the way that it experiences itself (in the case of people or of God). This internalization is done out of the capacity — requiring objective critical distance — to perform the ethical action that is required with respect to it.

We learn all this not only from the fact that Moses' struggles are resolved by the decision to accept the mission, but also from the short sentence in the story that interprets the substance of the knowledge derived from seeing and hearing everything as attributed to God: "I have *seen* well the plight of My people in Egypt and have *heard* their outcry because of their taskmasters; yes, I *know* their sufferings. I have come down to rescue them from the Egyptians and to bring them out of that land..." (3:7–8) God, who knows the pains of the people because He has seen and heard, knows in Himself what the people know about their situation. He feels in Himself what His people feels in its situation even though He transcends all these things. Thus the internalization is knowledge, and from it proceeds action. Moses His prophet is required to undergo the same internalization whose source is in seeing and hearing of God's feeling towards His people and God's will to redeem them that proceeds from it. That is Moses' mission. He cannot hide from it because he has seen and heard and knows not only the situation of the people, but also God's relation to their situation. It is impossible to hide from knowledge acquired through seeing, because a person cannot hide from himself, and also because a person cannot hide from his knowledge that God sees him and judges him.

Faith and its Basis in the Revelation of the Power of Divine Creativity that Governs Nature

The verbal tapestry that the Bible uses to depict the encounter of God and Moses at the burning bush is the natural expression of a viewpoint to which we might give the epistemological label of "prophetic phenomenology." This is a phenomenology of relationship: the relation of God to humankind and the ethical relationship of human beings to each other as individuals, families, communities and nations, follow necessarily from the relationship between an individual and his God that is formative of his ethical personality. This epistemology assumes faith in God as the creator and ruler of the world. The word "faith" is not mentioned in the encounter at the burning bush, but it is generated in that encounter through a revelation that arouses fear.

What is "faith"?[7] In the language of biblical narrative (recalling here the patriarchal narratives of Genesis that revolve around faith and its testing), the issue of "faith" is not whether there is a God governing the world, but whether human beings put their trust in God respecting their success in this earthly life. God's existence is assumed in the biblical narrative as a given that can be known from the human being's dependence on nature, from the marvelous creative powers manifested in it. Faith is the moral certainty that these creative powers — that are manifested in human nature also, but often take destructive forms as well — are directed to the good of human beings, who feel that the

---

7   The distinction Schweid draws here is similar to that made by Buber in his book, *Two Types of Faith*. (LL)

world is their home and wish to achieve mastery over it in order to derive their gratification from it. Faith is the moral certainty that trusts in the goodness of God the Creator and Ruler, and in His dedication to the good of His creatures — to the continuation of their lives, to their fulfillment, and to the creative power that flows through them. Faith is thus the knowledge that if the person is wholehearted in following God's will, this will be a guarantee of his prosperity in life.

According to the Genesis narrative, faith is implanted in the human being created in the divine image from the time of his creation, yet it is continually subject to test, for in the course of his natural existence a person encounters many incidents that he regards as evil from the standpoint of his prosperity and happiness. Keeping faith despite all this is thus dependent on the experience of life in whose course are revealed signs and proofs that testify directly to God's love and loyalty to the person. In Moses' first revelatory encounter, his faith is confirmed by the vision of the bush. Here is a dry desert shrub that could be consumed in an instant by an ordinary fire, yet it continues to burn without being consumed, as if the fire burns of its own accord without being sustained by the bush. This marvelous vision of the fire, which recurs later in the narrative in the form of the pillar of fire that guides the Israelite people on their journey in the wilderness, as well as the lightning-fire of the Sinai theophany, and the fire that descends from heaven to consume the sacrifices presented on the altar in the Tabernacle — this vision repeatedly identifies the divine presence as YHWH, the eternal, absolute Present-One in the world that He created.

The vision of God expresses a presence that is grasped by the senses as a power of reality so mighty that mortal flesh-and-blood could not withstand it if they tried to see it through a seeing oriented to knowing as opposed to fear, for it exceeds the capacity of the senses. Hence the fear that overwhelmed Moses in his eagerness to see what was too marvelous for him. Nevertheless the fire that is seen from a distance is not material like ordinary material things, not even like natural fire that has a subtle materiality that eludes the grasp of the senses. The divine fire is manifest on that evanescent boundary between material reality and immateriality, and thus it represents a spiritual-volitional power that is directed to creativity and beneficence on the one hand, and on the other hand to a zealous violence toward anyone who takes a stand against it. Moses, who was fearful of the heavenly fire of the bush, grasps in it the holy, otherly presence of YHWH, who can be seen and known only through the revelation of His wisdom and will in His creations. As for God Himself, humanity cannot see Him and live. This, we recall, was explicitly said to Moses in his second personal revelation, parallel to the first but surpassing it in directness, the encounter with which Moses was privileged during the crisis of leadership that he underwent after the sin of the Golden Calf, when he sought reconfirmation of his faith through the reestablishment of God's leadership in the midst of His people. (Exodus 33:17–23) Moses' request to know God's eternal being in itself was rejected, but instead he was allowed to see God "from behind." This enigmatic expression is elaborated in the narrative: seeing "from behind" is explained as seeing "all God's goodness." In other words, it is seeing everything of which God declared "it is good" on creating it. Before we continue with the narrative of the revelation to Moses, we should remark that from here derives the absolute prohibition that was proclaimed at the Sinai theophany against representing or imaging the Lord, the absolute Present-One, through representations or images that a person fashions and forms in his thought. God is revealed as the absolute Present-One, yet He remains hidden as the Source of all living creatures. He is revealed through His power that surges through nature, not through the lifeless imitation of living creatures that He Himself created, that testify through their lives to their transcendent Creator. Surely every attempt to emulate the rule of God through the lifeless imitation of His creatures — the work of man's hands and the fruit of his limited reason — is only sinful human hubris. This is indeed the sin that the Israelites committed under Aaron's guidance in the episode of the Golden Calf.

A Dialogue of Sights and Seeings, Utterances and Hearings

Let us summarize: The vision of burning fire in the bush attests to the eternal presence of the absolute Present-One in our world, even if human beings are not aware of it or try to hide from it, like Moses who is herding his flock "at the edge of the wilderness." The vision comes to remind Moses that even "at the edge of the wilderness" he is observed and remains appointed for the mission for which he was born. It comes to reawaken the faith that was impressed in him from birth, and it serves as the basis of the formative prophetic dialogue that takes place between Moses and the absolute Present-One, whose being transcends this particular vision. This is a dialogue comprising sights and seeings — i.e., apprehension of objective truths — as well as utterances and hearings — i.e., intersubjective reflections on truth — expressing the reciprocity between the Sender and the emissary.

Does this reading of the dialogue between God and Moses in the encounter of the bush deviate from the proper meaning of the narrative? We can test the validity of this interpretation by applying it to the account depicting the revelation that occurred at the same spot, when Moses has completed his first mission and brought his people to serve God at the foothills of the same mountain where he had received his charge:

On the third day, as morning dawned, there was thunder, and lightning, and a dense cloud upon the mountain, and a very loud blast of the horn; and all the people who were in the camp trembled. Moses led the people out of the camp toward God, and they took their places at the foot of the mountain. Now Mount Sinai was all in smoke, for the Lord had come down upon it in fire; the smoke rose like the smoke of a kiln, and the whole mountain trembled violently. The blare of the horn grew louder and louder. As Moses spoke, God answered him *be-kol* ["in the sound (of a voice)" or "in thunder"]. The Lord came down upon Mount Sinai, on the top of the mountain, and the Lord called Moses to the top of the mountain and Moses went up. The Lord said to Moses, "Go down, warn the people not to break through to the Lord to gaze, lest many of them perish. The priests, also, who come near the Lord, must stay pure, lest the Lord break out against them." But Moses said to the Lord, "The people cannot come up to Mount Sinai, for You warned us saying, 'Set bounds about the mountain and sanctify it.' " So the Lord said to him, "Go down, and come back together with Aaron; but let not the priests or the people break through to come up to the Lord, lest He break out against them." And Moses went down to the people and spoke to them. God spoke all these words, saying... [the text of the Ten Commandments]... All the people witnessed the thunder and lightning, the blare of the horn and the mountain smoking; and when the people saw it, they fell back and stood at a distance. "You speak to us," they said to Moses, "and we will obey; but let not God speak to us, lest we die." Moses answered the people, "Be not afraid; for God has come only in order to test you, and in order that the fear of Him may be ever with you, so that you do not go astray." So the people remained at a distance, while Moses approached the thick cloud where God was. (Exodus 19:16–20:18)

The parallel between the two theophanies — the one at the bush, and the later one at Sinai — can be seen from several prominent elements that appear together with those changes required for a public event at which all the people are present. Already at the preparatory stage for the public event we find reiteration of the warning that all the people must sanctify themselves, for every individual — women, men, and children — must be in attendance. Nevertheless, they must stand far back, at the foothills of the mountain. Even the priests who are dedicated to the service of God are not allowed to approach any closer to the place where God Himself — not through mediation of His angels — will reveal Himself. Only Moses and Aaron, who have been appointed to prophecy, are permitted and required to draw near. As prophets, they know how to keep their inner distance while drawing close, and to see in fear. This is the proper spiritual posture which the people will be able to emulate only through a more distant physical and spiritual approach. These differences from the encounter at the bush articulate the parallel, underlining these finer points. In the revelatory vision, the power of creation is revealed as a power of absolute sovereignty before which one cannot stand. Yet this revelation is also different by the criteria of its methods and its central focus. It is crucially important this time that it be seen by the entire people. Thus in addition to the fire, there are added the lightning, the thunder, and the heavy smoke that envelops the mountain. These were not necessary to call Moses into colloquy, but they are required in order to speak to the people while at the same time obscuring the numinous vision that the people could not withstand, and that they did not know to treat with caution even after being duly warned. The fear of holiness is aroused in them by being witness to the veiled vision while hearing the sounds that are not clearly articulated into words.

Here we approach the heart of the narrative of revelation: Whence came the words that are spoken to the people during the theophany cited above? If we attend to the story on the literal level, we see that Moses plays here the role played by the angel of God that spoke to him out of the burning bush. In the climactic theophany to the people, it is Moses who speaks, and God "answers in thunder/voice." In the second part of the Sinai revelation narrative, when Moses descends from the mountain holding the tablets of the covenant in his hand, he and his assistant Joshua hear the sound of "the people shouting." The same Hebrew verb *'anah* is used to describe the sound of God during the theophany (Exodus 19:19) and the people before the calf

(Exodus 32:17–18). In the context of the story, it should be understood as the sound of the people shouting to express acceptance and agreement. By the same token, the *'anah*-response of God to Moses' words is an expression of divine agreement that turns Moses' words into God's words in the eyes of the people, who observe Moses holding conversation with God. This, too, is how we can understand the surprising words, "All the people saw the *qolot* (voices/thunderings)." (20:15) We will come to the same conclusion if we examine the content of Moses' words to the people, when he reports the words of God to them. Eight out of the ten commandments are the divine laws that are commonly known among all humankind. They are general rules of conduct that Moses must already have taught to his people before the mighty theophany, when he was sitting and judging the people from morning to evening. (18:16) Even the commandment of the Sabbath was already given to the people at the time of the manna. (16:22–29) Thus the two commandments that are original with the Sinai theophany are "I am the Lord" and "You shall have no other gods before Me." These proclaim God's sovereignty over His people and impart force "from the mouth of the Omnipotent One" (as the rabbis said) to the rest of the commandments that were proclaimed. Indeed, these first two commandments are the message directly embodied in the fearsome power experienced in the theophany itself. Thus in the Sinaitic theophany itself, the dialogue between God and Moses — and through Moses' agency, to the people — is conducted as a dialogue of sights and seeings, utterances, voices experienced as visions, and hearings of the product of human thought.

In conclusion, ought we to assume that at the basis of the biblical narrative there was a settled theoretical doctrine, or ought we perhaps to assume that there was an inter-literary tradition of the insights of prophetic language permeated with reflection? We have no scientific way to answer this question, but we have no need of giving an unequivocal answer. It is important, rather, that these linguistic meanings offer us a key to understanding the central ideas that shape the biblical world-view as it develops form the narratives in Genesis of creation and the beginnings of human history, and those in Exodus and the rest of the Bible that set forth the history of Israel.

Creation, Making, Bringing Forth, Saying, Seeing and Knowing in the Creation Narrative

Many interpreters of the creation narrative — especially the philosophical commentators who adopted the notion of creation *ex nihilo* ("from nothing") — subscribe to the view that the creation of the world is a manifestation of the absolute divine will, expressed in a command that is uttered and obeyed: "He said, and it was so." The basis of this assertion is the Bible's description of the first being that was created by divine utterance: "God said, 'Let there be light!' And there was light." (Genesis 1:3) However, this interpretation ignores the fact that the text does not say the light "was created," but simply that it "was," while the "creation" that is mentioned as the first action ("In the beginning God created...") is not phrased as a command followed by obedience, but is asserted as an attestation of making on the part of God Himself. As the text does not say with what or out of what God created the heavens and the earth, the meaning of "created" remains enigmatic and in need of explication by way of the following description. It is possible to understand it as creation *ex nihilo*, in which case creation is the embodiment of the divine will itself, when it breaks outside of the willing "I" and becomes a separate reality. But it is also possible to understand it as "creation out of something," in which case creation is the carving out of heaven and earth from inchoate primordial matter. Either way, we have a divine making without speaking.

The continuation of the narrative attests to a combination of several activities in the process of formative generation: it says of the grasses and the trees that the earth "brought them forth" out of itself in response to the divine utterance; of the heavenly lights it says that God "made" them and "placed" them; of the great sea monsters, it says again that God "created" them; but of the ordinary sea life it says that the waters "brought forth swarms" of them by the divine word; and of the fowl of heaven, that they simply "flew across the expanse of the sky" at the divine word, without saying where they came from (maybe from the wind, which already in verse 2 was sweeping over the water?). Of the land animals it says that the earth "brought them forth," but the continuation also states that God "made" them, apparently out of the dust of the earth that had brought them forth. As for man, it first says that God "made" them — as it said of the animals in the second version — and then that God "created" them. This intentionally varied use of different verbs of generation in connection with the different beings permits a comparative interpretation of each of them.

"Bringing forth" is like birthing, which requires two partners. On the one hand there is the fertilizing divine notion, which is implanted through the begetting divine will; on the other hand is the earth, water or wind in response, out of whose component essence the generated beings emerge or are born. "Making" is the direct formative action of God. This is clarified further in the close of the creation narrative on the seventh day:

God had finished, on the seventh day, His work that He had made, and then He rested on the seventh day from all His work that He had made. God blessed the seventh day and declared it holy, for on it He ceased from all His work, that by creating, God had made. (Genesis 2:2–3)

We learn from here that "making" is the outcome of "work." What is work? We can learn its meaning from the description of the kinds of work in the making of the Tabernacle in Exodus (Chapters 35–38), which has instructive parallels to the depiction of the generation of the world as a product of artistic craft, based on a conceptual plan prepared in advance that God communicated to Moses. Work is thus the skilled making of various objects, each preordained for its own purpose.[8] "Making" in its various forms — including work — is the investment of human or divine energy in an action calculated to produce a thing in accordance with a purpose intended by the maker.

This leads us to interpreting the verb "create." The conjunction of "make" and "create" in Genesis 2:3 ("that by creating God had made") informs us that creating is a special kind of making. Wherein is it special? If we compare those elements that the earth, water or air produced out of their preexisting substance, those elements that God "made" in a formative action out of earthly or celestial matter, and those elements that God "created," it turns out that the created things are not contingent on something previously given. God produces them from the overwhelming flow from His inwardness of the generative life striving to come to expression. This understanding of "creation"

---

[8]   The Hebrew *mal'akh* (angel) and *mela'khah* (work) have in common the notion of mission — the angel is sent to achieve a goal, the work-object is constructed to perform a function.

is confirmed by the conjunction of making and creating in the case of humanity. According to the description of Adam's creation in Genesis 2, God "formed" man's body from the dust of the earth — the aspect of "making." Afterwards God "breathed the breath of life" (that came from the divine essence) into this earthly golem — and this is the aspect of "creation."

Let us apply this interpretation to the original creation of heaven and earth. After their creation, we are told that they were "unformed and void, with darkness over the face of the deep." (1:2) This description applies especially to the earth, though from the continuation of the story it becomes apparent that the heavens were only separated from the earth by the division of waters from waters on the second day. Thus the primeval chaos — the blob without any demarcating boundaries or distinguishable essences or qualities — embraced the totality of heaven-and-earth. From this we can infer that the first creation was the breaking-out of the power of absolute divine life out of a mighty desire that did not yet have any reasoned will.

This description of creation finds support from the depiction of the revelation of YHWH as an absolute power symbolized by fire, in the theophanies of the burning bush and of Sinai. To be sure, the name YHWH is not mentioned in the first account of creation, but it is disclosed only in the follow-up account of the creation of humanity. YHWH is veiled in the first chapter by the name *Elohim* (God), which describes His relation to the world but is not the proper divine name. But there is a similar phenomenon in the revelation to Moses at the bush: first "*Elohim*" speaks to Moses from the bush through an angel, and on the basis of this colloquy is later revealed to him the name of God Himself, the absolute Present-One. In this connection it is worth commenting on the mysterious plural form of the epithet *Elohim*, which is highlighted and elaborated in the first chapter of the creation narrative. At the creation of the human being, God says in the plural, "Let us make man." If one were to draw an analogy from the subject at hand — from the fact that humanity was created as one which turned out to be two — then the plural applied to the divinity should also mean two. From the narrative, this duality can only refer to the commanding divine will, which transcends the world and will be revealed in the next chapter through the name YHWH, and the "wind/spirit of God" which was said (1:2) to be "hovering over the waters," i.e., the aspect of God that is in contact with the world while connected to God, just as the hands of the potter are touching the clay that he molds, though they are a part of him. It is apparent, then, that the spirit of God performs the "bringing forth" and "making," while the actions of creation and will that impregnate through the power of the idea come from the transcendent will that is revealed through the name YHWH.

Meanwhile, the power of created life breaks away from the divine power in order to become an independent being in its own right, just as the fetus that splits off from the life-flow of its mother yearns to separate from her and have a life of its own. But there still continues the work of formation that inducts all the offspring into their proper functions in the same three ways that we described earlier — bringing forth, making, and creating — in order to establish the "good" creature. The "good" creature is the one that is complete unto itself, that has the power to live even when separated from the life of her creator, who still continues to look after her and relate to her as a parent to a child or as an artisan to his creation. We saw that in the same way God imbues the human beings created in the divine image with the gift of spirit, so that they can be not only a creature with an independent life, but a creature worthy and able "to rule" and to preserve the earth through their "labor," which is an expression of the independent creative power within them.

These distinctions open the way to defining the double viewpoint from which the creation narrative is projected. On the one hand it assumes the basic faith in God as the sovereign will manifested in the creative power of nature. In this creative power is also latent an explosive and destructive force, to which we are witness in the mighty spectacles of nature whose reason and purpose are beyond the human power of "seeing," and are experienced with "fear," as a surpassing mystery in which the secret of creation is embodied. On the basis of this faith, the original creation is described from the viewpoint of God, who is conceived as an artist who is at the same time the progenitor, the fashioner, and the finisher of the image of His creation until it has been made capable of its own life opposite Him, and He has become its God.

On the other hand, it assumes the direct and comprehensive viewpoint of the human being who knows by himself that he was born and was fashioned and did not create himself. In this respect he appears to himself as one of the marvels of God's creation, but he finds in himself the capability of rulership and creativity in the world, and he sees the world as the living environment in which he must survive, develop and fulfill his Creator's mission.

In this way the viewpoint of God the Creator is juxtaposed to the viewpoint of the created human being, who sees himself in the center of the world that God created both for His own sake as creator and for the sake of His creatures who are in possession of their own lives. The next step, building on the previous distinction, is crucial: these two viewpoints are opposite, but they do not exclude each other or contradict each other. On the contrary, they meet and complement each other in the persona of the Bible's narrator, who presents also the viewpoint of God, the progenitor-artist, as perceived from the human viewpoint. For example, the narrative depicts God and His relations to the created world in the third person, not in the first person of revelation. It is understood that the source of the narrative of Genesis, which is the first part of the Mosaic Torah, must be rooted in divine revelation. Only that can be the source of the seeing and speaking of things that can only be known from the viewpoint of their Creator, but in that capacity it presents only what a human being can see and know as a created creature to whom God reveals Himself through the marvelous spectacles of nature and through the marvel embodied in himself. The narrative of Genesis is thus a dialogical confluence of divine thought relating to humanity and human thought relating to God, taking into account the boundaries that limit the human being's ability to see.

We return to the narrative and to the cognitive process at its foundation. We saw that the creation on the first day was a making without an object that can be described as the fruit of an existential drive to express itself, to form an object that should stand against it, and that would thus enable the absolute Present-One to become God and to rule over His "kingdom." Only after the action that expresses yearning focused on itself, blind toward the "outside" toward which it is splitting off, comes the utterance that expresses the beginning of thought that is reflective and discriminating both inwardly and outwardly — inwardly, to transform the yearning into a rational will that strives to convert the subjective vision into an objective, self-subsistent reality; outwardly, to know the primeval chaos, the depths of the murky abyss and everything latent in it, which must be "brought out" of it and must be "formed" and "made" in order to impress the vision onto the inchoate external substrate and shape it into a cosmos.

Thus we can understand the meaning of the first utterance, "Let there be light." First of all, it is not in the mode of direct making but rather of command, i.e. expressing a will. Will differs from blind desire by virtue of the wisdom that is at the basis of will, the inquiring thought-process that defines a reason and goal for every action. Second, God can address the command "Let there be light" only to Himself. He is the only one who can hear a command before humanity exists. Surely the dark primeval world cannot produce light out of itself; the watery deep cannot illuminate itself any more than it can see. Third, the import of the command "Let there be light" is the expression of the will to see, to recognize, to know. Fourth, the command is fulfilled simultaneously with its utterance. Insofar as God wills light, there is light. This means that the very will of God to see is transformed into seeing, if only the seeing of the need to see, and in this sense God causes the light to be, out of the absolute being of Himself. He becomes identical with self-perception, the seeing that is directed at the seeing self on the one hand, and at the creation that He created on the other hand.

Support for this interpretation is found in the linguistic connection generated by the association between the words *ra'ayah* (seeing) and *ohr* (light). The sense of sight not only uses light for its purpose but it shares in the characteristic of light — namely, the transparency that reveals objects and brings them out of the hiddenness of being self-enclosed, unknown to others and to themselves. In other words, the first light is the light of divine knowledge through which looking becomes a mode of appraisal and self-appraisal: "God saw the light that it was good." (1:4) Thus light becomes the criterion of "good" in creation: an entity is good if it is distinct, visible, known, congruent with the vision for which it was created, and if it does not tend to conceal and hide from itself and from its Creator-Maker (as Adam and Eve hid from themselves and from their Creator after they sinned). There follows immediately the first act of seeing that is manifest in the light of the first knowledge: the separation and differentiation between diverse things, the connection and relation between them, and their evaluation with respect to each other, is the faculty that sees and discerns objective truth — "God separated the light from the darkness."

As light is the touchstone of good, so darkness is the touchstone of evil. In this distinction is rooted finally the origin of time-awareness, which measures actions that are external to the absolute eternal being of God, and which sets up an opposite mode of being, which by virtue of its essential characteristic that differs from the Creator-God is always "becoming" through perpetual renewal, just as the light always "becomes" and is subject to perpetual renewal: "God called the light day, and the darkness He called night." (1:5) In consonance with what we have said so far, "day" is the time of deliberate action, action that is directed at whatever is good, separate, distinct, visible and judged; "night" is the time of concealing things in the obscurity of primal chaos, that shrinks from being seen and being judged. When things come out into the light and are revealed, they are good; when they sink into obscurity, they are bad. This distinction between day and night is also the first awareness of worldly time, and this will merit a separate discussion.

Is There Science in the Bible?

Modern philosophical commentators argue convincingly that in the depiction of the creation of the world in Genesis there is no science and not even a pretension to science, neither in the empirical mode of ancient Greek philosophy nor in the modern experimental mode. Every attempt to find imagined agreement between the description in Genesis and the scientific picture of the world is in their view a flight of arbitrary homiletical fancy that fails to do justice either to scientific inquiry or to serious religious thought. In the light of everything that we have said so far, we can endorse this judgment wholeheartedly, but with a qualification. We have seen that the depiction of Genesis is of a philosophical-phenomenological character — descriptive, but not causal-analytical. It is based on a faith that is rooted in "seeing" the spectacles of primordial nature as the revelations of a creative divine power, and in a sweeping vision of the world as an integrated whole, a totality that only the human being can see in the manner that its Creator sees it. In these respects, the Genesis narrative indeed contains a faithful enough depiction of the world as a person still sees it today when he considers it as it presents itself directly to his senses. The narrative describes the parts of the visible universe: heaven and earth, land and sea, the rhythms of time, the forms of life that were known at that time, the heavenly lights, the functional relations among creatures, and especially their functional relations with respect to the human being, who sees himself at the center of thing by virtue of his ability to create a cultural order unique to humanity in the context of nature and building on its foundation. Thus the human being is viewed as a living creature within nature but also standing apart from it as one created "in the image of God."

In this respect, it is possible to discern in Genesis's depiction of the order of the world a scientific aspect. Moreover, it would be possible to elaborate this description further in a scientific vein by focusing the scope of observation on each area of natural reality in turn. However, the Genesis narrative refrains from doing so, and this seems to have been a considered decision. A survey of the world's creatures and the relations between them is for the narrator preparatory to investigating the questions arising from his faith. One might defend the claim that the Genesis narrative considers the possibility of science, but it chooses rather the philosophic vision that asks the existential questions of the human being, those that pertain to his destiny, his morality and the meaning of his life: Why is there a world? Why humanity? For Genesis is the first part of the Torah, whose principal concern is to teach the laws of life.

Human Destiny According to the Creation Narrative

We made some general remarks earlier about the human being's place in the world according to the creation narrative: He is placed in the center of the created world. The description of the world up through its creation is made from the point of view of a human narrator, on the basis of his looking at the world as a general living environment and on the basis of the truth that was revealed to him when he contemplated with a profoundly piercing vision the evidences that attest to the presence of God in the nature of the world and in the human soul. From man's knowledge of the connection that is the basis for his faith in God flows the knowledge of his own destiny — to govern the earth in accordance with the divine command, in the same way that God governs the heavens. This is the meaning of his being described as created "in Our image and likeness" (Gen. 1:26). This expression compares humanity's status vis-à-vis animals in very different terms than the text compares animals' status vis-à-vis the birds and the fishes. In order to characterize the meaning of human uniqueness, we must distinguish between the human ambition to become like gods — the danger that indeed lies in wait for him — and his being created "in the divine image and likeness." Man is like God inasmuch as his position on earth represents God's direct sovereignty in heaven. None of the rest of the world's creatures can know God, but they can have sensory-creaturely knowledge of man, who is an animal like them, and know their ruler in him. Humankind is thus created to represent the kingship of the heavenly God on earth.

Two imperatives are incumbent on him to carry out his task. The first is embodied in his animal nature, and like the animals he is blessed/commanded: "Be fruitful and multiply and fill the earth." (Gen. 1:28) The second has its source in the divine spirit that was breathed into him: "Subdue the earth, and rule the fish of the seas and the fowl of heaven and all living creatures that crawl on the earth." This second formula does not spell out the meaning of human subjugation of the earth, but Chapter 2 elaborates: "There was no man to till the earth." It follows that subduing the land is expressed in the labor of cultivating the land, to make it a garden luxuriant with sustenance from which humanity and all other animals will eat and be satisfied. Support for this explanation will be found first of all in the end of Chapter 1, where only the seed-bearing grasses are given as food to man and the other animals, while the fruit trees are given as food to mankind, and secondly in what is told in Chapter 2:

The Lord God planted a garden in Eden, in the east, and placed there the man whom He had formed. And from the ground the Lord God caused to grow every tree that was pleasing to the sight and good for food, with the tree of life in the middle of the garden, and the tree of knowledge of good and bad. (2:8–9)

The Hebrew word *gan* (garden) denotes a protected (*mugan*) place, in other words, a civilized region that humanity requires in order to maintain itself, be fruitful and multiply, to fill the land and live a proper life on it according to the divine command. God planted the garden and caused fruit trees to sprout in it in order to signify and instruct mankind what is his task as "tiller of the earth" from which he was physically created. It is incumbent on him to take care of the products of the land and work them so that it will be a fitting living environment for him. He must do this out of a sense of kinship with all the rest of the earth's creatures, while observing the ethical conditions required for his social life.

The "tree of life" and "tree of knowledge of good and evil" that were planted in the center of the "garden" symbolize man's obligation to the land which he must till because his physical life depends on it, his responsibility to other human beings (represented in the conjugality of man and woman), and his responsibility to all other living creatures to whom the earth yields its produce. There is a reciprocal relation between these three obligations. Man's moral failure involves his failure as cultivator of the earth for his own good and the good of all its inhabitants. In place of brotherhood, which is the condition for the prosperity of the human rulers of the earth, quarrel and enmity prevail, transforming benign governance into despotism. Human governance over the earth is maintained on condition that they obey the imperatives of God, who rules in heaven and earth for their benefit. But the human creative power operates freely. Like God, man knows good and bad. He can choose, therefore he must choose. But his freedom is maintained only when he chooses to obey the divine imperative, which is in harmony with his true destiny. When he rebels against the divine command in order to prove his egoistic independence, he surrenders his spirit and eventually his body to his animal drives. From the learning of this lesson and onward begins (according to the biblical narrative) the history of the human being as one responsible for his garden before God.

The meaning of the Eden narrative — the temptation, sin and expulsion, after which man must bear the full weight of the task to till the soil and build up civilization — is the struggle of Adam and Eve, the first couple, to realize their destiny. We shall devote special analysis to this episode in our chapter of the male-female relationship. What we have said so far will suffice for our current topic of the philosophy of the biblical narrative. We must make the transition from the ontological dimension of creation (the formation of all species of existence) to the dimension of the historical process that unfolds in time, which is the basis for the Bible's understanding of history, expressed biblically as "these are the generations of…"

The Dimension of Time: Transition from the Coming-into-Being of the World to Historical Time

The awareness of time in the creation story originates with the first act of creation. This is the beginning of the objective knowledge that determines the conscious relation between God, the eternal being, and the world, which exists separately from God in a state of perpetual becoming. The distinction between day and night expresses the time relation first implicitly and then in the explicit statement: "There was evening and there was morning, one day." (1:5) The text employs the cardinal "one" in contrast with the ordinal "second, third," etc. for the other days, because in Hebrew the word *rishon* ("first") would echo the first word of the text *bereshit* ("in the beginning"). This underscores that the "beginning" is that unique moment on the threshold of time and eternity. As for the "one" of the first day, it does not signify the succession of events or time-units in a continuous progression, but rather a whole unit standing alone. Thus "one day" refers to the time-span of a day as a measure of time. A close reading of the creation narrative will show that each day was the occasion for one complete action, and occasionally (where the refrain "it was good" is repeated) two actions with a conditional connection. Thus, in the creation narrative, time is conceived as the measure of duration of an action completed from beginning to end — as long as the action is continuing, it is regarded as an event that occurs in the present, which is the current "day." When the defined action is concluded and another succeeding action starts, a new "present" begins. This is the new "day," and the previous becomes "past." Just as the past gives way to the next day, the progression toward the completion of all the works and fulfillment of the vision of creation in the days yet to come — this progression goes beyond the present and from that standpoint anticipates the days foreseen as the future.

Nevertheless we must emphasize that the transformation of "today" into the past or anticipating the transition from "this day" to the future do not cancel the "day" whose creation activity was completed. After the night that intervenes between one day and the next, everything that was done before the new day is renewed in anticipation of the new day and the new activity that will distinguish it. It turns out that the past and future are not only boundaries of different days, but the one is parent and the other its child, for they include the "day" as units of a time that is growing ever longer, becoming a temporal continuum embracing activity that strives for ever more inclusive periods: the week, the month, the year, and eventually the Sabbatical of seven years and the Jubilee of fifty years. This is the source of the direction of time's flow in the biblical narrative: it has a cyclicality of calendric periods and generations that is in sync with the rhythm of renewal of vegetable and animal life in every generation, but it also moves in stages in the direction of creative addition and progress toward a future that will be glimpsed in the vision that will find fulfillment in "the end of days," that will be as a Sabbath not only for the formation of the material-bodily constituents of the world, but also with respect to the ethical relations of all living creatures, especially of human beings.

The day and night that are mentioned in the creation narrative are the time-units of the creative process, as we said: each day is the span of one creative action from beginning to end. It follows from this that at least until the fourth day, when the celestial lights are created "to separate day from night, and to serve as signs for the set times — the days and the years, and to serve as lights in the expanse of the sky to shine upon the earth" (1:14–15) — the days do not necessarily designate the familiar days of our post-creation lives, from sunrise to sunset. It is almost certainly the case that the rest of the days of creation, through the Sabbath of creation, are not calendric days either, even though they signify the post-creation cycles of time in a paradigmatic way, as we shall see later. The day of the creation narrative is measured by a different standard — by God's review of the world in its process of creation and formation. The classic statement "there was evening and there was morning" at the end of each stage of creation is indeed said for each of the six days, until the Sabbath that brings creation to its culmination, beyond which there begins the life-time and activity of mankind on earth. This does not, however, refer to the rising and setting of the sun, but to the beginning and conclusion of a particular stage of creation. Only after the Sabbath of creation, that brings the narrative of formation of the terrestrial world to its completion, do the calendric days, weeks and years make their entrance, for from this point on it is not the time of divine activity, but of human activity.

This change is underlined by the duplication of the creative narrative itself. In point of fact, there is hardly any actual duplication. A close reading will show that the second story is a second beginning, actually a continuation. There will be several more new beginnings in the history of humanity and of Israel to come. For instance, this second narrative begins, "These are the generations of heaven and earth when they were created, when the Lord God made earth and heaven..." (2:4) All seven days of creation are included in this sentence as if they were one day, and what is told afterwards is the narrative of the history of heaven and earth, including the first man and his descendants who are called his "generations" — the same Hebrew word (*toledot*) being used for generations and for history.

From this we learn that the rhythm of time after creation is the rhythm established by its "generations," while the rhythm of time of creation follows its unfolding events that are tied paradigmatically to the time of generations. The morning signifies the first activity of the day, the activity of what was already created, and the beginning of the new formation that was unknown in the prior days. The evening signifies the completion of the day's activity. The night is the cessation of that activity whose process requires successive stages. The morning is signaled by the increase of light that displays reality in its full solidity; it shows everything as if new. In the morning all creatures exposed to the light of day open up in all their glory to the observer. Their inner essence is not bashful, but rises to the level of certainty in our minds. With the evening, the light that reveals the world starts to dim, and the world starts to become gathered to the dark abyss from which it originated; for even in daylight the deep waters are hidden and mysterious. But with night, when the world is not visible — as if to say that it is not present before God who saw it and desired it — we experience the primal chaos. Its darkness is not merely the absence of light, but its opposite. The world is gathered to its hiding place until darkness completely envelops it, and it is as if it does not exist. In the creation narrative, the night-world is nowhere to be found, for to be is to be present to sight. The material, earthly world lacks self-awareness, and the animals and human beings who experience it have not yet come into the picture. If God stops seeing the world, for whom does it exist?

In support of this phenomenological understanding of the notion of existence in the creation narrative, let us recall here the story of the ten plagues in Egypt. The plagues destroy by stages the whole terrestrial existence of Egypt, in a process that starts with the water, continues on the dry land, and then in the air, and ends in the heavens, from which God observes His creation. The final step is the darkness, in which Egypt seems to vanish, because God does not see it, though He continues to see His own people Israel. From God's point of view, Egypt no longer exists, and this is a sign of her eventual destruction, before her king and army are drowned in the sea, just as when the earth and all its creatures were drowned in the flood of Noah and sank into the primordial slime.

In the cycle of the days of creation, every "morning" is therefore a renewal of what was created previously, in order to add to it the creation of the next stage. When evening descends, sight is again obscured, the world flickers, fades, and goes out, until all creation is completed and "finished" in the hallowed time of the Sabbath. This is still not the cycle of calendric times. Time is the time of coming-into-being. The concept of days, weeks, and years — the periods and occasions of our time — does not apply to them, because it is not their measure. This is another time, the time that we now distinguish as physical time that flows in one direction and is expressed in processes of generation and destruction in the world, in the tendency to development. These processes and their time are not dependent on man and his knowledge of them, but man is dependent on them. Calendric time, that measures the development of creatures and especially of human beings through maturation and decline until death, is different. It measures the unfolding of things from the perspective of the human being who was created in God's image. Like God, he sees the created world and himself in the world, but only from his limited perspective, conditioned by the world and its time on the one hand, and on his Creator-God on the other.

Day and night of human time differ from the day and night of creation not only by their continuity and their definite measure, but by their relativity. Man leaves off his work and sleeps in his nighttime, but all the time that he lives, his consciousness does not cease, and he sees in the night also. So do all the other animals feel and go about their pursuits at night. The creation narrative sets forth this distinction in the transformation from the first light of creation, which implies an absolute distinction between day and night, to the celestial lights of the fourth day. From the time that God put "the greater light to rule the day and the lesser light to rule the night" in the heavenly firmament, the distinction between day and night is relative and not absolute. The fuller reality is still the daytime existence — bright, visible, and well-ordered. Night is the time of falling apart and sinking into sin and its ally — death. From here on, this is the cyclical rhythm of the human workdays. In the human Sabbath, which sanctifies creation, is symbolized the eternity for which man yearns, but it is not to be attained in this earthly existence. The terrestrial Sabbath-day is a day like all other days. It is made special by being sanctified as a symbol that expresses the aspiration, that in the "end of days" will be realized the full accord between the vision of God that guides human activity and the ability of humanity to realize it.

From the creation narrative we have derived two notions of time: material becoming, and the development of living species in nature; and calendric time, that captures the cyclicality of human life within the cyclicality of the motion of the large bodies in space in relation to each other. What we said about the earthly Sabbath points to a third notion of time, which begins after the expulsion of Adam and Eve from Eden — historical time.

We saw that calendric, cyclical time of days, weeks and years is also directed to a culmination that is the completion of work: from morning to night, which marks the beginning and end of a day's work; from the first weekday to the Sabbath, which "finishes" the works of the days of the week. Calendric time can be extended into the cyclicality of historical time in two complementary ways: first, by extending the regular cyclical progression of weeks beyond the months and years into cycles of seven years (Sabbaticals) and seven-times-seven years which are rounded off into the 50-year cycle of the Jubilee. The other way is to extend the regular cyclical progression of the annual seasons — marking the renewal of the earth's produce, which sustains the animal world and humanity, thus renewing the futurity of their lives — into the successive progression of human generations — each generation and the novelty that it contributes when it tends the "garden" of humanity and fulfills its task to subdue the earth and govern it.

From the standpoint of history, which recounts the generations of the "garden" (culture) that rests on the foundation of working the land and the proliferation of its products and the other constituents of the terrestrial world, and on the foundation of the formation of the orders of society (interpersonal, familial, tribal, ethnic and political) — from this standpoint, the extension of the regular progression of weeks into sabbaticals and Jubilees is conceived as cyclical with respect to the Torah's legislation that requires the renewal of the social and political order that is connected with the just distribution of the land's resources. These are the resources that God prepared for human beings when He created them. It is He who provides for their just distribution through providing or withholding the water that primarily comes not from earthly sources but from the storehouse of the heavens to fructify the earth. (We recall what is recorded of the work of the second day: "God made the expanse, and it separated the water which was below the expanse from the water which was above the expanse. And it was so." [Genesis 2:7] We recall the importance that the biblical narrative attributes to the years of blessing and the years of drought, by whose means God rewards or punishes according to the righteousness or sins of the peoples.)

According to the Torah's legislation, the Sabbath, the Sabbatical year and the Jubilee take back from man's hands the dominion that God granted them over the land and its resources, so that they may sustain themselves from it in fairness. The land returns to the original domain of its Creator, who is its true master. On the Sabbath, the Sabbatical year, and the Jubilee year, all working of the land for the need of human sustenance is forbidden. These times are set aside for the "service of God" alone. It thus becomes possible for human beings to fulfill the general mandate of God and to repair periodically the deviations from the social and ethical norm, a kind of inevitable wear and tear of the just social arrangements that God established for humanity on earth in the covenant of Noah and his sons, and to the Israelites in the covenant of Sinai. Every family returns to its ancestral inheritance; obligations that result in servitude of one person to another are cancelled; those that were sold into slavery are freed; the produce of the land, which grows of itself in the Sabbatical and Jubilee years as God's free gifts without human intervention, are distributed equally to all the land's inhabitants. (Exodus 23:10–12, Leviticus 25, Deuteronomy 15:1–18) This is the "redemption" of the land and all who dwell on it, the meaning of which is (as we said) the restoration of the proper order of life that God legislated to humanity. For God requires that there be accord between the laws of the renewal of creation, that hold sway in the cycles of the produce of the land, and the laws of ethical life that God legislated to people as families, tribes, and nations in order that they shall represent the rule of God on earth.

Indeed, according to the continuation of the narrative in Genesis, the cycle of the generations takes the form of actual generations of human individuals divided into families, tribes and nations, whose connections of origin tie them together when they settle in their lands, each nation in the ancestral land that God appointed for it so that it should survive and maintain its "garden" there, thus carrying out its part in the general task of humanity to "subdue" the land and govern it. It is important to note that with the conclusion of the creation narrative, the book of Genesis continues as a series of generational accounts — the "generations" of Adam, the generations of Noah, the generations of Abraham, the generations of Isaac and Ishmael, and the generations of Jacob and Esau. They are all connected one to the other, and so together they comprise a single book whose topic is the "generations of humanity." But they also stand apart from each other, for each nation has its own way in its own ancestral land. Thus every people has its own connection to God, under whose governance it establishes its own kingdom. (The distinction between the gods of the nations and the God of Israel on the one hand, and between both of these and idolatry on the other, is a complicated matter, and this is not the place to deal with it.)

What, then, does each "book of generations" include? First, the relation of the generations to the families, tribes, and peoples by their various names, where each patriarch is considered to be the founder of a nation, and his direct descendants are the founders of its families and tribes. Second, the famous deeds that the founding personalities performed, which are the deeds which have foundational significance in the lives of the nations, especially the covenants and their observance or violation. Unlike the cycle of Sabbaticals and Jubilees, these (with the exception of the covenant of Noah) do not involve the renewal of the order that God created human beings in his covenants, but they do involve deeds that signal progress or retreat with respect to the fulfillment of the mission with which God invested humanity. In other words, did these deeds express fidelity to that mission, or do they express rebellion that strives to establish a kingdom of idolatry, which is the opposite of the true kingdom of God and expresses man's sinful, egoistic yearning for mastery? The generational narratives include the covenant of Noah and his sons, the calling of Abraham, the trials he endured and the covenants that he concluded, which have legal implications for the future. They include also the calling of Isaac and Jacob, Joseph and Judah, the obstacles that stand in their path when they attempt to establish their people's foothold in the land through the covenants that they enacted, their successes and failures to advance the great promise that is bound up with their calling as a nation that will come forth from their progeny, and that will extend by their means also to the other peoples in whose midst they dwell.

This is also the criterion by which were chosen the stories of the history of the Israelite people in the rest of the Pentateuch and in the narratives of the early and later prophets, Ezra, Nehemiah and Chronicles. Analyzing the connection between the creation narratives and the criterion by which the historical narratives were chosen — those included in the history of the generations of the nations generally and of Israel specifically — will lead us to understand the philosophical meaning of the Biblical term *divrei ha-yamim* — literally "the matters of the days" — which the ancient Greeks (and the Western world following them) called "history." We saw above that the concept of "day" in the week of creation was established as the duration of the present in which a particular thing (*davar*) was created, generated or made, constituting a further stage in the becoming of the world. These days are worth mentioning because whatever was created, generated or made in them remains and endures, and God takes notice of it as a fundamental element of life on earth for the fulfillment of the task of humanity. The same applies to the "days" whose stories are included in the historical books of the Bible. Here too the "day" is not the calendrical unit from sunrise to sunset, but the span of an intentional action carried out from its beginning to its conclusion, an action that once performed endures, and cannot be confused with another action that corrects or furthers it. Even after it is fixed or passes, it has a progeny of deeds, such as those that further or correct what was perverted through commission of a sin, and those that spoil the "garden" of the people and the "garden" of humanity through the devolution of its sins culminating in its collapse. In this case a new beginning is made, with fresh hope for progress.

All this deserves deeper and more detailed examination of the stories themselves, which will come later. For understanding the term *divrei ha-yamim* it is worth emphasizing that we are speaking of deliberately planned deeds that add substantially to the created world or detract from it, that have a continuing effect on what follows and thus do not merely slip into the oblivion of time. In this sense God sees and knows them in the same way that He sees and knows all the stages of creation that accrue day after day, inasmuch as they give rise to one another, are based on each other, and become the archetypes of the succeeding forms in the flow of living creatures on earth, especially humanity. If during the days of creation God establishes His kingdom on heaven and earth, then in the days of the "generations" human beings — as families, tribes, and nations — establish their cultures on the foundations of the earth's resources. Therefore these too are worthy of being seen and known to God, and their human descendants are commanded to remember them in order to draw forth from them the "progeny" that will shape the image of their garden for time to come. Therefore the calendric "day" in which a foundational deed is completed that has consequences for the future — especially when we are speaking of an event or deed which reveals God's aid to His people to be redeemed from their bondage, to overcome their sins and to arrive at a new stage in the realization of their calling among the nations — this day is set aside and distinguished from other days and is set in the calendar of the year as a festival that will recur in the cycle of time. It is not a sign of what is renewed cyclically in nature and in human life as a natural phenomenon, but rather an expression of the addition and progression that takes place in culture in the march from the past to the future. Therefore on this day is recited the "new song" that is a kind of verbal memorial, fixed in the collective memory of the people and passed on from one generation to the next, as a reminder to preserve the achievement of the past in order with its help to outline the further accomplishment for the future.

Crossroads of Human History:
From Covenantal Morality to Idolatrous Mores

The generational narratives that comprise Genesis relate to the history of all nations. The first covenant, enacted directly between the Creator-God and the family of Noah, relates to all humanity. Its purpose is to lay the foundation for the ethical, social and political orders that are fitting for the "gardens" of all nations, who are commanded again — after the whole earth has been submerged in the waters of the flood — to be fruitful and multiply, to fill the earth, to govern it and to establish on it social orders by which may be prevented the destructive behavior that caused the flood, so that there will be no more need to bring on the world the punishment of annihilation. God learned the lesson of His first failure and has made His peace with a given reality that cannot be totally undone but perhaps can be reformed by stages if humanity will agree to cooperate: "The devisings of man's heart are evil from his youth." (8:21) To start the process of reform, God enacts a covenant that is the basis of a government that will prevent or at least rein in the destructive tendencies. The first principle of this covenant is a lesson learned from the story of the first murder that occurred after the expulsion from Eden, when the children of Adam and Eve started to seek their own way and to set up with their own powers the garden necessary for their sustenance.

According to the biblical narrative, the attempt to return to the reality of the lost Garden of Eden, or to establish another garden by dint of independent effort, to subdue the land and extract from it whatever is needed for human life — even with accommodation for what the earth with its limited abilities can yield for mankind without becoming depleted and desolate, and with accommodation for what mankind, with limited powers, can attain through their labor without becoming subjugated and losing the divine image that justifies their life and their dominion — this attempt became the first step on the road that led to corruption. We shall return soon to the story of Cain and Abel, who presented the challenge on the plane of interpersonal ethical relations. With respect to the covenant enacted with Noah and his sons as heads of tribes and nations, this story of the quarrel of the brothers who took two opposing paths offers the following lesson: in order to prevent the destruction of the garden that man can establish by his independent powers, and to insure that a proper life should be maintained in it for the one created in the image of God, one must prevent that most heinous of ethical sins, the sin that is the grandfather of all sins in both interpersonal relations and human-divine relations: murder. "Shedding the blood of man by man." In the Ten Commandments too, the first ethical-social imperative is: "Do not murder."

The covenant of Noah is founded on the recognition that the souls of all living beings, and especially of human beings created in the divine image, are holy, and therefore no one has the right to take the soul of another. According to the language of the covenant, the soul of the animal and the human being are identified with the blood, and therefore it is absolutely forbidden to shed human blood. (9:1–17) The basis of this prohibition on man's being created in the divine image establishes around it the absolute recognition that is at the foundation of the covenant: subordination to the authority of God who is the creator of the world. In respect of this exclusive subordination, all human beings are equal in the relationship that God has to each and every individual — all are equal before Him in the sanctity of their lives and in the application of the divine law to each of them. For all human beings are God's possessions. A man who murders his neighbor has seized jurisdiction over God's holy treasure, that cannot be waived by God who created him. Only the Creator-God has jurisdiction to take the soul of a person because He breathed it into him, but only in a just and proper manner.

The far-reaching conclusion that follows from this — one that the Sinaitic Torah draws explicitly — is that the essential opposition is not just to murder but to slavery, that turns the person himself, his life, his soul, his will, and his physical and spiritual powers into the property of another. On the basis of this legislation, that makes all human beings subordinate to the authority of the one God who created them, the book of Genesis establishes the notion of humanity. All families, tribes and nations that comprise it are the descendants of one couple: first Adam and Eve, and afterwards Noah and his family who were rescued from the flood. All human beings are kin. It is forbidden for them to kill one another, and it is forbidden for them to subjugate each other, whether as individuals or as nations. In this sense, the covenant of Noah is the universal religion on whose basis all religions are founded. It unites the descendants of all nations under the service of the God of heaven, the one God, the Eternal, the Creator who reigns over heaven and earth.

However, humanity's unity does not stand in contradiction to its destiny to spread over the whole earth and to impose its governance on it — the governance of God that it represents. Humanity is obligated to separate out into nations, each of which will establish its own special "garden" in its ancestral land. The book of Genesis assumes, though, that in the way of nature it is the nation — a kind of family of tribes, each of whose members speak the same language and are naturally disposed to see and know each other as kin and treat each other as neighbors — that is the largest social collective in which it is possible to maintain a common government based on covenantal ethical values. Genesis presents this as a fact without giving any explanation. However, as a basis for maintaining covenantal morality the Torah's legislation added to the prohibition of murder the following positive injunctions: "Honor your father and your mother, that you may long endure on the land which the Lord your God is giving you." (Ex. 20:12) "You shall not take vengeance or bear a grudge against your kinsfolk. Love your neighbor as yourself." (Lev. 19:18) This explains how the establishment of human society on the basis of nations that develop from families, ancestral houses and tribes is possible — through the honoring of parents and the love of neighbors that unites human families and builds nations, and that is how they are maintained.

The biblical story condemns, however, the aspiration that flows from the will to power, to unite all humanity as one political power on the basis of "the same language and the same speech." (Genesis 11:1) From the story of the Tower of Babel we learn that the aspiration to establish human autarchy that would seem to insure the conditions of the independent survival of the human race on earth and thus restore the reality of the Garden of Eden — this aspiration constitutes a rebellion against the will of God, that humanity should spread out over the whole earth and separate into nations. From it developed afterwards the ambition to try to ascend to heaven to wrest sovereignty from God's hands. This aspiration is a terrible stumbling-block to human beings themselves, because they are setting up a tyrannical regime that will end up oppressing and enslaving them under its yoke. They will no longer be the subjects of God, but of a tyrannical regime that they have set up with their own hands. The story of the Tower of Babel does not spell out this aspect of the quest for human power, but we will deal with it later in connection with the story of Joseph and the Exodus. The story of the Tower of Babel comes to tell us of God's will that humanity should spread out over the whole earth, and it concludes with the confounding of the rebellious plan. The confusion of languages signifies the unraveling of the internal solidarity that was the basis of the autarchical regime, and then God's design comes to fruition: each people takes charge of its own land, develops its own language, cultivates its own garden. Each people establishes its own covenant and nation-state. The logic of the story requires that the covenant that was enacted between God and Noah and his sons shall be the basis of all these covenants, but the original family covenant included only general principles, whereas nation-states require detailed covenants that organize all domains of activity and social relations, as per the example of the covenant that was enacted between God and His people at Sinai. According to God's plan — that requires the separation of the peoples and their independent existence in their own lands — every people requires a covenant that is uniquely its own and appropriate to its life-conditions, its needs, and its goals in its land.

Splitting the one covenant into as many covenants as the nations of the earth creates a variety of relations to God, with whom these covenants are enacted. Indeed, according to the narrative in Genesis, each nation established its covenant with its own designated god. It is surprising at first sight that this view, which reflects historical reality after the fact, is not brought as a criticism and is not presented as a contradiction to the view that the heavenly God, who created the world, is the one and only sovereign, and that all humanity are subordinate to Him. A consideration of the distinction we drew earlier between the generic-functional meaning of the word "god" and the absolutely individual signification of the proper name YHWH will help resolve the surprise. We recall that in the story in the first chapter of Genesis of the placement of the heavenly lights in the firmament, their task was "to give light to the earth, and to rule in the day and the night, and to separate light from darkness." (1:17–18) The task of ruling is identified in these short sentences with the task of light and seeing, with distingishing between light and darkness, which is also the distinction between good and evil, and thus the providence over the orders of life that hold sway as the rule of law and order that God ordains for creation. This is the conceptual basis for the hierarchy of domains through which is later drawn the distinction between the gods of the nations that exist under the rule of the heavenly bodies that were appointed over them, and the God of Abraham and his progeny whom the Creator-God chose to be His special people. That is the people that will preserve through its ways of life in its land the testimony to the direct sovereignty of the God of heaven on earth. Thus the people that takes its descent from Abraham is established as the central axis of the biblical narrative of the generations of humanity.

How, though, are the gods of the nations distinguished from the idols, whom it is a sin to worship? We shall consider this philosophical-ethical distinction in depth when we turn our attention to the fact that in the biblical narrative the Israelites are also accused of idolatry. Not only when they worship the gods of their neighbor-nations in place of the one God who entered into a covenant with them, but also when they are apparently worshiping the God who brought them out of Egypt, but in a sinful way, in a way that includes "taking His name in vain." The proof-case of this is the story of the Golden Calf. The sin is expressed outwardly in the casting of the molten statue, which Aaron identified with the God who brought the people out of Egypt, in contravention of the stringent prohibition against making a statue or image. But a close reading of the details of the story reveals that this sin committed by Moses' brother Aaron does not bring about his being punished. It is considered a serious error but not a brazen sin. On the contrary. Aaron's defense, in which he pleaded that he acted in the only way that he knew to pacify the disorderly people who had taken leave of their senses because of Moses' prolonged absence — this defense was accepted.

Moses' anger was first kindled when God told him that his people had "dealt corruptly." The intention is to the behavior of the people described in the words, "the people sat down to eat and drink, and they rose to make merry." (Exodus 32:6) The Hebrew *le-tzaḥek* implies dances with lewd connotations. Afterwards, when Moses has come down the mountain with his assistant Joshua, Moses hears the "sound of song" of the celebrating people, and he sees the calf and the dancing. (32:19) All these appear to Moses as an absolute deterioration of the morale and ethical fiber of the people, that hold it together and stand as its sole bulwark against its enemies: "Moses saw that the people were out of control — since Aaron had let them get out of control — so that they were a derision to their enemies." (32:25) It is worth noting the linguistic similarity between the word *pera'oh* ("he let them get out of control") and *Par'oh* — Pharaoh, who represents the people's enemies, whose challenge renders it mandatory for them to deploy their full moral strength. This is the sin that brings Moses to impose the most severe punishment that he has inflicted on his people, in order to prevent the even more severe punishment awaiting them from God: destruction of the people in the wilderness, probably at the hands of its "enemies," because that is the likely result of their moral deterioration.

Idolatry is recognized, then, in the character of the forms of worship arranged around the gods of the nations, their moral connotation, and the status ascribed to the idols as instruments of a certain kind of rule. In the story of the calf, the moral degeneracy of the idolatrous worship stands out. Indeed, if we consider Egyptian idolatry as it is depicted in the Exodus narrative — in the contest between YHWH, mediated by Moses and Aaron, and the reigning world-view of Pharaoh and his magicians — we can consider its ethical and political aspects.

Egypt, like Babylon of the story of the Tower of Babel and like Sodom and Gomorrah whose upheaval is recounted, is a land that lives by the water from the river (in contrast to Canaan which "soaks up its water from the rains of heaven" [Deuteronomy 11:11]). Situated on the banks of the Nile, Egypt is a land that is to all appearances blessed with the conditions required for establishing a garden similar to the Eden from which Adam and Eve were banished. Eden was also located at the source of the mighty rivers (the Tigris and Euphrates) where natural abundance is assured. The dream of Eden to which people are inclined to dream of returning as of yore, and the land of the Nile blessed with its relatively secure resources, nevertheless differ somewhat in that the resources of the latter are not indeed totally immune to occasional stoppage and calamity. The Joseph story in Genesis tells that Egypt once experienced seven years of drought, that brought it to the point of famine. And according to the exodus narrative, the ten plagues originated first of all from the Nile, then from the dust of the affected soil, from the pasture-land surrounding it, and from the locusts and hail that descended from heaven.

To these must be added the envious human enemies contiguous to Egypt, from whom it was necessary for them to protect themselves, preferably through conquest and oppression, just as the Pharaoh who "knew not Joseph" took preemptive action against the Israelites who were likely to ally themselves with Egypt's enemies in case of war. Second, and more essentially, the "garden" that was planted not by God had to be established and maintained continually by grueling hard labor, with sophisticated tools, through division of labor, with the help of strict planning, organization and leadership that impose discipline and absolute concentration on the work, in other words, by means of power not only over the natural resources, but over the most important resource — human labor. In fact, power over human labor is power over man himself. Through sophisticated planning and effective implementation — in the manner that Joseph operated in Egypt when he struggled with the danger of famine — it is possible to create an administrative framework that is authoritative for this purpose — at least relatively so. We recall that the internal and external dangers represented by the plagues and enemies are real and long-standing. They pose a challenge to the power of the government, but this also raises the real possibility that it will grow more rigid until it falls apart because of internal rebellion. The price of authority of the whole system is that tyranny that enslaves all living individuals to its purposes and turns them into slaves. The authority is embodied in the ruling class — Pharaoh and his magicians. They seem to benefit from an Edenic reality, but even they — as we learn from Pharaoh, who hardens his heart even as he sees Egypt collapsing under him — are enslaved to their addiction to power, as power becomes for them not only their goal in life, but a compulsive need.

This internal contradiction that is embodied in the logic of the tyrannical state — this is finally Egypt's undoing. That is the secret of Moses' success in bringing his people out of the clutches of the unraveling authority, but for our purpose it also reveals the essence of idolatry, that seeks to maintain the social-political outlook of the tyrannical state. Pharaoh apotheosizes himself as the son of the Egyptian gods, and his magicians are the priests of those gods, who are identified with those forces of nature on which Egypt's sustenance depends: the Nile, the sun, the moon. Together they see themselves and represent themselves to their people not just as the "servants" of the gods, but as the embodiment of their power, which is the power that justifies their position of authority in the eyes of their people. In their ceremonies they pretend to prove through their magical acts that they control those powers and know how to activate them at will.

This claim is at issue in the contest between Moses on the one hand and Pharaoh and his magicians on the other, a contest that is conducted through actions rather than words. In this confrontation the question is reiterated: Who really rules over the forces of nature on which Egypt depends for its sustenance, and on which its state is established — Pharaoh and his magicians "who performed these actions with their devices" — in other words, who pretend to be masters of magical knowledge, or maybe the God of heaven who is the true Lord? In contrast to the magicians who made a show of producing the "signs" by their own powers, Moses emphasizes that it is not he who brings the plagues but the Creator-God, the one who reveals Himself as "I Am that I Am." God rules the forces of nature. He also rules over the gods of Egypt whom the magicians have turned into idols. The prophetic irony that is conspicuous in the story is pronounced in the climax when the Egyptian magicians use their magical knowledge to enhance the plagues that emerge from the Nile — the god of Egypt — against their own persons, until they admit that the matter is not in their hands but "it is the finger of God." (Exodus 8:15)

According to this description, idolatry consists in relating to the gods who represent the forces of nature — which in the view of the biblical narrator indeed act and rule in the world, but subject to the will of the God of heaven who made them and delegated them — as if to fateful powers that man can control by his knowledge and impose his will on them. Indeed, it is the purpose of idolatry to justify the reigning principle of the slave-states, based on violence and wickedness, and to claim for the tyrannical authority an absolute divine mandate. This is of course an imagined mandate, but it achieves its objectives so long as the citizens that are subordinated to it believe in it. This is the reason why God "hardens" Pharaoh's heart. It is His purpose to break the idolatrous delusion decisively and to free the Israelites from fearing it. Afterwards, when Moses has brought his people forth from physical and spiritual servitude, he will establish the alternate authority based on the principles of the Noahide covenant. It follows that this was the fateful crossroads at which humanity stood after the expulsion from the Garden of Eden, facing the task to establish its garden and to bear responsibility for its life and its governance of the world.

We return now to the story of Cain and Abel, which represents the parting of ways in its interpersonal, ethical-political aspect, in the same way that the story of Adam's and Eve's sin poses the problem of conjugal relations that is the basis of the family, the fundamental unit of social and cultural life. The story of the first brotherly feud deals with the question: What brings man, created in the divine image and likeness, to commit the most heinous social sin? As we said before, human society is said to be founded on the basis of familial love, and here from that very source springs forth the most terrible hatred, that brings about the most destructive act, the act that stands in the most absolute contradiction to man's status as one created in the image of God! If good is identified with life and evil with death, then murder is absolute evil. Yet it is precisely man, who is created in the divine image, who brings murder into the world, and murder breaks out precisely within the family that gives life to its members, and precisely between brothers who are children to the same parents, brothers who are supposed to love each other and to honor their parents and to obey them lovingly!

It is important to note that the outbreak of murder within the family does not disturb the biblical outlook that the family is the fundamental unit of covenantal society based on love. But precisely for that reason the question is posed without evasion or concealment. As we saw, the story of the Noahide covenant attributes the wickedness that brings about murder to "the *yetzer*[9] of man's heart" that is "evil from his youth," and this is said specifically of "man's heart," of the one who was created in the image and likeness of God. Why? Is man's *yetzer*, that arises in the context of the animal characteristics that are perpetuated in him, manifested only in him and uniquely special to him from among all the animals to which he is similar, who also are born from parents and perpetuate themselves in flocks? If we examine the urges themselves — the urge for self-protection, the sexual urge, the acquisitive urge, the urge for power and aggrandizement — these urges are manifest in all animal species similar to humanity. In them, too, we see that these urges sometimes bring them to war and even to war-to-the-death. Nevertheless, the urges of the other animals are

---

[9]   *Yetzer* — This key word means "devisings, product" in its Biblical context and "urge, libido" in its rabbinic sense. In the former meaning, the human being is wholly free, but it is an observed fact that the product (*yetzer*) of the human heart is evil continually, from youth on. In the rabbinic view, the human being is subject to temptation or urges from a hidden source — the *yetzer* — and must devise strategies to resist it. Schweid's analysis here is an integration and mediation of these two approaches. See Genesis 6:5, 8:21. (LL)

not regarded by the thoughtful observer as falling into the category of evil, because they lack the element of conscious deliberation and considered decision that raises these actions to the ethical plane. On the contrary, the urges of animals are good because they serve them in the natural struggle for survival. Through them they preserve themselves to the best of their ability, and thus they preserve their species. Not so the human being, who was created in the image of God and who must live in a human family and in a human society. The animal urges can be a stumbling-block for him if he does not know how to control them and direct them, through conscious choice based on ethical deliberation.

The observation that the *yetzer* of man's heart is "evil from his youth" implies this distinction. The sexual urge of Adam and Eve was evil in their first experience as a couple, and it brought them to the sin of mutual exploitation and domination. This sin later generated enmity, which was perpetuated as long as they did not learn to control their urge for the sake of the objective for which it was created: siring offspring and raising them. The same applies to the urges for individual life and survival, which prevent a person from collaborating to form the "garden" that is necessary for collective survival under the harsh conditions of earthly existence. It is therefore incumbent on human beings to learn to control their urges that can lead them to the most serious of sins that can bring about their ruin. This is the deeper lesson of the story of the first brotherly quarrel that culminated in murder.

In the narrative of human history, Adam's and Eve's two sons, Cain and Abel, represent the first generation that had to grapple with the problem of existence outside the Garden of Eden. Cain, whose mother boasted of him "I have gotten a man from the Lord," (Genesis 4:1) chooses to be a tiller of the soil (4:2). Abel, whose name is given no significance, and did not inspire the same pride in Eve as did her firstborn son, chooses to be a keeper of sheep. These are two ways to live off the land after the expulsion from Eden. If we examine the choices of the brothers in light of the lessons of the Eden narrative, it is clear that Cain, the "man" in whom Eve takes pride, is the son who followed seriously the divine injunction, for already in Eden Adam and Eve were appointed "to work the land." The only difference is that with the expulsion from Eden the land was cursed and the labor of tilling it had become hard and burdensome. Nevertheless, Cain accepted the judgment and went out to till it, while Abel preferred to live as if the reality of Eden still survived, as his name indicates.[10] He preferred to live from what the land gave on its own, and to be content with it. The tangible advantage of this was that he did not subordinate himself to the land and its toil. Cain knew, though, that right was on his side, for he was the one who was carrying out the will of God and of his parents. But "after some days" — when Cain reaped his harvest and Abel's flocks delivered their young — when the two brothers brought their offerings to God, each from the blessing with which he had been blessed, the Lord showed favor to Abel and his offering, "but to Cain and his offering He showed no favor." (4:5)

The art of the biblical narrative allows the reader to probe deeper and to discover for himself what is the significance of Cain's penchant for evil, for the story itself does not elaborate on this. Perhaps we should start with the question, how did the two brothers know whose offering was preferred? The answer is suggested in Cain's angry reaction, namely that his face fell. It is likely that Abel performed his sacrifice and returned to his flocks cheerful and joyous. He felt that his works had been blessed, and he received the return on his labors that he had hoped for. That is how a person knows that God has heeded his offering, for if his works have not been blessed he knows that God has paid no attention to him. But Abel felt that his works had been blessed. He did not complain about God, nor about his parents, nor about his brother Cain. Cheerful and joyous, he celebrated what the land had yielded of its own accord, and what the flocks had bestowed on him of their fleece and milk (for according to the creation narrative eating meat was forbidden from the outset, and Abel could only present an offering from his flock to God).

On the other hand, Cain — whose name (which means "blade of steel") suggests not only the meaning of "acquisition" that his mother derived, but also that he was a master of tools that can be used either to work the soil or as weapons for defense against enemies and also for murder — Cain was not satisfied with what he had accomplished, and he had his complaints. A tiller of the soil hopes to extract from it by his labor more than it would have yielded by itself — a lot more. It was for that purpose that Cain invested much toil and "canny" ingenuity in devising his tool-kit, but the results fell short of expectation. Hence his fierce envy of his brother. Abel had not wearied himself, or hoped

---

10   The name Abel (*Hevel*) in Hebrew means "breath," "wind," "vanity." See below — "Abel passed away like the wind, without leaving an impression." (p. 89)

for more than he received, and was satisfied; he was not consumed by worry for the morrow, or concerned that someone would steal the property that he did not have. That is why he was so cheerful and joyous. But Cain refused to live like Abel. He was not modest in his desires, and he wanted to provide security for the future; he aspired to unlimited abundance. But he achieved neither security nor abundance, or maybe he achieved a little and was not satisfied. Hence his jealousy of his celebrating brother. It is even likely that he was angry for if Abel had only invested his energies in the field in which the one tended his sheep and the other plowed and sowed in order to increase their yield, they could have achieved together what Cain was unable to achieve on his own.

For all these reasons, God did not favor Cain. We now compare the story of Cain to that of Noah. Noah was also a "tiller of the soil" (9:20) but his name[11] indicates that he was easygoing with others and with himself, working the land but walking wholeheartedly with his God and satisfied with what the land gave him, for that constituted his "righteousness." God favored Noah and even extended grace to him because he was righteous in his generations, whereas He said to Cain:

Why are you distressed, and why is your face fallen? Surely, if you do right, there is uplift; but if you do not do right, sin couches at the door; its urge is toward you, but you can be its master. (4:6–7)

What, though, did Cain "say" after this to his brother Abel when they were in the field? Here the text is not explicit but only suggests that he said something, i.e. that he started an argument that ignited the jealousy that was simmering inside him, though it was clear that it had been simmering even before he brought his offering. Sin was already crouching at the door then, and that is another reason why God did not favor his offering. The result was murder, accompanied by Cain's piercing plea against the divine judgment: "Am I my brother's keeper?" (4:9) As if he cried out in lament: "Was my brother my keeper? Did he assist me in my labor so that we might achieve together what I could not achieve on my own? What do I owe him?" But even in this evasive reply, which reveals his sin through the attempt to conceal it, as Adam and Eve had tried to conceal theirs — even in this reply,

---

[11] Hebrew *noah* means "rest, relief" in Biblical Hebrew; "easygoing" is one of its many meanings in modern Hebrew.

Cain knows that he is indeed his brother's keeper, and has betrayed his responsibility. Murder has no justification. There is no forgiveness for murder, because it is impossible to undo it and its consequences as if it had never happened. The blood cries out from the ground. Cain himself knows what God is telling him:

> Hark, your brother's blood cries out to Me from the ground! Therefore, you shall be cursed from the ground, which opened its mouth to receive your brother's blood from your hand. If you till the soil, it shall no longer yield its strength to you. You shall become a ceaseless wanderer on earth." (4:10–12)

According to the divine decree, Cain has forfeited his right to be a tiller of the soil. The land, out of which God formed the body of the human being, must refuse to provide its strength to Cain the murderer. He has betrayed it. He has abused his responsibility and therefore he must hide himself in shame not only from God who judges him, but also from himself.

But this is not the end of the story, because despite his awful sin, Cain was the man who chose the right way, to be a tiller of the soil, the founder of the first "garden" after the expulsion from the Garden of Eden, whereas Abel passed away like the wind, without leaving an impression on the earth. Therefore God gave Cain, who bears his punishment by acknowledging his guilt, protection against vengeance. Moreover, Cain, the man of tools, marries and begets Enoch who built the first city. (4:17) From Cain's line descended Lamech, who like Cain was guilty of murder — even double murder — but his descendants invented several important crafts that are still basic for maintaining the human "garden": "Jabal was the ancestor of those who dwell in tents and amidst herds; his brother Jubal was the ancestor of all who play the lyre and the pipe; and it was Tubal-Cain who forged all implements of copper and iron." (4:20–22) It follows from this that learning the lesson from the first moral failure, which may have been inevitable from the outset, can bring about reformation. But even in his success, man should not trust in himself, for as God said to Cain, "sin couches at the door; its urge is toward you, but you can be its master."

The moral to be learned from this as a lesson for the future progress of human civilization is two-sided and complex. On the one hand we are bidden to learn from it what motivates human beings to fashion their "garden" on earth, and on the other hand we are bidden to learn what brings them to destroy it with all their might. The libidinal instinct that motivates people in their activity is revealed in full force in their creative labors but also in their murderous actions. What stands at the basis of the force peculiar to human beings, that is manifested not only in their dealings with strangers but even more vividly in their dealings with their closest and dearest? We see that this is the urge for acquisition[12], the desire to possess not only what is truly necessary for a person for his living today, but also what might be useful to him tomorrow or the next day. This is an appetite in which possession itself bestows the pleasure of power, mastery and control. From this appetite is born envy[13], which is the desire to possess and have mastery of everything that a person lacks, precisely because it belongs to someone else. Most likely for this very reason a person tends to be jealous of those closest to him, whom he needs and is obligated to love, with whom he must share what he has acquired by his labor and talent for the sake of his life, his happiness, and his prosperity with them: his brother, his spouse, his parents and children. Hence the severity with which the biblical narrative and legislation deal with the passion of envy, that indeed incites people to achievement, but if left uncontrolled ends up destroying everything.

As we said, the vital lesson that is learned from the story of Cain and Abel is incorporated in the covenant of Noah and his children as the foundation of covenantal morality. The same applies to the Ten Commandments (Exodus 20:13): the prohibitions against murder, adultery, theft and bearing false witness against one's "neighbor" are prohibitions of the sins whose deeper source is envy. The legislation of the Ten Commandments thus addresses them directly, and it concludes with the double prohibition: "You shall not covet your neighbor's house; you shall not covet your neighbor's wife, or his male or female slave, or his ox or his ass, or anything that is your neighbor's." (20:14) The clear reason is that envy — the desire that something which your neighbor enjoys should be yours and not his —

[12]   Acquisition: *kinyan*, from the same linguistic root as *kayin* (Cain).
[13]   Envy: *kin'ah*, possibly a distant etymological cousin of *kayin* (Cain). But the 16th century commentator Ephraim Luntshitz noted that Ecclesiastes 4:4 suggests that Abel may not have been free of envy himself in his dealings with his brother: "I have also noted that all labor and skillful enterprise come from men's envy of each other — this, too, is vanity (*hevel* = Abel)!" (LL — see *Keli Yekar* on Genesis 4.)

is the source of jealousy, which begets all those sins that tear and fray the delicate fabric of relationships which is the basis for the continued existence of human society.

Vision and Fulfillment: Pattern of a Second Beginning

From reflecting on the historical narrative of the creation of heaven and earth, the doings of Adam and Eve and their descendants, and the generation of Noah, we put together a developmental framework that reflects the goal of human history according to the biblical narrative: to fulfill God's vision of creation wherein the "heavens and the earth and all their array" (Genesis 2:1) should stand on their own as God desired and intended in His plan, for their own good and for the glory of God's kingdom. The first chapter of Genesis describes the divine vision through its actualization in the divine actions of creation and making. Yet even here when mankind is created in the image and likeness of God, it is hinted that the earthly hosts — the animals and other creatures — are liable to degenerate and not stand firm as God had desired, unless they are regenerated each day from the chaos to which they return and subside in the nighttime, and unless God appoints a ruler from among them in whom will pulsate an independent ability to advance himself and the other earthly creatures in fulfillment of the divine vision — the human being.

As we saw above, already in the second chapter of Genesis there is offered a second beginning of the creation narrative, similar to the previous and yet different. This beginning relates to the problem of the fulfillment of the divine vision by viewing earthly reality through it. In this view, it becomes clear that only the heavens, their host, and the earth itself — the land and sea — take a stand and persist in being as God wished and intended for them, whereas the earthly host is waiting for the blessing of the rains that come from heaven, and for the labor of the human being so that they can fulfill their being according to the plan of creation. It also becomes clear that the human being is indeed graced with the spiritual ability to collaborate with his creator in bringing forth the creatures of the earth (= *adamah*, for which Adam is named). It is he who knows how to call them by names that define their essence, the names by which they will be known not only to humans but to God. (Genesis 2:19–20) He knows to call himself "Adam," i.e. the Earthling;

and he knows to call his wife — after he has known her as a helpmate befitting for herself and for him — "Eve" (*havva*), for she is the mother of all life (*hai*). Yet it becomes clear in all this that the human being is not able to maintain himself at the spiritual-moral level and in the task that his creator intended for him, and so his mission is directed first of all at himself — he must create the conditions necessary for him, and to advance his spiritual capabilities and his morals so that he may be worthy of his creation in the divine image and worthy to rule over the creatures of the earth.

With this as background, there enters the historical narrative another concept that becomes formative for it: the "test" or "probation." This notion is also hinted at in the creation narrative. After the creation or making of each thing, God examines it to see: is it good? Did it turn out to be what God wanted and intended? Only when God sees and knows that "they were good," does He bless the new creatures, by giving them the power to be fruitful and multiply, thus insuring the survival of the species on their own. However it is in the second chapter, which deals with the creation of Adam and Eve and their education for their special task, that the concept of "test" in the full sense takes center stage in the concerted effort to fulfill the vision of creation. The test becomes the central theme of the story of the history of the first human beings and their descendants. The first test which God set for Adam and Eve consisted of the "tree of life" and the "tree of knowledge of good and evil" that God planted in the Garden of Eden, along with the prohibition against eating from the "tree of knowledge" that was a delight to the eyes and enticing to eat from its fruit; not to mention the role of the cunning serpent, embodying the awareness of temptation, who presents to the couple, who do not yet know the substance of their task though they have heard tell of it, the fatal challenge.

This test has a double purpose. God wants to know whether the man and his wife are "good" enough to carry out their mission on earth. At the same time, he wants Adam and Eve to come to know themselves through this test, so that they will understand their purpose and learn to identify with it. It is clear that the second purpose is the main purpose. A close reading of the story of the first sin will bear out that God knew from the outset that the couple would not pass the test: their sexuality and earthly-libidinal sensuality is ripened, but the knowledge of its meaning and purpose beyond the enjoyment and pleasure that it brings — namely, to procreate and bear children, to raise and educate them in a relationship of mutual respect — this knowledge has not come to fruition yet. Therefore they will disobey the divine command and sin, not against God alone but against themselves. Only when they attain the awareness of death, that is connected to the satisfaction of sexual desire, will they understand the importance and significance of continuing life through their progeny. And only through experiencing sin will a person learn what sin is, and what is the path of right that stands in contrast to it, not in the manner of hearing a received lesson but the intimate knowledge that comes from direct contact. Only when one has been enticed by the intoxicating pleasure of the senses, the Edenic bliss that is pleasure for its own sake without thought of its price, arising from mutual egoistic exploitation — only then will a person learn what is the responsibility of sexual love that is intended to bring life to the world, and continuity of the enterprise of life and creativity. From this one will learn also the mutual relation of marital partners who are intended to be helpmeets for each other in raising their children, and one will know what is the labor that devolves from responsible parenthood and its sense of obligation. In other words, only from the experience of sin of the "innocent" (who is not innocent in the ethical sense) and the naked[14] (who is rather cunning, seductive and exploitative) — only thus shall the members of the first couple learn to pass the second test and thus atone for their sin and fulfill their mission. Had they preferred to eat from the "tree of life" and live forever in their Edenic state, they would not have come into the world or fulfilled the assignment implicit in their blessing: to be fruitful and multiply, to fill the earth, subdue it and rule over it.

From the idea of a test whose purpose is pedagogic and teleological comes the corollary that completes the pattern of the historical narratives of the Bible: Every later test will result in success to a certain degree, but will end ultimately in failure, which will stand as evidence that the gap between the vision of divine creation and the ability of earth's children, as individuals, families, tribes and peoples to achieve it through their moral, social, and political efforts has not been bridged. Nevertheless, it will have achieved something positive that may be viewed as "righteousness" or in rabbinic language "merit," that gives promise of another test that is like a second beginning, a corrective beginning, a beginning that can reduce the gap from both sides: from

---

14   Schweid here plays on the homonymity of *'erom* (naked) and *'arum* (cunning), a central verbal motif of the Genesis Eden story (see Genesis 2:25, 3:1 and 3:7).

the side of God, who loves His creatures despite their weakness, who understands the limitations of human ability and reduces His expectations; and from the side of human beings, who show more self-knowledge, more responsibility and devotion, more fortitude and perseverance in their personal education and the fulfillment of their mission.

After their sin and punishment, Adam and Eve have the chance of a second beginning, turning from the visionary to the realistic, to become a family that raises its offspring under the conditions of the earthly existence that was intended for them. Together they produce the son whose name proclaims "I have gotten a man from the Lord" — Cain, who was ready to accept the assignment to work the land. Cain is also tested by a divine trial: he chose the right path, but God did not favor his offering. He failed and sinned. But he, like his parents, was also given a chance for a second, restorative beginning: he raises a family, begets and raises the founders of the first city, and in the succeeding generations his descendants initiate the crafts that help build the earthly "garden."

But the full pattern of the historical probation-narrative — partial success, failure, punishment, a second restorative beginning — is depicted in the story of Noah and his sons. The full development of this pattern is recognizable in that this story, more than the story of Cain and Abel, departs from mythic-symbolic formulation and approaches closer to a genuine historical narrative, depicting a world of reality that is close to our everyday experience.

The story of Noah grows out of the narrative of the preceding generations, that of the descendants of Cain and the descendants of Seth, the third son of Adam and Eve who was born after the episode of Cain and Abel and apparently learned its lesson. The second beginning given to Adam's progeny succeeds insofar as the "garden" is established on earth in accordance with God's will. The climax of success is associated with the generations of Enosh ("at that time they began to invoke YHWH by name" — Genesis 4:26) and Enoch ("Enoch walked with God; then he was no more, for God took him" — 5:24). But success expressed in earthly prosperity eventually leads to moral and political corruption, and the deterioration is very swift. God saw "how great was man's wickedness on earth, and how every plan devised by his mind was nothing but evil all the time. And the Lord regretted that He had made man on earth..." (6:5–6) In great sadness He decides to wipe out the human being that he created together with all the terrestrial animals, whom he was appointed to represent and to rule over them. But God's sadness testifies that despite His deep regret that He created humanity and breathed His spirit into them — making them His children — His love for them has not been quenched. God sees that even though humanity as a whole has become corrupt, there remains one man who has stood the test:

> Noah found favor with the Lord. This is the line of Noah — Noah was a righteous man; he was blameless in his age; Noah walked with God... (6:8–9)

Precisely because all other humans had sinned but Noah had not sinned, this man was especially precious to his Creator and found great favor with Him. God does not release all humanity from their punishment, but by the merit of this one single righteous person who found favor in God's eyes, the human species is given a chance at a second restorative beginning.

The story of Noah and his sons is a second beginning of the entire creation narrative, despite (or because of) its transition from the mythic plane to the historic plane. The flood returns the earth to the primeval chaos of the first creation: the waters under the earth and the waters descending from heaven burst forth from both directions, combining and covering the land. All the land creatures are wiped away from it. But Noah, who thus becomes the second Adam, is saved in the ark that he was commanded to build, and in it he saves all the species of land animals with him, for he is their choicest, their representative and their ruler. Like Adam, Noah has no independent existence without an obligatory relationship to them: the human being bears responsibility not only to himself, but to the whole biosphere of which he is a part!

When the flood is over and the waters abate and return to their sources, the dry land appears, the fruit trees that bear seed (the olive!) return to life, and the grasses sprout and provide food to earth's creatures from the earth — or the creation that had been submerged is renewed, and Noah and his sons are "born" from the ark like newborns. They start over the story of Adam and Eve with the hope that this time it will be successful, and indeed, this time it is the return of the natural descendants of Adam and the natural descendents of the first animals. This is not their mythological creation, but their actual creation. Noah also plants a garden — he, the tiller of the soil, and not God — after the reestablishment of the earthly covenant between him and God.

This is the second beginning of this time, and we have already seen that God — who regretted the creation of man, but regretted also His tragic decision to do away with him utterly — has made his peace with reality. The new divine maturity is expressed in His realistic recognition that "the *yetzer* of man's heart is evil from his youth," and therefore it is necessary to set up a curb to the human *yetzer* through laws enforced by a political institution. God promises to Noah and his children that the flood will not be repeated, but in return He requires a government possessed of obligatory authority, based on divine mandate, to put an end to human moral degeneracy. This government will be established through the aid of laws, whose transgression shall result in punishment. This is the source of the hope that the gap between the divine vision and human ability to fulfill it can be reduced. However, the continuation of the story teaches us that granting authority to human government can result in the rule of men who see governmental power as their prerogative, and that is the corruption of idolatry.

The parallel between the story of Noah and that of the creation is complete. It continues also through the story of the fruit of the "tree of knowledge of good and evil." This time the tree is the vine, in other words the vineyard that Noah planted for himself, whereupon he made wine and drank himself into a state of intoxication and oblivion. (Genesis 9:20-21) This is the joy of the imagined return to the lost Paradise — the joy of fulfillment of the dream of the human animal — to live in happiness in the sense of full surrender to one's desires, utter satiety, absolute sensual pleasure and enjoyment in a never-ending present. This promises liberation from cares and anxieties, from responsibility to oneself and the other, to the point of losing all shame before the one who will see him in the expectation of obtaining his care and leadership. Noah the righteous, who merited and took on the probative test bound up with saving the human and animal species and passed it, reaps his reward in this manner and fails. Thus he realizes the danger of egoistic corruption that lies in wait as a result of success. It is liable to bring him to profanation and degradation of the divine image that is in him.

Noah's punishment comes to him through his son Ham, who found the opportunity to vent the feelings of jealousy and malice that he harbored toward his father. He gets back at him and shames the sexuality from which he was born. Thus he descends to a lower moral depth than his father, whose moral failure involved no malicious act. The moral failure of Ham, the father of Canaan, represents (according to the biblical story) the purest expression of man's evil urge that is "evil from his youth." From it comes idolatry of the malicious, reprobate, Amalekite kind, that finds pleasure in evil for its own sake, drawing on its own libidinal urge. Hence the curse laid on him and his son Canaan, to whom the biblical story attributes participation in the sin. But the two other sons of Noah, the firstborn Shem and the younger Japheth, passed the test. They had compassion for their father and were careful to preserve his honor after he had disgraced himself, and their kindness perpetuates their father's righteousness. By their merit was resumed the expansion of the human race over the face of the earth to establish their gardens as they had been commanded.

But the pattern repeats itself. After fortune smiled on the human race and they accumulated might and power, there started the rebellion documented in the Tower of Babel story (Genesis 11:1–9). The Hamite-Canaanite idolatry came to power again as before the Flood, and nevertheless God stood by His promise to Noah — not to bring on humanity the punishment of annihilation, so the punishment for this rebellion is the downfall of the offending kingdom through the destructive logic of its own wickedness. The citizens of the kingdom who aspire to power through the might of their unity, undo it when they have arrived at their goal. The egoistic motivation that united them becomes a divisive factor when they fight for their share of the power. This is the meaning of the confusion of tongues. The ironic result was that God's plan to disperse humanity throughout the earth in order to rule it in justice and equity was fulfilled not by the will of these people, but despite it: the mutual hostility that was generated among them brought about the dispersion of the nations, each in its own land. But the motivating force continued to be the appetite for supremacy and the sinful idolatry of power, which did not find its satisfaction in Shinar. The result was thus an increase in the gap between the divine vision of creation and the power and readiness of human beings to fulfill it.

This time, too, a second restorative opportunity had to come from the one individual who stood fast in his righteousness like Noah, except that the task laid on him would be immeasurably greater. As the sinful idolatrous kingdoms did not disappear but remained strong and do-minant, the chosen individual would have to leave them and establish a regime that was different in its entire substance. It would be a regime that would realize the vision of God at creation and within which God would dwell, thus demonstrating to a humanity sinking into idolatry that God is the true ruler in heaven and on earth. The righteous person on whom the task rested to save the future of humanity must therefore withdraw from it in order to realize the vision on his own, and through his exemplary realization he will restore it and lead it back toward improvement.

From the standpoint of the Creator-God, this will be an additional step of reduction of the gap between the vision and the human ability to realize it. God renounces His aspiration to raise all humanity in a single stroke to the moral-religious level that He expects of them, and He chooses instead to establish from the seed of His only lover a single people that shall be educated to be God's "special treasure": the host in whose midst God will appear as king in His world. But has He not raised the bar of expectations of this chosen individual and special nation above what can be expected of any human being? Surely he will have to put them through extraordinary probationary trials in order to educate them and prepare them for their task, and surely the lesson of the successes and failures of Noah and his descendants will require of God and His chosen ones to exhibit much greater historical patience than was manifested in the establishment of the covenant with Noah! Both God and His chosen Abraham and his descendants to come know that the vision will not be realized in the near future, not in their generation and not in the next. The road will be long, and every stage will be attained only when the time is ripe.

In order to encourage his chosen lovers, God establishes covenants with them and promises them prosperity and worldly happiness in the future, after they fulfill their mission. But He is not shy about warning them that the promises will be fulfilled in the distant future if they stand firm in their obligations to follow God's ways and fulfill His commandments. The highest quality required from them, however, is faith. They are trained in it through their frequent probative trials, and it is the central lesson to be drawn from the stories of the patriarchs in Genesis and from the story of the Exodus from Egypt in the rest of the books of the Pentateuch: faith in the fulfillment of God's promises in the agreements that He made with them. Even if the time be long, even if the obstacles are many and great, even if by the circumstances of the present the chances for fulfillment of the promises seem nil, they should still know: if they stand fast by their obligations to keep God's commands and follow in His ways, they will be able to overcome all the obstacles, and the promises that they received will be fulfilled in some "end of days."

These words seem to lower the bar of expectations for all other peoples in their relation to God and Israel, and to raise the bar of expectations for Israel. In order for the patriarchs and their descendants to meet all these expectations, another instructive change occurs in the narrative. Prior to His choice of Abraham, God does not intervene directly in the affairs of His chosen ones, but from Abraham onward He intervenes a great deal in shaping their destiny. In moments of great transition, faced with threats that ordinary mortals cannot withstand and overcome with their meager powers, God exercises His absolute supreme power as Creator of the world, whether directly or through His "angels." In the patriarchal narratives they appear without prior mention as creatures of the "host of heaven" who perform God's word on earth and thus mediate between heaven and earth. The more that the task of bridging the gap between the divine vision of creation and its fulfillment by human beings appears to surpass the meager powers of humanity, the more God's readiness for direct intervention increases. But it is proper to emphasize that the biblical story insists on a clear boundary in everything connected to intervention in the destiny of God's chosen ones: God dispels threats and releases His chosen ones from situations that they could not overcome on their own, but He never lightens their load or assists them in anything concerning the fulfillment of His commandments, i.e. whatever is connected with their struggling toward ethical, social and political perfection of their earthly existence. In this task they must stand on their own. This is especially noticeable in the Exodus narrative: God performs many supernatural signs for His people to bring them out of Egypt and sustain them in the wilderness, but they must conquer the land of Israel on their own, and they must establish their sanctuary and their kingdom on their own, according to the divine command.

From the inception of Abraham's career in Genesis Chapter 12 onward, the story of the patriarchs and of the people descended from them becomes the central axis of the history of humanity in the Bible. The narrative does not ignore the history of other nations. On the contrary, their story continues to be a focus of interest, but always from the standpoint of their relation to the patriarchs and their descendants: do they help and assist them out of fidelity to the Noahide covenant that was established with all humanity, or do they obstruct them on account of their immersion in sinful idolatry? The pattern that we described above — probative test, partial success, failure, punishment, and restorative second beginning — recurs several times in the history of the Israelite people up to the destruction of the first Temple, the Babylonian exile and the return to Zion. The feeling that despite all these efforts the gap between the vision and its fulfillment continues to widen and deepen — especially the gap between the destiny of the people of Israel, which despite its sins remains the only people faithful to God's Torah, and its persecution by the gentiles whose idolatry serves them and affords them supremacy on earth, making the destiny of Israel dependent on the caprices of their sinful will — this feeling brought about finally the awakening of the wishful hope sustaining the late prophets, that God would intervene more, that He would impose His rule as Creator to close the gap that keeps growing and never gets any smaller. It appears that as long as terrestrial nature, animal nature, and especially human nature does not change for the better, as long as the human *yetzer* that is evil from youth does not reform itself to fulfill God's commands, as long as the land does not reform itself and deliver its yield to humanity without their having to submit to a lifetime of labor and always worry about the morrow, so that they can devote all their energies to their ethical mission — until then, the gap between the divine vision of creation and its fulfillment will not be abolished, and the history of Israel and of humanity will not have achieved their goal.

Canaan and Israel

In Rashi's commentary to the first verse of Genesis, he says (à propos of Rabbi Isaac's objection that the story of creation ought not to have been mentioned in the Torah, except to justify the conquest of the land of Canaan by the tribes of Israel): God the Creator is the lord of all the earth and He gives it to whoever pleases Him. Given the preceding discussion of the ideas implicit in the creation narrative and its ramifications for the history of the nations, this apologetic assertion seems far-fetched. However, if we examine it in the general context of the historical narrative as a narrative that documents man's way to fulfill his task to realize the vision of creation in the world, it seems to aim at a point of truth. The story of the patriarchs' attempts to gain a foothold in this particular land, which already belonged to the Canaanite nations and was named after them, is an advanced stage in the struggle to fulfill humanity's task — to conquer the earth and rule it according to God's commandment in order to realize the vision of creation. But in that case, the obstinate attempt to implant a young people that emerged from the great civilization of Mesopotamia, the Land of Two Rivers (backdrop for the story of the Tower of Babel), precisely into that land that was already the possession of a much older people, in order to displace it — this obstinate obsession raises a major ethical problem. It is this people's task to further the mission of all humanity to spread over the whole earth that God created and to conquer it in order to rule it in justice and equity in accord with God's commandments. How is this task compatible with seizing the territory of another nation by force?

The Biblical narrative raises this question in unvarnished candor. It justifies the patriarchs' attempts to settle in the land by concluding treaties that were proper and beneficial to both sides, or by purchasing plots of land in customary fashion, as Abraham did in acquiring the cave of Machpelah in Hebron, though preserving strict social and political separation from the Canaanite rulers. The patriarchs marry only their familial cousins from the old country — Haran — and they do not mix with "the people of the land." Thus they confirm their view that the local inhabitants are idolators (and idolatrous practices defile the land over which God's eyes keep watch), as well as their aspiration to set matters right in good time by changing the national ownership of the land and dwelling in it in place of the Canaanite nations. This farsighted plan is explicitly laid out in the covenant enacted between God and Abraham "between the pieces of the sacrifice" in Chapter 15, where Abraham is promised that four hundred years later, after an extensive exile, his descendants will take over the land from its current masters who now dwell rightly on it, "for the iniquity of the Amorites is not yet complete." (15:16) This promise emphasizes the purpose and the reason, but also the moral problematic. The historical narrative does not ignore that the peoples of Canaan had a right to live there. God granted this land to them, and it is their rightful legacy.

In this connection we should point out that in all the books of the Bible without exception, the promised land is called the Land of Canaan, not the Land of Israel. This is a crucial point. It is the way of the Biblical narrative to refer to lands by the name of the nations that established their rule there. The presence of a state determines legitimate national ownership over a territory. In conformity to this principle, the name "land of Israel" occurs only three times in the Bible, referring to that territory in which the "kingdom of Israel" held sway, in parallel to the "land of Judah" where the kingdom of Judah ruled. The "land of Israel" by this criterion is not the whole territory promised to the patriarchs. That larger domain continues to be called the "land of Canaan." This indicates recognition that originally the peoples of Canaan had a legitimate claim of legal ownership over this land. Moreover, this is evidence that through the time of the return to Zion under Cyrus, or more precisely up to the establishment of the Hasmonean dynasty, the tribes of Israel did not succeed in obtaining clear title by the terms of their own Torah — which expresses universal standards of justice without favoritism even to Israel — to the land which was promised to them.

But this does not eliminate the fact that the land was indeed promised to them, and the promise itself has full juridical force that obligates God to His covenant. The patriarchal narrative attests to this several times, and the "covenant of the sacrifice" that was cited above is only one such instance. The covenant that promises Canaan to Israel was repeated to each of the patriarchs, and then to the entire people at Sinai, as is documented in Exodus and again just before the conquest in Deuteronomy. But it seems clear that in order for the promise to be fulfilled, the people must gain a foothold in the land and establish their rule there in justice and righteousness, as the prophet Isaiah said, "Zion shall be redeemed in justice, and her repentant ones in righteousness." (Isaiah 1:27) This means that from the divine viewpoint — represented by the patriarchs and the prophets — the promise to Israel becomes legitimated not only through the good behavior of the people worthy in God's eyes to dwell in the land holy to Him, but it is intended to correct idolatrous sin in the center of its most corrupted and hardened concentration in order to raise all humanity to the level of its mission on earth. From this divine perspective, the fulfillment of the mission is for His sake and the sake of all humanity, not something rooted in egoistic motives.

But if this is the case, the moral problem with which the biblical narrative grapples is compounded, for from the standpoint of the patriarchs and their descendants the realization of the mission for God's sake and humanity's sake is also their justification as a people, which although chosen still aspires to worldly prosperity and happiness like all peoples. This is the case in God's eyes too, and so it is said to Abram when he sets out on his journey:

Go forth from your native land and from your father's house to the land that I will show you. I will make of you a great nation and I will bless you; I will make your name great, and you shall be a blessing. I will bless those who bless you and curse him that curses you; and all the families of the earth shall be blessed through you. (Genesis 12:1–3)

Fulfillment of the command in its entirety heightens the complementarity of Abraham's blessing and that of the gentiles: through its worldly prosperity Israel becomes a blessing to all the families of the earth.

It is a wonderful promise, but it will be hard for the people to realize it. To succeed on their path, the patriarchs and their descendants must first reform themselves. It is not their job to reform the sinful inhabitants of Canaan, but rather themselves, in a land where the prevailing contrary example may present several obstacles and temptations. There may be no contradiction from God's standpoint between seeking the people's own good and their mission on behalf of humanity. But the biblical narrative is quite alert to the fact that from the patriarchs' and their descendants' standpoint this is the substance of the great test that embodies the gap between the vision of creation and its realization: from the standpoint of human nature, with its congenital evil impulse, and from the standpoint of the nature of the land, which does not automatically give man all that he needs for prosperity and happiness, there must develop, in the process of realizing the mission, a contradiction between Israel's national egoism and its ethical mission. For only with its entry to the land and the establishment of its commonwealth will this people become a nation like all the nations, and this means that only there will it be able to prove that it is worthy of its land, though originally it is not better than other peoples. On the contrary, it has quite a few weaknesses and failings. In the course of coming into the land, all the ethical, social and political problems in need of solution will come to the surface, and it will be very hard to find a just solution to them, much less to implement it. It will therefore be a long road, hard and convoluted. Its failures will exceed its successes, and its declines will outnumber its ascents. The prophetic narrative of the Bible foresees this in advance. Without guidance and direct assistance from on high, the travelers will not be able to reach their destination.

The moral problem embodied in the choice of the land of Canaan for realizing the mission of the patriarchs and the people descended from them receives all its ramifications from the circumstances and conditions of its realization: Is it an accident that God granted this very land to the Canaanite nations? Is it an accident that precisely there the fiasco of idolatry found its most extreme expression? Is it an accident that precisely there was found the chance to deal with this sin and overcome it for the sake of Israel and humanity? Close reading of the patriarchal narrative shows that all these are not accidental. The land of Canaan was singled out originally from all other lands. This is the chosen land, just as the people descended from the patriarchs is the chosen people. This is the chosen land not necessarily by being preferable to the other lands in its prospects for material prosperity and happiness, but because of the choice demanded of the people that possesses it in order to merit the prosperity that it expects — the choice between the way that God commands and the way that the primordial evil impulse drives him to follow. The land of Canaan is a land in which life is a continual test that requires again and again that one make the right choice.

What distinguishes this land in its qualities and its locale? The first hint is already given in the language of the command spoken to Abram: "Go to the land that I will *show* you [*asher ar'eka* — that I will *make you see*]." Recalling the significance of *seeing* in biblical language will suggest to the reader the precise significance of this announcement, which at first sight seems general and undefined: where should Abram turn? How will God show him the way? Abram does not hesitate. He knows immediately which is *the* land (with the definite article) that on approaching it he will see it *as God sees it*. Then he will recognize its special quality: this land is the land that God sees, and whose inhabitants are seen by God. In other words, God judges them by their deeds and intentions. This interpretation of the command "Go forth" is confirmed in the story of the binding of Isaac where the same command appears. There the destination is "the land of Moriah." (22:2) This name has a rich meaning. It is "the land that I will tell you." It is the land of the Amorites, but also the land of instruction and epiphany.[15] The third meaning is explicitly emphasized at the end of the account of the Binding of Isaac narrative. God says to Abraham, "Now I know that you are a God-fearing man," (22:12) and Abraham responds: "Abraham

---

[15] The verbal play of these notions in Hebrew is strongly suggestive. *'Amar* (tell, say) has the same root as *'Emori* (Amorite); epiphany (*ra'aya*) is of the same root as *ra'ah* (see) and *ar'eka* (I will show you), while phonetically resembling *hora'ah* (instruction) — of the same root as "Moriah."

called the name of that place *Adonai-yir'eh* [YHWH will see], concerning
which it is said today: 'On the mount where YHWH is seen.' " (22:14)[16]
Indeed, the outlook that the land of Canaan or the land of the Amorites,
the hill-dwellers of Canaan, is the land that God sees and on which
His providence is manifest, recurs repeatedly in several variations
throughout the patriarchal narrative, and is attested by all the covenants
that the patriarchs who tour the land to see it enact in several cultic
centers — they offer a sacrifice on the altar, and God responds to them
with a direct personal revelation, which has no parallel in any story of
revelation from the generation of Noah to Abraham. The appearance of
angels from God to human beings to impart His command and prepare
their way is also repeated for Abram when he comes to Canaan. But
the clearest, most explicit story testifying of the land that God observes
and rules it continually, is the dream of Jacob at Beth El on his way to
Haran, before leaving the boundaries of Canaan:

He had a dream; a ladder [stairway] was set on the ground and its top
reached to the sky, and angels of God were going up and down on it. And
the Lord was standing beside him and He said, "I am the Lord, the God of
your father Abraham and the God of Isaac: the ground on which you are
lying I will assign to you and your offspring. Your descendants shall be as
the dust of the earth; you shall spread out to the west and to the east, to the
north and the south. All the families of the earth shall be blessed through
you and your descendants. Remember, I am with you: I will protect you
wherever you go and will bring you back to this land. I will not leave you
until I have done what I have promised you."
Jacob awoke from his sleep and said, "Surely the Lord is present in this
place, and I did not know it!" Shaken [by fear], he said, "How awesome is
this place! This is none other than the abode of God, and that is the gateway
to heaven."…He named that site Bethel [house of God]; but previously the
name of the city had been Luz. (Genesis 28:12–19)

All the years that Jacob dwelt in Haran he was not privileged with another
revelation like this, though God's providence never left him; but as
soon as he returned to the border of the land promised to him and his

---

16   In other words, Abraham and Isaac's sacrificial communion with God's
presence at that site prefigures the regular communion that would take place
in the Temple which would be built on the same site, and where Israelites
would go on pilgrimage thrice annually "to see [or appear before] the face of
the Lord YHWH" (Exodus 23:17, 34:23).

descendants he again encounters an angel of God (32:2–3), and at the ford of Jabok he wrestles with an angel of God and is blessed. (32:25–31) We learn from all these examples that the land of Canaan is the land opposite which the gates of heaven are opened, through which God spreads forth His hidden sovereignty over the land. Gaining control over that land, and the possibility of maintaining oneself on it materially in personal and political freedom, are directly conditional on obedience to the commandment of God who rules over it and watches it, though hidden from the view of those whose evil impulse veils this from their sight.

From the time that Abram arrives in the land of Canaan, he is the first person who sees, knows, experiences and testifies to this hidden divine rule. (Perhaps another witness is Melchizedek the king of Salem, who was a priest of God Most High, and who blessed Abram in the name of "God Most High, Creator of heaven and earth." — 14:18–19) This is the bedrock of the faith of Abraham and his descendants in the covenant enacted with them and its sweeping promise, even though its fulfillment is delayed. But why was this land chosen to be the place opposite which the gates of heaven are opened, and through which is formed the connection between heaven and earth? The biblical-prophetic explanation unfolds through the stories of the trials through history: Canaan is a hilly land located between two lands based on river economies — Mesopotamia and Egypt — home to a series of great historical empires, who tried continually to recreate the usurping idolatrous regime described in the story of the Tower of Babel, and to unite all the peoples of the world under their dominion. The two characteristics of the land of Canaan — its hilliness and its intermediate location — contribute to its unique status. First of all, it forms a connecting bridge between its two powerful neighbors. They have the potential of making peace with one another, of developing commercial ties leading to their own prosperity and that of Canaan. But they also are liable to compete and fight with each other over which one will bring the other peoples under its rule. The second way is of course the way toward which the idolatrous impulse drives them. From the standpoint of the small nations caught in between, this reality means that their own survival depends on keeping peace between the two major powers. When war breaks out, their own land is subject to conquest, or they may enter a treaty with one of the powers against the other to buy their own protection. These alternatives are both bad, and even in peaceful times there is the danger of adapting to the social-ethical, political, and religious standard of the neighboring idolatrous powers, allowing the ethical-Messianic vision to fall into disrepair. Thus destruction lurks from either direction.

The only alternative promising national freedom is to abstain from becoming involved in the game of Realpolitik between the competing powers, and to be on watch against being influenced by their social ethics, their methods of rule and their idolatrous worship. It is possible to achieve this abstention and watchfulness only by relying on faith in the rule of God, which is hidden from sight of the idolaters but which can be revealed to those servants of God who keep faith with him, for He rules heaven and earth, and His power surpasses the power of the sinful empires. This is the choice which comes up repeatedly, through which the people who wish to dwell peaceably on their land in Canaan and to enjoy a free and prosperous existence must be tested.

In addition to suffering an intermediate location between two empires, this land has a hilly terrain, so that its ability to sustain the people dwelling on it is directly dependent on the God of heaven:

> For the land that you are about to enter and possess is not like the land of Egypt from which you have come. There the grain you sowed had to be watered by your own labors, like a vegetable garden; but the land you are about to cross into and possess, a land of hills and valleys, soaks up its water from the rains of heaven. It is a land which the Lord your God looks after, on which the Lord your God always keeps His eye, from year's beginning to year's end.
>
> If, then, you obey the commandments that I enjoin upon you this day, loving the Lord your God and serving Him with all your heart and soul, I will grant the rain for your land in season, the early rain and the late. You shall gather in your new grain and wine and oil — I will also provide grass in the fields for your cattle — and thus you shall eat your fill. Take care not to be lured away to serve other gods and bow to them. For the Lord's anger will flare up against you, and He will shut up the skies so that there will be no rain and the ground will not yield its produce; and you will soon perish from the good land that the Lord is giving to you. (Deuteronomy 11:10–17)

What, then, is liable to lure away the heart of the people who live in Canaan to serve other gods, as indeed it did so many times? Why is this stiff warning called for, that the prophets sound so often? It seems that in the answer to this question we will also find the answer to the question what falls to the lot of the people of Canaan when they descend to the depths of sinful idolatry precisely when they dwell in the chosen land. The Torah repeatedly warns against the danger of temptation of the worship of Baal and Astarte that are full of abominable lewdness, promiscuity and prostitution, which were practiced by the Canaanite inhabitants. These were rituals whose purpose was to bring down the rains and increase the abundance of the harvest through influencing the gods who were thought to rule over the storehouses of water that come down from heaven and are collected in the terrestrial reservoirs of the springs and wells. The way to influence them is the way of base sexual seduction that was thought to impregnate the land, and other magical methods. The congenitally evil impulse of the human heart tends to give credence to these methods. They seem "scientific" to him because they imitate his own natural reproductive processes, and he projects his own sexual desires onto the gods that represent the forces of nature. Against this, how is it possible to rely on the claims of the prophets that following the path of ethics will bring abundant harvests, prevent the injustice perpetrated by the rich against the poor, and restrain Israel's wicked enemies from engaging in a war of conquest? What is the natural-causal web that connects ethical behavior with rainfall, and observance of interpersonal injunctions with the growth of the land's produce?

The historical narrative of the patriarchs and their descendants in the Torah and the historical books of the Bible emphasizes the providence of God over His land as expressed in bestowing and withholding the rain, while the historical narrative of Israel on its land in the literary prophets emphasizes the expression of divine providence in the power struggles between the imperial powers: Egypt from the south, Assyria, Babylon and Persia from the north. And yet both of the characteristics of the land of Canaan — its hilliness and its central location — which show anyone who has eyes to see that the gates of heaven are open over it and the God of the heavens watches over it Himself — these characteristics are thematized in different ways throughout all the chapters of the historical narrative: starting with the narrative of Abram, who migrates from Ur of the Chaldees and from Haran, but continues to see them as his birthplace, and goes down to Egypt because of the drought in Canaan but is expelled from it and returns to Canaan; through the story of Isaac, who remains tied to the land but marries a wife from Haran, sends his son to marry in Haran, and like his father Abraham sojourns in the land of the Philistines because of the drought; and culminating in the story of Jacob, who flees to Haran from his brother Esau, marries and has children there, but returns to Canaan and tries to settle there, but finally descends to Egypt with all his family after his son Joseph because of the drought. The medieval commentator Nahmanides said: "The life-events of the fathers are a sign for the children." In Egypt the people of Israel developed from an ancestral clan to a nation, and it then returned to Canaan and tried to become permanently established in the land but failed. It became involved in wars between Egypt and Assyria and later between Egypt and Babylonia, and it was driven off its land. As Canaan was the chosen land, it is the key to understanding the history of the chosen people, which vacillates between exile and redemption.

Personal Development of the Patriarchs, and Development of the People toward the Fulfillment of their Destiny

The recognition that bridging the gap between the vision of creation and its fulfillment through the actions of human beings must be an extended gradual process that requires a person to accept his mission and prepare himself for it, undergoing many changing trials on its behalf — this realization occasions an additional development in the mode of the biblical narrative. We pointed out earlier the transition from the mythic-symbolical mode of the story of creation to the quasi-historical mode of the narrative of the descendants of Adam and of Noah and his children. Now we must point out an additional transition from the mode of the concise narrative — presenting one character or two contrasting characters, complete and developed in their traits, characters who do not change or develop, seen in one quintessential action that presents a problem or a stance — to that of the long narrative with a complex plot that unfolds gradually, with many twists and turns, whose characters develop in their personal traits and their ethical stances, in their faith and their world outlooks — sometimes from worse to better, and sometimes from better to worse. These are characters in whose life-stories is reflected not only a quasi-historical reality but the destinies of realistic human beings like me and you.

The most complete narrative of this kind in the Bible is that of Joseph and his brothers, or more precisely Joseph and Judah. The story has several subplots and several rises and falls that develop the characterization of the heroes. The Joseph whom his brothers come to know as Pharaoh's viceroy is different from the Joseph whom they knew when they cast him into the pit and sold him to the Ishmaelites. The brothers see him and hear his voice and are able to ascertain from his words to them that he understands them even without the interpreter between them, and knows more about them than they had told him. But despite all the hints that he lets drop, they do not recognize him even when the idea that their misfortune must be a punishment for their selling their brother occurs to them. But when they have settled in Goshen and become accustomed to see him as the noble brother whom they did not know how to appreciate properly in his youth, he has already become the powerful Egyptian to whom they turn in fear after their father's death: a totally different person from the one whom they knew whey they came to Egypt. Not the man who rescued the Egyptians and neighboring peoples from death by famine, but the exploitative tyrant who bought up all the land of Egypt and turned its inhabitants into slaves to Pharaoh and his magicians. There was good reason for them to fear that after their father's death he would behave toward them as he had behaved toward all the citizens of Egypt — he could revoke their rights over the land of Goshen and turn them also into slaves, or drive them out of his land.

But Joseph also saw the change in his brothers when they came to him in Egypt. Of course he recognized his brothers — their language, dress and general manners had not changed, and he waited impatiently for the moment that they would recognize him and be persuaded of the veracity of his dreams — but it is clear that in his memory he harbored the image of the men who hated him, belittled him, and in their blindness set him on the path that led to the verification of his dreams. He had to learn through his dealings with them, and especially from the dealings between him and his brother Judah, how much they had changed, and how much he himself had changed with respect to them. Therefore, from the moment he made himself known to them, the denouement of vengeance that he had anticipated became transformed into one of weeping, compassion and atonement.

What awakened in Joseph the emotional urge to break his silence and not to wait until his brothers recognized him and stood face to face with their guilt that was beyond forgiving and their blindness surpassing atonement? (Genesis 45:1) It was the speech of Judah — the brother who in their youth took the lead of the brothers who were debating Joseph's fate, who cast Joseph into the pit and sold him into slavery for monetary gain. Now he stood before him as the man who again stood up to lead the confused brothers, and who took the whole responsibility on himself. (44:18–34) On the one hand Judah showed Joseph the respect that was his due as an Egyptian ruler: he repeatedly referred to himself and his brothers as "your servants"; he repeatedly addressed him as "my lord." Thus he indirectly acknowledged that he and his brothers had erred in their estimation of him, while fulfilling Joseph's dream that his brothers should bow as servants before him. But in another respect, here stood the brother who was his equal in his struggle for righteousness. This was no longer the calculating man who saved him from death in order to sell him for profit, but the leader of his family who represents to him his obligation to his father. The reader of the narrative knows what Joseph cannot know: the episode of the relations between Judah and his daughter-in-law Tamar, an episode that transformed him into another person, who knows how to judge himself and another fairly and to accept responsibility for his misdeeds in order to repair the damage he has done. (Chapter 38) But Joseph saw before him a man who yields on point of honor and acknowledges the authority of one who stands above him, submitting properly to his superior, yet who does not tremble or abnegate himself but demands the responsibility that goes with mastery. It is the ruler's duty to act justly, and Judah demands that justice be done. The lord must be honest and faithful to the promises for which the brothers had risked themselves, endangered their father, and brought Benjamin with them.

The moral that arises from this confrontation is the very heart of the whole story: Joseph and Judah each developed on his own trajectory, and in them we see represented two types of rulership that became embodied in two dynasties, one descended from Joseph and the other from Judah. On the one hand is the "kingdom of Israel," at whose center stood the tribe of Joseph's son Ephraim, and whose style of rule and religious worship imitated Egypt of the Pharaohs. On the other hand is the "kingdom of Judah," at whose center stood the tribe of Judah, and whose style of rule was faithful to the tradition of sovereignty established by popular covenant, one whose kings stand under the covenantal law and not above it.

The ethical-political world of ideas embodied in the Joseph narrative will occupy us later on in another context: the relation between Joseph, who laid the foundations for the Pharaonic regime that enslaved Israel, and Moses, who laid the foundations for the Torahitic law of freedom in Israel. In this context our interest is mainly in the method of the narrative: a line of development with many surprising turns, including the amalgamation of two story-lines that at first sight have no connection (as in the transition from the story of Joseph to that of Judah). But when we examine the whole story from its end to its beginning, its consistent logic is revealed, directed at an ethical-religious moral. This logic follows from the connection between actions whose source is in the decision of human will and the ethical consequences that follow from that decision, over which a person has no control, until they arrive at a distant result from which the next decision will have to be made, that will either repair the situation or aggravate it further. In this way the narrative reflects the ways of divine providence over the education of His people, manifesting the fulfillment of the divine purpose on the one hand, and the expression of human nature in human individuals on the other hand.

The biblical narrative is unique in that its characters represent general existential human situations and individual ethical problems, yet each of them is a unique personality with his or her own name and unique destiny. Each character is thus a unique person and not a symbol. This realism of the biblical narrative is the source of its educational influence over its readers, for in every generation the reader can see in them his companions, his counterparts, his antagonists, or his exemplars. He can put himself in their place, identify them or judge them on the basis of his own life-experience, and thus he judges himself from a distance and derives the proper lessons in his own way into the circle of his life.

These remarks apply to all the historical narratives of the patriarchs and leaders of the people, for with respect to their humanity that is swayed alternately by their congenital impulses and by their destiny, they are the same as every human being. Even Moses, the greatest of them all, is no exception. He arrived through struggle to the highest rank of ethical leadership that a person can attain, yet he too failed through his sins, and every new trial by which he was tested threatened to topple his achievement.

From Sin to Destiny:
Stories of Abram/Abraham and Sarai/Sarah

One of the literary devices that biblical narrative uses to direct the reader's thought to its lessons is the names of its heroes. The mother usually gives her child a name that expresses her feelings, hopes and expectations. She thus delineates for her offspring a destiny that is a factor in their personal formation for the future. Thus, for instance, the first man gave the names Adam and Eve to himself and his wife, and Eve named her sons Cain and Abel. The names Noah [relief] and Nimrod [rebellion] have meaning in connection with their destinies. When we arrive at the narrative of Abram and Sarai, we see a new subtlety in this respect: the prefigurative names given them by their parents are changed by God at a certain stage. This is evidence that they have undergone a great transformation that has raised them in their level of mission — they have succeeded in reshaping the personalities and destiny that were molded by the given factors of their birth, without disrupting the continuity of their identities. They are no longer those persons called by the names given by their parents — Abram has become Abraham, and Sarai Sarah. The new names express an enlargement of their destinies and coming closer to God, for the letter *hei* added to their names is derived from God's name YHWH. Perhaps this transformation involves liberation from the sin that had kept them from fulfilling their destiny. We find a more dramatic example of the revolution expressed by the name-change in Jacob's acquiring the name "Israel" when he returned from Haran to Canaan on the way to his confrontation with his brother Esau. The name "Jacob," that expressed his devious nature — crooked, crafty, coming from behind and grabbing onto his brother's heel — that generated hostility between him and his brother, was exchanged for a name that expressed his transcending his nature to the point that he could have straight dealings with his brother, who was more material in his nature but at the same time more open and straightforward than he.[17] There is great significance to the fact that in the subsequent narrative he is variously referred to as Jacob or Israel in keeping with his moral failure

---

[17]   The name *Ya'akov* has a common root with *'akev* (heel — as per the biblical etymology in Genesis 25:26) and *'akov* (curved, crooked), with the connotation of "deal crookedly" and "supplant" (hence Esau's complaint in 27:36). The associations of the name *Israel* are many. Though the biblical etymology in 32:29 plays on *yasar* ("to wrestle"), there is also the prominent connection with *yashar* ("straight, upright") which Schweid emphasizes here. See also the name Jeshurun (Deuteronomy 33:5 and elsewhere), and Isaiah 40:4: "Let the rugged ground (*'akov*) become level (*miyshor*)" — an apt metaphor for Jacob/Israel's personal transformation alluding to both of his names. (LL)

or fortitude in respect of the trials that he encounters. The older names of Abram and Sarai do not recur once they are changed, indicating that they succeeded in overcoming the sin that encumbered them on the way to fulfilling their destiny.

What do we known about Abram in his beginnings? From the name that his parents gave him[18] we learn that he was destined for greatness, to be the father of a people descended from him. From God's revelation to him we learn that the destiny held out for him by his parents was rooted in the tradition of the line of Shem that derived from the covenant of Noah and his children. The members of Abram's ancestral clan remained faithful to the service of the God of heaven who rules also on earth, though the surrounding people, with Nimrod, sank into idolatry. We nevertheless see that Abram's father Terah and all the members of his family were influenced by the idolatry of their compatriots. How do we learn this? From the motive for which Terah set out with his son and his daughter-in-law, who was barren, toward the land of Canaan. (11:31) The reader may surmise that there is a connection between Sarai's infertility and the migration, for how will Abram become an "exalted father" if his wife is barren? This happens before God's revelation in Haran to go to "the land that I will show you." This also explains how he knew immediately to which land he should go.

Do these first narrative data harbor any hint of the cause of Sarai's infertility and to the choice of the land of Canaan as a land of destiny where it might be overcome? This question remains for the present without an answer, but it arouses the reader's curiosity to know the continuation of the story. Only thus will be clarified the secret of this couple who were appointed to found a people that should be descended from them: Abram who is destined to be an "exalted father" and Sarai who is destined for "royalty" were brother and sister, the children of the same father. Could not this sin of incest, a practice of idolators, be the cause of Sarai's barrenness? It appears that uprooting the family from its Chaldean origins and its journey towards Canaan — where the worship of the God of Heaven still survived (as attested by the presence of Melchizedek, priest of God on High in Salem) — had its source in the hope that by worshipping God on High on altars erected anew to His name in His land, their sin might be purged and they might succeed in realizing their destiny together.

---

[18] Abram: *Av* [father] *ram* [exalted], with a suggestion of *'am* [people/nation].

We shall see that it is not easy to become liberated from the chains of sin. The family set out, but they stopped half-way at Haran. The story does not tell us why, but from the continuation we can learn that the dallying in Haran had its source in the same reason for which Abram later went down to Egypt a short time after they arrived in Canaan (12:10–20) — survival needs, and the lure of easy riches. However, once we understand the data of the beginning of the story, we may note something else that arises from comparing it to previous biblical stories. As with the story of Adam and Eve, yet different from the story of Cain, Abel, Noah and his children, this story does not focus on a single individual, but on a couple. Moreover, it relates to each member of the couple as a separate person striving individually toward her own destiny, though the fulfillment occurs in common.

This description of the relation between two persons who have become a couple shows up clearly in the trial in which their secret is revealed when they go down to Egypt, and even more so when the same trial is repeated in Gerar: "When God made me wander from my father's house [Abraham explains in exculpation to Abimelech, king of Gerar], I said to her, 'Let this be the kindness that you shall do me: whatever place we come to, say there of me: He is my brother." (20:13) When they set out on the path that will lead both of them to the fulfillment of their personal destiny, they establish a covenant that is evidence that each of them decided to set out on the journey at his or her own initiative and responsibility. This is not a decision that was arrived at by the husband whose will compels his wife. Abram does not "rule" his wife, but she goes in order to realize her royal destiny, that depends on her succeeding in bearing a son. Since Abram endangers himself when he sets out on a long journey with such a beautiful woman as she — who knows as well as he the powerful attraction emanating from her! Who knows as well as he that libidinal men are not likely to withstand temptation in her vicinity — much less adherents of the idolatrous ethic! Therefore he requests of her — and she agrees graciously to bear the responsibility for the results of their common undertaking. The whole matter of the relations between Abram/Abraham and Sarai/Sarah up to the birth of Isaac can only be interpreted properly if we understand that the members of this couple struggle, change and develop until they arrive at the fullest expression of selfhood of each of them through a relation of reciprocity that follows from the covenant of equals that they entered into before God. May we infer from this that the difference between the peoples that developed from the mating of Adam and Eve, and from Noah and his anonymous wife, versus the people that descended from Abraham and Sarah, is rooted in this special conception of the relations of the father and the mother?

The comparison to the story of Adam and Eve raises a new insight. As the first couple, Adam and Eve were both brother-and-sister and husband-and-wife, and the beginning of their way as a couple was rooted in the sin for which they had to atone in order to rise to their destiny. Should we infer from this that every beginning of purposeful development in the creation of national cultures is rooted in a fateful sin that is rooted in the libidinal nature of man that is congenitally evil, and that from it comes the drive to improvement and purification, as well as the temptation to decline and corruption? The repetition of the sin of incest in the story of Lot and his daughters — that branches off from the story of Abram and Sarai — from whom were descended the nations Ammon and Moab that were cousin-nations to Israel, strengthens this assumption. Indeed, looking at the history of Abram/Abraham and Sarai/Sarah from the end to the beginning suggests that this is its moral: they turned their sin to moral leverage in order to overcome their congenital evil impulse that caused them to sin, and to turn their sin into righteousness.

We return to the start of the story. We have uncovered two motives for Abram and Sarai to set out on the way to Canaan: the command of God, to which they responded out of the sense of destiny that their parents had implanted in them, and the sense of sin, that prevented them from fulfilling this destiny. Abram was seventy-five years old (the story is careful to record the age of its heroes at each stage of their journey) when after the death of his father in Haran he heard a prophetic command to continue the journey that his father had started. With him goes also his nephew Lot, who will soon play an important role on his journey. Like his father, he goes not as an isolated individual but as the head of an ancestral clan. This is the the responsibility of a leader who bears responsibility not only for the continuity of one private family but for an ancestral clan that seeks to become a nation, or even a family of nations. This is the meaning of the name *Abram*. When they arrive in Canaan, Abram passes through two ancient centers of worship of YHWH, and he worships his God there in order to merit His beneficence. These are Elon Moreh that is next to Shechem, and Beth El. (12:6–9) Afterwards he continues to "journey by stages toward the Negeb" in search of living quarters for himself and his entourage.

In the two centers through which he passes he builds altars to YHWH. Is he answered? Only with an obscure general promise, much more modest than the one he had received in Haran: "I will give this land to your offspring." (12:7) When will he have offspring? How will the land be given to him? What must he do in order for the promise to be fulfilled? The words are vague. It is possible to say that the God who commanded him to go and promised him rich reward hides His face from him in the expectation of seeing what he is ready to do for the realization of his destiny.

The severe famine that overtook Canaan on his arrival confirms this assumption. God sets up the same test that his father failed on his journey. Abram does not withstand it any better. On the contrary, his decline was double: leaving the place where his God dwells, and settling in a rich, corrupt land, whose inhabitants have sunk deeper into the depths of idolatrous corruption more than the inhabitants of Canaan of the same period. Abram and Sarai jeopardized their marriage and the realization of their common destiny. They risked being drawn into idolatrous worship that would be a betrayal of their spiritual destiny. But the pressures of existence (was it indeed impossible to stand up to them out of readiness to suffer?) and the temptations of wealth grew apace. Were they trying their God who was trying them? Did they express thus their anger and their disappointment? Did they want to force God to extend them a helping hand because they thought that the trial in which they were placed was greater than the power of a human being to bear?

We may infer that God, who tried His chosen ones, understood that they were still far from the necessary level to withstand these tests with the extraordinary perseverance that is based on the power of faith, and in order to salvage the faith that they had, He extended a helping hand to them, smote Pharaoh's house with terrible plagues, freed Sarai from her royal captivity and enriched Abram with the freely-offered gifts of the smitten Egyptians. (12:16–20) All the traditional commentators point out the parallel between this story and the story of the descent of the Israelite tribes into Egypt and their exodus from there, and this interpretation is also convincing in its educational lessons. But to understand the continuation of the story of the couple on trial, we should emphasize that in this chapter of the story Sarai begins to fulfill the independent role for which she is appointed, and that Abram and Sarai learned from their rescue the lesson that they did not know how to learn from the trial that they underwent: if their descent expressed the weakness of their faith in respect of their egoistic impulse, the story of their miraculous rescue aroused in them the self-criticism and hence the understanding, which path they ought to have chosen in the first place instead of going down to Egypt. Thus, after their rescue, their sin became leverage for moral growth and empowerment.

The result can be seen immediately in the two tests that came up for Abram upon his return. From his conduct in these tests it appears that he was indeed transformed into another man. This is expressed in both aspects of conduct in which he failed in Egypt: eagerness for wealth, and taking responsibility to grapple with the obstacles of worldly life through combative self-reliance instead of depending on God or on mortal rulers. These two trials were bound up with Abram's relations with his nephew Lot (13:5–18), and in consequence also his relations with the inhabitants of Canaan (14:1–24). These were tests of political leadership, and Abram passed them with flying colors. He resolved the quarrel between Lot's shepherds and his own fairly through separation — giving the choice of pastureland to Lot — which turned out economically beneficial as well. But it is more important that Lot chose to return to the rich river valley, similar to Egypt from which he had just returned, even though the people there were extremely wicked, demonstrating that he had not derived the proper lessons from his sojourn in Egypt, whereas Abram turned to the hill country that depends on divine providence. The correctness of his choice is proved immediately afterwards, when Lot is taken captive by the conquerors of his city. Abram rushed to assist him, rescuing him and his compatriots, and showed magnanimity by declining his share of the spoils:

But Abram said to the king of Sodom, "I swear to the Lord, God most High, Creator of heaven and earth: I will not take so much as a thread or a sandal strap of what is yours; you shall not say, 'It is I who made Abram rich.' " (14:22–23)

We recall that the man who said this is the man who had just returned from Egypt, with the spoil of the gifts that enriched him — the fruits of his sin in going down to Egypt — in his hand. This is convincing evidence of the great transformation that took place in him, in respect both of his faith in God and his independence and ethical responsibility.

After these events, Abram is privileged with another audience with God. He is found worthy to receive the first covenant (the "covenant between the pieces"). In this covenant he is promised that his two momentous requests will be granted: he will have a son who will inherit after him, and the land will be given as a bequest to his descendants. But it is a covenant with strings attached. If we examine its conditions, we see that more than being a reward for passing the previous trials, it is a setup for a double trial to come, one that will test the quality of the relations between him and God, and between him and his sister-wife Sarai, as we shall see shortly.

As for his relationship with God, the question was whether the faith that had been manifested, and his readiness to act on his initiative, to mix in as a citizen in the promised land and thus to bring blessing to his family, to his ancestral clan and to the neighboring peoples — whether all these proceeded from his obligation to his destiny to "be a blessing" to all, or from his selfish expectation to enjoy reward from his God?

Two promises given to Abram were absolute, but at that point they did not seem achievable in the natural way: Abram and Sarai were already an infertile couple. (15:2) Abram was still able to sire offspring, but Sarai was on the verge of menopause. If the promise were not realized immediately, it could no longer be realized in the natural way. As for the land of Canaan, nations dwelt there who occupied it by law. Abram could be convinced of this by the conduct of Melchizedek towards him. How could God, who ruled justly, take the land back justly and bestow it to his descendants? To this question, Abram received the answer that the promise would be fulfilled only in a far distant future, when the guilt of the Amorites is complete. But even regarding the fulfillment of the promise that a son would be born to him, which Abram could still regard as possible (though barely so), he received no immediate confirmation.

This was the background for the trial in the continued relationship between him and his sister-wife Sarai. He believed that even if the promise were delayed, it would be fulfilled eventually, but Sarai could not believe it, unless her believing husband would betray her and sire a child by another woman whom he would marry right in front of her eyes. From this prospect derived Sarai's decision to carry out her maternal imperative in a way that would not require direct sexual relations on her part, which were starting to appear ludicrous:[19]

---

[19]   "Ludicrous" (*matzḥikim*). Schweid invokes the theme of laughter/play/sport that will occur in various forms — including sexual — with Isaac, Ishmael, and the marital relation of Isaac and Rebekah (see Genesis 17:17, 18:12–15, 21:3–6, 21:9, 26:8), as developed below.

Sarai said to Abram, "Look, the Lord has kept me from bearing. Consort with my maid; perhaps I shall have a son through her." And Abram heeded Sarai's request. (16:2)

Here they have come to agreement again. But it was a severe test of the covenant that the two had established before God: Sarai gave Abram her maid Hagar to have a son through her, not to allow her to supplant her! If Abram still had manhood enough to consort with Hagar and make her pregnant so that she could bear his son, then he could still be swayed enough by his senses to start to see in Sarai's maid his own beloved wife, which strengthened Hagar in her feeling that — now pregnant — she could usurp her mistress! Abram's faithfulness to the covenant between himself and Sarai was now tested by his congenital sexual nature which had not yet been tamed: "Sarai said to Abram, 'The wrong done me is your fault! . . . The Lord judge between you and me!" (16:5)

Abram judged rightly and immediately carried out his obligation to Sarai. He returned the maid to Sarai's authority so that she could deal with her as she saw fit. But he thus sinned against the younger woman and against his son whom she already carried in her womb — Sarai took her revenge on the uppity maidservant, abusing her and endangering the fruit of her womb. The maidservant fled from her, thus endangering both her own life and her infant's. Only God could help deliver Abram from the two equal sins that crouched at his doorstep. "I will greatly increase your offspring, and they shall be too many to count," says God's angel to the fleeing Hagar to induce her to return to her mistress; thus he promises her that she will in her own right be mother to a nation related to Abraham. (16:10–15) Thus justice is done to Sarai, to Hagar, and to Ishmael.

Let us pay attention: according to the promise to Hagar, Ishmael is considered her own progeny. Sarai thus succeeded in maintaining her authority, but her hope to acquire progeny through her handmaid is disappointed. Such was not God's intention, nor would it have done justice to Abram and Sarai. Their promised son must be theirs in all respects, their successor and heir both physically and spiritually, i.e., he must be conceived and born naturally through marital relations that take place between them. Abram was 86 when his son Ishmael was born to Hagar, but only thirteen years later, when Ishmael was 13 and he was 99, did God consider Abram and Sarai worthy as a couple that had withstood their trial and expiated their sin. Only when they had not abandoned faith after all this time did God reveal Himself to Abram again, repeating the blessing with which He had blessed him when he left Haran: he will be the father of a multitude of nations, and his descendants will possess the land of Canaan. (17:4–9) This is finally confirmation that Abram and Sarai are worthy of fulfillment of the promise that they will have a son.

But we may well ask: Why was fulfillment of the promise delayed until then? What did God expect of Abram and Sarai? What more was demanded of them that they should be transformed and rid of sin? Perhaps the lesson of the story of Hagar and Ishmael provides the answer to this question. We saw that in that trial their loyalty to their own marital covenant was tested. But if we delve deeper we will find that in addition to their relations with each other, there was raised the question of their relation to the son who would be born to them. Had they overcome the egotism expressed in siring children who continue the lives of their parents as flesh of their flesh? Had they overcome the demand to see in their son their redeemer from the humiliation of barrenness, their deliverance from people's gossip over the reason for their infertility, or the source of their esteem and reputation? Clearly they failed this test. We see, though, that when Ishmael turned 13, when the time came to enter him into the covenant with God, and when Abram and Sarai both had reached old age, they despaired and gave up on their egoistic aspirations. Their whole desire now was to fulfill their destiny and mission as parents of the people chosen to God. This marked their victory over the desire that had caused their sin, and it no longer posed an obstacle to them.

The substance of the change that occurred in their spirit and body is expressed by the two commandments that Abram was commanded. First, the change of his name from Abram to Abraham — and Sarai's to Sarah — marks the change in their spirit. We noted before that the change of a name marks the change in a person's standing before God. The addition to both of their names of the Hebrew letter *hei* — taken from the name of YHWH — attests that their desire to bring a son into the world stems from their faith and fidelity to God's commandment and from God's endowing them with His spirit. Second, the commandment of the covenant of circumcision stamps onto the organ of generation the sign of destiny that demands mastery over the congenital libidinal urge, sanctifying it and transforming it from an urge steeped in pleasure for its own sake into a desire dedicated to fulfilling the command of procreation. Looking back at the story of story of Adam and Eve we see that this was the difference between their first mating ensnared in a sin rooted in physical lust and the second mating that was called "knowing," from which a man was "gotten from YHWH." The covenant of circumcision engraves on the man's organ of generation the sign that the progeny of Abraham and Sarah are appointed to be holy to God, and thus they will find their physical and spiritual happiness: "Thus shall be the covenant between Me and you and your offspring to follow, which you shall keep: every male among you shall be circumcised." (17:10)

And yet the change that attests to their liberation from the clutches of sin is ironically absent from these two texts — namely, their prodigious age. They no longer have marital relations, and the congenital libidinal urge has died away! This sad reality turns the wonderful prediction into an incomparably excruciating trial. For in order to produce a child Abraham and Sarah must resume marital relations but in a chaste spirit, as brother and sister without sinful thoughts:

Abraham threw himself on his face and laughed, as he said to himself, "Can a child be born to a man a hundred years old, or can Sarah bear a child at ninety?" And Abraham said to God, "O that Ishmael might live by Your favor!" God said, "Nevertheless, Sarah your wife shall bear you a son, and you shall name him Isaac; and I will maintain My covenant with him as an everlasting covenant for his offspring to come." (17:17–19)

Abraham withstands the test with difficulty, and in the sequel it is told that Sarah has similar problems. If the natural, egoistic standpoint must decide, perhaps it is better that the son promised to the couple who has already passed beyond the age of fertility should not be born at all. Indeed a child who is born after the quenching of the parents' desire and their sexual attraction for one another will be a laughing-stock and make his parents an object of ridicule to all their acquaintances. Even Abraham and Sarah laugh inwardly when they think of this commandment that they will have to fulfill in sanctity!

One may say that if Abraham's laughter expresses his shame, God's commandment expresses the divine sense of humor. Abraham, who feared the laughter of ordinary people, expresses the change he has undergone, one that God had anticipated: the egoistic yearning of His chosen ones for a child has vanished as if it had never been. If the ninety-nine year old Abraham will agree to beget a son of ninety-year-old Sarah and she agrees to bear him, then indeed whoever hears will laugh at the thought that these two nonagenarians succeeded in carrying out marital relations. But the fact that the laugh-provoking son was born and is living and thriving, while testifying with his whole physical and spiritual being that he is his parents' son, would transform the wicked, lascivious laughter that had accompanied the earthy brother and his gorgeous sister throughout their lives into holy laughter, rejoicing for the promise that came to fulfillment. This is the meaning of God's response to Abraham, and later to Sarah, that the son that they will produce together in their old age will be called Isaac/laughter. He — and not they who hear the circumstances of his birth — will laugh, and it will not be the laughter of derision but a laughter celebrating the blessing of his life.

Inasmuch as Abraham and Sarah acted in concert, and Sarah was an independent woman who made her own decisions, it was proper that the announcement that would require her to resume marital relations after becoming "withered" should be conveyed to her directly. This consideration leads us to the next chapter of the story: Abraham was sitting in the entrance of his tent at the heat of the day, after entering into the covenant of circumcision with his son Ishmael. He was still suffering the pain of the operation in his aging flesh, when he was honored by the visit of three guests. He sensed on their appearance that these were no ordinary men. Enthused with wonder, he felt a surge of youthful alacrity and ran to serve his guests and give word to Sarah in the tent: "Abraham hurried to Sarah in the tent and said, 'Quickly prepare three se'ahs of fine flour; knead them and make cakes!" Abraham then ran to the herd..." (18:6-7)

Abraham was in quite a rush. Was this out of fear that his guests would escape from his tent? Or was his running a fulfillment of their first mission? Maybe it marked the necessary change in Abraham from senility to youth? And if that was the case with Abraham, then so too with Sarah. The angels' second assignment was to give her the news, for the news itself might rejuvenate her vital pleasure. "Where is Sarah your wife?" the angel asks. "Here in the tent," Abraham replied. "I will return to you in a year's time, and Sarah will have a son." (18:9-10) It is a promise, but it is uttered like a command.

Sarah was listening at the entrance of the tent, which was behind him. Now Abraham and Sarah were old, advanced in years; Sarah had stopped having the periods of women. And Sarah laughed to herself, saying, "Now that I am withered, am I to have enjoyment — with my husband so old?"

Then the Lord said to Abraham "Why did Sarah laugh, saying 'Shall I in truth bear a child, old as I am?' Is anything too wondrous for the Lord? I will return to you at the time next year, and Sarah shall have a son." (Genesis 18:10–14)

Another announcement that sounds like a command, this time to Sarah, that she should be responsive to her elderly husband; for otherwise, how will it be possible for her to have a son in a year's time? We now examine the short exchange that follows between Sarah and the angel: "Sarah denied, saying, 'I did not laugh,' for she was afraid. The angel replied, 'No, you did laugh.'" (18:15) Whence comes this submissive reverence of Sarah, who but a moment earlier laughed defiantly? Now she is obedient. Maybe her words reflect the action of that other laughter, not in mocking of her and the husband of her youth, but the laughter that they knew in their youth, the laughter of desire and flirting?

The angels who came to visit Abraham had a third assignment. The first two brought about the physical transformation of Abraham and Sarah. The third represented the concern for fulfilling the spiritual assignment. Abraham and Sarah were designated to be a blessing for all the nations of the earth:

"...Abraham is to become a great and populous nation and all the nations of the earth are to be blessed through him. For I have singled him out, that he may instruct his children and his posterity to keep the way of the Lord by doing what is just and right, in order that the Lord may bring about for Abraham what He has promised him." (Genesis 18:18–19)

These open and emphatic words need no esoteric interpretation. The clan of Abraham, that will be established through Isaac's birth, is appointed to bridge the gap between the vision of divine creation and its realization in human societies and states. The bargaining between God and Abraham over the judgment to be meted out to the cities of the plain of the Jordan (Genesis 18:17–32) is a test of Abraham's thinking as a leader and righteous judge of all those subject to his leadership, including his ally Lot to whom he is duty-bound to come to his assistance.

Did Abraham pass this ethical-judicial-political test that God brought to his doorstep? It would seem so. It seems that God accepted Abraham's opinion that was proffered in the manner of a lawyer defending his client. Like a lawyer, Abraham sought a legal basis for protecting Sodom and Gomorrah from execution of a swift, annihilative judgment. He did not dispute the proposition that the cities of the plain were evil and sinful and deserved to be wiped off the face of the earth, if one judged them as cities or states by the sum of their sins. In that respect, they were indefensible. But would not a summary condemnation be an injustice to the individuals who did not sin?

The judicial issue that Abraham the advocate argues before God the judge is: how many righteous must be found in Sodom in order that their merit may be weighed against the sins of the majority and bring about a lifting of the general sentence? Fifty? Forty? Thirty? Twenty? Through careful advocacy he arrives at the minimum number: ten! God, who agrees to the claims of his advocate without contest, already knows that there are not even ten righteous in Sodom, and its doom is sealed. He is also completely aware of Abraham's logic, who is trying so hard to defend the people of Sodom and Gomorrah in order to save his ally Lot, who indeed sinned by choosing to dwell in that wealthy city of sinners, but he also knows that Lot did not sin in his family life. He must admit that Lot's family life had not the idolatrous stain that was present in his own life.

It stands to reason that the angels were sent to Sodom to carry out the verdict that had already been sealed and to rescue the lone righteous man who had not sinned. For unlike Abraham, God recalls the merit of individuals — like Noah, like Abraham himself: even if they are not free from all sin, they strive to the best of their human ability. Therefore the hope of bridging the gap between the vision of creation and its realization depends on them. Abraham, who now felt himself as a righteous person who had purified himself from all his sins, did not remember this. Instead of arguing vigorously for sparing the righteous because most of their deeds were good he brought on his nephew and ally Lot a test that he could not pass, just as he himself had not passed it. Worse yet, the consequence of Lot's failed test was to set up tests that his wife and daughters could not pass.

Was Lot able to escape scot-free from the dilemma posed to him, whether to protect his guests or his daughters' virtue — who were more innocent than he, since they bore no responsibility for being born into the wicked city? Had the Sodomites not refused his offer by their excess of evil, and had the angels not miraculously rescued Lot, he would not have survived in a state of virtue. Still, by his very suggestion he sinned against his two daughters, who heard his words; he sinned against his paternal responsibility by expressing willingness to surrender them. Was Lot's wife able to withstand the test of the hectic departure from the city, without looking back as she realized that her whole life's enterprise was being demolished together with the city and she would not be able to reconstitute it anywhere else? Could Lot's daughters have behaved otherwise than they did with their father, after their trust in him had been destroyed and they saw no other way to realize their destiny as mothers? (Genesis 19)

God was lenient in judging all these sinners, whose intentions were for the best, and He rescued them despite their unavoidable sins. In His eyes, they were among the righteous who preserve His hope that people will rise above their urges. Still, if we take into account all these consequences of the recommendation that Abraham advocated before God, we will see that he did not pass his first test of pursuing a policy of true justice. Indeed, this is the connection between the story of the angels to the following story of Abraham's and Sarah's sojourn in Gerar, a story that seems to Biblical scholars like a mere retelling of the story of their adventure in Egypt, out of context here.

Indeed? Recognizing that the story of Abraham and the angels provides no perfect happy ending to the ongoing human comedy will lead us to the contextual meaning of the other story. Abraham did not pass his "true justice" advocacy test, and God did not adopt his verdict. The adventure of Abraham and Sarah in Gerar, where they sought, as a happy, rejuvenated couple, to find a fitting place to raise the son who was to be born to them — comes to remind them who they are and where they came from. This is the way of God — or of the masterful narrator — to allow the heroes of his story to recognize their error, so that they will appreciate the full responsibility of the task of leadership that rests on them when they educate their son to face his destiny. Thus Abraham and Sarah were placed again in a test similar to the one that they failed at the start of their journey, but this test was doubtless immeasurably easier than the test that the "righteous" Abraham brought upon his ally Lot. In Gerar Abraham had a chance to judge whether he withstood it better than Lot.

With the story of the king of Gerar, we shall turn back to examine the outcome of the events in order to extract its special meaning. But before that, in connection with the approaching birth of Isaac, we should pay attention to the full complexity of the stories of the destruction of the cities of the plain and the fate of Lot and his family. From these stories we learn of a great revolution that took place in the whole region of

Canaan, and in Canaan itself, from the time of Abram's and Sarai's arrival to Canaan and the birth of Isaac. The flourishing cities of the plain, whom Abram aided militarily on his return from Egypt in order to rescue Lot, were devastated in a great earthquake. In the hill-country of Canaan there appeared new Semitic peoples, close in kin to Abraham and Sarah and tied to the same political legacy, but touched with idolatry, and of these, our story mentions the Ammonites and Moabites, two nations that maintained close and complex relations with the people that descended from Abraham and had a major impact on their situation. Within the land of Canaan there was an increasing influence of the kingdom of Gerar, whose source was in the Philistine migration from the Greek isles. Gerar became economically and militarily more powerful, as becomes clear in the sequel from Abraham's efforts after Isaac's birth to negotiate a lasting treaty with them. (Genesis 21:22–34) Isaac conducted the same policy when his time came, and he was even thrust into a similar encounter in Gerar with his wife Rebekah (26:6–33). Furthermore, from the story of the acquisition of the cave of Machpelah in Hebron (Chapter 23) it turns out that the Hittite power also had an established presence in the land. The vision that all the land of Canaan would belong to him seemed quite remote; and Abraham, as a political leader who sought to integrate the ancestral clan that he led into its immediate and remote surroundings, had to give thought to his relations with his neighbors and find a place for himself and his son among them. He had to negotiate treaties that would secure the right for him and his son to dwell in the land of Canaan, on which several peoples, old and new, had cast their eyes, until his descendants would increase in it and the promise of inheriting the land would be fulfilled.

This, then, is the full background for the episode of Abraham and Sarah in Gerar (Genesis 20). The story is indeed parallel to that of the descent into Egypt, but if we pay attention to its particulars, it differs in important details. First, there are the motives of the sojourn. Abraham is seeking a place where he can maintain his family and raise his son who is about to be born, in peace and security within the borders of the land of Canaan. In the south, between Kadesh and Shur, he finds open space where he can settle legally without infringing on anyone's territory or taking anyone's property. In Gerar he can be a *ger* (resident alien), with the recognition of the law of the land. In all these respects, we cannot suspect him of looking for trouble, especially as he and his wife Sarah were still quite old despite their belated rejuvenation. Abraham's primary motivation becomes clear from the rest of the story: he chose to dwell in Gerar in order to prepare the groundwork for concluding a treaty with Abimelech. He wanted to learn up close the manners of the community in order to determine whether "there is fear of God in this place" (20:11), in other words, whether he can trust the king and his people that they are law-abiding and stand by the treaties that they enact. For this purpose he came to sojourn — as Lot had sojourned in Sodom — confident that God will protect him in his virtue.

It seems that this time it is God who has thrown him into this test and not for his benefit, i.e., as a response to the test that he forced on Lot. If Abraham was punished for his failure by this situation into which he was thrust, then this would increase the laughter and derision of the gossipers, both concerning the sexual attractiveness of old Sarah, that seduced Abimelech into taking her into his harem, and concerning the possibility that Abimelech, rather than 100-year-old Abraham, might be the true father of her child. But by the same moral principle that led to Lot's rescue, here too God would refrain from blaming His chosen one for his failure in a situation where it was forbidden to endanger his life: for just now has begun the period of his responsibility as a father for the future of the son who will be born to him.

By the end of the story Abraham knows from his experience what he wanted to learn in the first place — that he can trust Abimelech the king of Gerar. It was therefore possible to put faith in him and enter into a covenant in order to insure for his son a future of security and peace. But in order to understand the procedure of the covenant between Abimelech king of Gerar and his army commander Phichol after Isaac's birth (Genesis 21:22–34), we should note that in respect of the justice required in inter-human relations — according to the way by which Abraham was obligated to mend the world — from his experience in Gerar Abraham ended up indebted to Abimelech, for Abraham's principal sin was that he misled the king, who turned out to be righteous and fearing God. The king rebuked him for this, but once he received his apology he sent him away honorably and with impressive generosity:

Abimelech took sheep and oxen and male and female slaves, and gave them to Abraham; and he restored his wife Sarah to him. And Abimelech said, "Here, my land is before you; settle wherever you please." And to Sarah he said, "I herewith give your brother a thousand pieces of silver; this will serve you as vindication before all who are with you, and you are cleared before everyone.

"They Shall Keep the Way of the Lord, by Doing What Is Just and Right" (Genesis 18:19)

The stories about the lives of Abraham and Sarah after Isaac's birth revolve around Abraham's efforts to insure the future of his son Isaac as heir to his possessions in Canaan, heir to the promise of the land of Canaan to his progeny, and heir to his spiritual mission. The third legacy, which is the end-goal to which the prior two are means, requires that all of Abraham's preparations for the future from this point on shall be done in the Lord's way, by doing what is just and right, which is the way of progress toward closing the gap between the vision of creation and its realization. The first step that was required turned inward to his family: prevention of a struggle between Abraham and Sarah, and between Isaac and his half-brothers — Ishmael and the other sons whom Abram-Abraham begot of his concubines. This was not told previously, but from the description of the distribution of the inheritance it becomes clear that Abraham had several concubines and that they bore him several sons. He cared for all of them, for it was through them that he became the "father of a multitude of nations," but they all received their inheritances outside the land of Canaan, which was designated for Isaac and his progeny.

As to judicial equity, the most problematic aspect was the inheritance right of Ishmael, for Hagar was no ordinary concubine but became Abram's wife specifically in order to bear him a son. Thus Ishmael became Abraham's first-born, with the right of primogeniture. We may additionally assume that if there survived in Abraham after Isaac's birth any egoistic love, the love of flesh and blood for his bodily progeny, this love would be for Ishmael. It was him that he begot in his natural prime, of a young woman whom he loved physically. Ishmael, who is described briefly in clear and bold strokes, was a very physical boy: healthy, lustful, full of life, strength, waywardness ("his hand against everyone, and everyone's hand against him" — Genesis 16:12), and exuberance ("making sport" in the righteous perception of Sarah who was returning to her role of supremacy — 21:9). Because of these traits Sarah was not able to bear the thought that Ishmael would grow up with her son Isaac — clearly if they grew up together, the older and stronger lad would jeopardize the preferred status of her son.

We have here a conflict of emotions between Abraham and Sarah. But for our purpose, the legal aspect of the conflict is important. We recall that Sarah's status in Abraham's family was not the normal status of a woman whose husband "ruled" her, for by the covenant that they made between themselves she was a "princess" (= "Sarah") and equal to Abraham also in respect of the authority to grant the inheritance. When Sarah demanded of Abraham, "Cast out that slave-woman and her son, for the son of that slave shall not share in the inheritance with my son Isaac" (21:10), she spoke in anger and jealousy, but also with legal authority that is perceptible in the words "slave" and "son of that slave-woman." These come to emphasize the difference in legal status between her and Hagar, and thus between Ishmael and Isaac. For Abraham this was a serious emotional and ethical trial: "The matter distressed Abraham greatly, for it concerned a son of his" (21:11) – and indeed he knew that Sarah was within her rights. Furthermore, this was the will of God, and therefore proceeded necessarily from His way, the plan for mending the world: Isaac, not Ishmael, was designated to be the father of the chosen people descended from Abraham, who would inherit the land of Canaan and the ethical-spiritual mission contingent on it.

In this context, God in his speech to Abraham emphasizes again a sentence whose importance will be considerable for the continuation of the story, for it foreshadows the binding of Isaac: "For it is through Isaac that offspring shall be continued for you." (21:12) The emphasis is on the phrase, "for you," i.e. not only for Sarah who is demanding Ishmael's expulsion. For this reason, Abraham accepts the judgment. Still, we should emphasize that accepting the rightful exclusivity of Isaac's inheritance of Canaan does not negate the right of Hagar, much less the right of Ishmael. He remains an heir, and Abraham must give him and his mother protection. This, too, is God's judgment: "As for the son of the slave-woman, I will make a nation of him, too, for he is your seed." (21:13) The emphasis is again on "your seed." How, then, did Abraham fulfill his ethical-legal debt to Ishmael?

The story conceals the part that Abraham played and gives credit for the solution to God, who took on Himself the protection of the slave-woman and her son and guaranteed their welfare and their future. From his side, Abraham expelled Hagar and her son with some bread and a skin-flask of water in her hand. She wandered in the wilderness of Beersheba, and an angel of God rescued them from death by thirst (Genesis 21:14-19). But we should note that the manner of depiction of these events again foreshadows the binding of Isaac: "Abraham rose early in the morning and took bread and a skin of water. He gave them to Hagar, putting them on her shoulder together with the child." (21:14 — see 22:3) It is as if Abraham offers his love for his son as a sacrifice to God, who demanded the deed while taking on Himself the role of protector. In this way, Abraham entrusts his son into God's hands, and Hagar becomes his agent by placing the boy on her shoulder. (This must be a ritual act: a fourteen-year-old boy can walk on his own two feet, and Hagar could certainly not carry him the whole distance on her shoulder.)

Thus Hagar goes on her way, similar to Abraham on the way to the binding of Isaac. Like him, she later hears the angel announcing that God has heard the voice of the lad, and he opens her eyes to see the well that was already in front of her eyes, just as Abraham was shown the substitute-ram that was already prepared in the thicket.

What happened next? According to the story of the Binding, Abraham returned with his son to his home. Like him, Hagar got up in front of the well after she drank and gave water to her son, and went on her way. Prior to this, though, she "wandered," and it appears that she knew where she was heading. After finding the well, her first stop, she finds her way to her final destination. The story does not spell out where she went or where the angel led her, but from the continuation it becomes evident that they dwelt in the wilderness of Paran, and the boy grew up in freedom and became a bowman. We learn from this that Hagar, who from Sarah's standpoint was simply expelled, knew from Abraham where she should go. From his standpoint she was not expelled, but sent forth to a place of protection that was ready for her where she could raise the boy to fulfill his destiny as a continuer of Abraham's line. Our assumption that Abraham, by fulfilling God's command, was caring for his slave-woman and her son Ishmael is strengthened by the fact that he took care to give gifts to all the sons of his concubines "and he sent them away from his son Isaac eastward, to the land of the East." (Genesis 25:6)

After Isaac's right of primogeniture to future inheritance of the land of Canaan was insured on behalf of the people that would issue from his seed, we are told of the securing of Isaac's actual landhold in the present. This is the interest in the story of the covenant enacted between Abraham and Abimelech and his army commander Phichol concerning Abraham's status in the land where he dwelt. (21:22–34) We should note again that this is the land where he is a resident alien, not a patrimony or national possession. From the national-legal standpoint it is defined as "land of the Philistines." The emphasis in the story is placed on the legal aspect, and we learn from it the full significance of a covenant enacted between equals. First, both parties enter the covenant of their full free choice, on the basis of common interests:

At that time Abimelech and Phichol, chief of his troops, said to Abraham, "God is with you in everything that you do. Therefore swear to me here by God that you will not deal falsely with me or with my kith and kin, but will deal with me and with the land in which you have sojourned as loyally as I have dealt with you." And Abraham said, "I swear it." (Genesis 21:22–24)

The initiative is from the side of Abimelech and Phichol on the basis of their claim of prior right: Abimelech dealt kindly with Abraham and granted him permission of residency in his land, therefore he and his people are entitled to expect the same relationship of fidelity and kindness from his side. In this kind of approach we find at the outset the assumption that both sides have an interest in the covenant, and that it is of equal benefit to both. Indeed, Abraham expresses his agreement. He acknowledges that the expectation of his prospective covenant-partners is correct, but he sets forth a counter-claim in response: "Abraham reproached Abimelech for the well of water which the servants of Abimelech had seized." (21:25) It is now Abimelech's turn to apologize and to pledge his responsibility to return to Abraham his full rights in the land.

Second, the covenant is a definition of mutual responsibility between equals in respect of their legal status, in a way that defines the responsibility of each side in terms of the rights of the other, in full reciprocity. As long as each one stands by his responsibility, he obligates the other side to stand by his. Third, the responsibility is made effective by oath, and it thus becomes the responsibility of each of the partners to God, who is thus made an additional partner of the covenant. If they break their oath, they sin before God as having sworn falsely. We recall that it was for this reason that Abraham wished to determine if there was "fear of God" in the king of Gerar and his people. Fourth, after the oath — that is enacted between the two participants, with God listening — a ceremony takes place that is a kind of public testimony before human witnesses who are not involved in the covenant and can witness to its enactment: "He said, 'Take these seven sheep from my hand so that you can be a witness that I have dug this well." (21:30) Fifth, a memorial is established as witness for the generations — in this case, the naming of the well where they swore: "Therefore the place was named Beer-Sheva (the 'Well of the Oath'), for there the two of them swore." (21:31) Similarly: "He planted a tamarisk in Beersheba and called there in the name of the Lord, God of Eternity." (21:33) Finally, it is worth noting that the covenant was enacted not only between the individuals who initiated it, but also their descendants after them for three generations. Thus Abraham secures not only his own landhold but that of his son and his heirs after him in the land where he dwells. Therefore he was careful that the covenant be enacted in a way that it should remain in force and be perpetuated for generations.

We now come to the story of the Akedah, the Binding of Isaac, that is regarded as the most important and problematic trial that Abraham underwent, both with respect to the fulfillment of his mission and with respect to the future of Isaac and his descendants in perpetuity. This is attested not only by the exceptional ritual expressive of supreme sacrifice, but also by the place chosen for the Akedah — Mount Moriah, the place where the Temple would later be built. The first question that we must determine from the literary context is: What did God command Abraham to do? More precisely, what did Abraham understand God to have commanded him? Did he set out on his way in full readiness to slaughter his son? Or perhaps did he know in advance that this was not the intention?

Let us first examine the language of the command: "After these things" (referring to the expulsion of Hagar and Ishmael, and the covenant with the king of Gerar; from a literary standpoint we should see this as the narrator's directive to understand the following story in the light of these two previous) —

After these things God put Abraham to the test. He said to him, "Abraham," and he answered, "Here I am." And He said, "Take your son, your favored one, Isaac, whom you love, and go to the land of Moriah, and raise him up there as an *'olah* [elevation-offering] on one of the heights that I will point out to you." (Genesis 22:1–2)

Three directives are here present, linked to one another: (1) taking his designated son intentionally, to dedicate him to his destiny; (2) going to the land of Moriah, to the mountain whose pointing-out defines the meaning of the name Moriah (= "instruction") — "one of the mountains that I will tell you," i.e. the mountain that will be the site of the telling of God's word and His instruction to Abraham then and for later generations; finally, the instruction that is the end-goal: *raising up* Isaac as an *'olah* to the Lord. What means this "raising up an *'olah* to the Lord"?

According to Leviticus (1:1–9), an *'olah* is a sacrifice that is offered up on YHWH's altar for atonement and sanctification, i.e. for elevation. He who offers the sacrifice lays his hands on the animal's head and confesses his sins, and thus the animal becomes a substitution and representative for himself. Afterwards the animal is placed on the altar over the wood-pile, it is slaughtered and cut up into sections and burned to YHWH in its entirety. By means of this sacrifice, the sins of the offerer are atoned, and he is dedicated to God. It is worth noting that from the standpoint of the relationship between God and the person, offering up the *'olah* expresses the person's standing before God as judge of all the earth in order to be purified an dedicated before Him from his sins. This is the general principle underlying the sacrifices in the Temple. In a later time, this became the major principle underlying prayer: a person should consider himself being judged before God for his sins in order to achieve purification and sanctification and thus be deserving of his life, which is a gift of divine grace. Thus he should follow God's ways and keep His commands.

To be sure, an ordinary *'olah* is the offering-up of an animal on the altar in place of the worshipper, as a symbolic substitute for himself. In order to consider the unique significance of the command to offer Isaac himself on the altar, we should examine the ceremony of ordination of Aaron and his sons to become priests before YHWH in the Tent of Meeting (Exodus 29). This is a complicated ritual, which includes several symbols that have the effect of identifying the worshippers with their sacrifices. At the climax, they are instructed: "Place all these [i.e., the selected pieces of the sacrificed ram and their accompanying meal-offerings] on the palms of Aaron and his sons, and offer them as an elevation offering before the Lord." (Exodus 29:24) The raising of the pieces is a symbolic act that signifies the elevation of the priests themselves onto the altar. In this way the significance of the dedication of the priests who minister before God is enhanced by their being acquired by God as His servants. They are themselves offered and elevated in order that they should be deemed worthy to offer the sacrifices of all Israel to God. Once they become God's sacred chattel in this manner, it is forbidden for them to leave the domain of the sanctuary, lest they profane their sanctity.

All of this helps explain the significance of the commandment that Abraham was commanded: he was required to take his son, to bring him to the place where YHWH's Temple would one day stand in the land of Canaan, and elevate him symbolically as an *'olah*, in other words, dedicate him as a priest to YHWH. From Abraham's standpoint, he symbolically transfers the title that he has as father to his son to God. This is right and just: God gave Abraham his son as a special, supernatural gift, and so it is altogether proper that he should give his son to God so that he might serve him in the land that may be considered God's sanctuary. This interpretation of the command is confirmed by the continuation, when God says to Abraham, after the symbolic elevation of Isaac over the wood of the altar and the symbolic taking of the knife (paralleling the symbolic elevation of Aaron' and his sons' hands over the altar): "Now I know that you fear God, since you have not withheld your son, your favored one, from Me." (22:12) We learned of the meaning of "god-fearing" from the episode of Abraham and Abimelech in Gerar, that it does not refer to one who obeys God's command as an order, no matter what it may be, but to one who reveres God as judge of all the earth, as a judge who sees all a person's deeds and inner thoughts and judges each one fairly as he deserves. The phrase "you have not withheld your son, your favored one, from Me" confirms that the significance of the entire action was to transfer the father's rights in his son to God, who had bestowed him in His great kindness.

We may now ask, whether Abraham could have thought that the divine command to "elevate" his favorite beloved son as an *'olah* meant that he should slaughter him on the altar and kill him? If we pay attention to the "things" after which God tested Abraham, it follows that just as this thought could not have arisen in God's mind, it could not have occurred to Abraham either. We return to the story of the expulsion of Hagar and Ishmael, which prefigures the Akedah. Abraham received two promises before he agreed to Sarah's demand, which he had regarded with suspicion: first, that no harm would come to Ishmael — on the contrary, he would grow up and become the progenitor of a nation that would come from his seed. Second, that Abraham would have seed through Isaac. If God promised that Ishmael would suffer no harm but would live, grow up, and become a progenitor of a nation from Abraham's seed, how would it occur to Abraham that God would require him to slaughter his son Isaac on the altar? Would it be conceivable that God would abrogate His promise that was given in a covenant that God had guaranteed? As a God-fearing man who walked in God's ways, the ways of justice and equity, Abraham would have had to refuse such a command, i.e. to see it as a test to which absolute refusal was the correct response, for that is what "the way of God — doing what is just and right" would require.

Confirmation that Abraham did not set out on his way with the thought of slaughtering his son is found in the conversation that took place between him and Isaac on the way:

> Isaac said to his father Abraham, "Father!" And he answered, "Yes, my son." And he said, "Here are the firestone and the wood; but where is the sheep for the burnt offering?" And Abraham said, "God will see to the sheep for His burnt offering, my son." (Genesis 22:7–8)

One should understand these words in their plain sense: Isaac's question flows from his confidence that his father is not going to slaughter him. Therefore he wonders, where is the sheep? Abraham replies that God will see to the sheep for the burnt-offering, and the simple meaning is that the two of them will see it when they arrive at the place where they are going. It is hard to interpret that Isaac understood his father's words in any other way, and it is hard to conceive that Abraham deceived his son at that moment. It is certainly possible to regroup the words "the sheep for His burnt-offering, my son" but only in another sense: "the sheep that God will provide will be your substitute, my son," and that is why you are carrying the wood for the burnt-offering. In this way, the ceremony receives its full ritual significance: it combines three participants in an exalting ceremony of mission full of joy of elevation and sanctification. Each of the three participants contributes the portion that represents himself: Isaac bears the wood symbolically on his shoulders; Abraham carries with him symbolically the firestone and the knife; and God will contribute the ram of His own in exchange for acquiring Isaac. "And the two of them walked on together" — together in knowledge, together in understanding and together in agreement, for a ceremony of this kind can only be carried out with the knowledge and free will of all participants, as is required in enactment of a covenant.

Analysis of the description of this action of offering an *'olah* also confirms this understanding. Abraham builds the altar, arranges the wood and binds Isaac on top of the wood. This is a symbolic action that expresses his absolute readiness to give his son to God, and Isaac, who is bound willingly, expresses by that deed his willingness to be offered to God. Thus the two of them did everything required from their side. Now comes the time for God to contribute His portion. When Abraham stretches forth his hand to the knife to complete the symbolic movement of offering the *'olah*, the angel of God who calls to him from heaven points him to the ram that was already made available in the thicket beside the altar: "When Abraham looked up, his eye fell upon a ram, caught in a thicket by its horns. So Abraham went and took the ram and offered it up as a burnt offering in place of his son." (22:13) All happened as Abraham had foreseen and predicted to his son when they had set out on their journey.

This interpretation of the story of the Akedah removes the moral problematic, along with the heroic dimension that the prevalent Jewish and Christian interpretation attaches to it. The source of the other interpretation is to be found in the rabbis, and we may assume that it originated in the experiences of martyrdom that the Jewish people underwent after the destruction of the First Temple and the Babylonian Exile:

All this has come upon us, yet we have not forgotten You, or been false to Your covenant. Our hearts have not gone astray, nor have our feet swerved from Your path, though You cast us, crushed, to where the sea monster is, and covered us over with deepest darkness. If we forget the name of our God and spread forth our hands to a foreign god, God would surely search it out, for He knows the secrets of the heart. It is for Your sake that we are slain all day long, that we are regarded as sheep to be slaughtered. (Psalm 44:18–23)

Because of the experiences of sacrifice of the Jewish people, the story of the quasi-sacrifice of Isaac became a symbol of Jewish destiny, the chosen people bearing on itself, as the Suffering Servant of YHWH in Isaiah's prophecy, the sins of all the peoples, thus being a "sheep led to slaughter, like a ewe, dumb before those who shear her, he did not open his mouth." (Isaiah 53:7) We should not be surprised that the paradox of Jewish existence was associated with the story of the Akedah, which thus became the primary source for demonstrating Israel's special merit before God as a basis for pleading that God be merciful in His judgment of them. Yet it should be clear that originally the meaning of the story was the reverse.

As we said, the original intention of the story was to establish the significance of the worship of God in the Temple, whose essence lies in the person's standing before God the Lord of creation and judge of the whole world: to be judged before Him, to atone for one's sins, to sanctify and devote oneself to Him by walking in His ways. Thus a person will find grace in God's eyes and merit long life, happiness and honor. And what is the significance of dedicating the son as a priest who ministers in the sanctuary by transferring title of him to God? This, too, is a precept that was perpetuated for generations, first through dedication of the first-born of every family in Israel to the priestly office, and afterwards through appointing the priests of the line of Aaron as representatives of the first-born of all Israel. (see Numbers 3:40–51) This was a way of symbolizing the choice of the people of Israel to be a kingdom of priests and holy nation, the people who were the "special treasure" of God, His possession and glory.

This conception of the status of the people in relation to its God has implications also for its status in relation to the land of Canaan, which was also God's special possession in perpetuity. The people, who are God's possession, are thus bound to the land that will be God's land forever. Indeed, in respect of the point in the narrative where the Akedah is incorporated, among the episodes of Abraham after Isaac's birth, this implication has essential importance: through the Akedah, Isaac is bound to the land, and the land is bound to him. He will never leave the land of Canaan even to marry the woman who was designated for him from the ancestral land of his father Abraham. This was his obligation under the covenant; God's obligation was to grant the land to Isaac and his seed in perpetuity, on condition that he and his seed fulfill what is incumbent on them and acquire the land dedicated to God by dwelling on it in ways of justice and righteousness.

From what has been said above it may be understood that the absolute acquisition of title of the land of Canaan for Isaac and his seed from God's side still does not make the land the possession of the people. In order for the promise to be fulfilled, the people must take physical possession of its land in a way that will be proper according to the divine law, which has been declared to be the law of all peoples that fear Him, i.e. the law of righteousness that applies equally to all human beings and all nations, and will therefore be acceptable by their judgment. This is the background for the episode in which Abraham takes part after the Binding of Isaac and after Sarah's death in Hebron — the purchase of the field of the cave of Machpelah from the Hittites, who are its legal owners according to the law of God and man. The significance of acquisition of this site, to be the eternal resting-place for his wife Sarah, for himself, and afterwards for Isaac and Rebekah, Jacob and Leah is expressed in the elaborate legal procedure of the transaction. It is a model of how to practice justice and righteousness when the promise is implemented to give the land of Canaan to the people of Israel.

Let us first compare the political framework of the negotiations for the purchase of the field with the prior negotiations with Abimelech and Pichol over Abraham's residency in the land of the Philistines. The earlier negotiations were with the king of Gerar and his army chief, who ruled in their land subject to the divine law. In the negotiations, these two represent their nation, for authority is invested in them. But they do not exercise it arbitrarily, but by the rule of justice ("fear of God"). In Hebron, the negotiations are carried out "in the presence of the Hittites, of all who entered the gate of his town." (Genesis 23:18) Here, too, the narrative description emphasizes that we are not speaking of a private negotiation between Abraham and Ephron the Hittite (who was the owner of the field and the cave) but of a public negotiation between Abraham and the "people of the land", [20] among whom Ephron the Hittite sat.

From these remarks we learn something about the governance of the city, in whose gate the popular assembly is gathered. Authority is held directly by it, and therefore Abraham turns directly to it: "I am a resident alien among you; sell me a burial-plot among you that I may remove my dead for burial." (Genesis 23:4) Only after the essential consent of the notables of the people to grant him a burial-place in their land does Abraham request of them to approach on his behalf Ephron the Hittite who sits among them, in order to negotiate with him concerning the purchase of the field-plot and cave that are in his ownership. Still, Abraham continues to conduct his negotiation in the sight of all those present in the gate of the city, and he thus emphasizes that the purchase that he transacts in Hebron has a political significance: Abraham is not a private citizen, but the head of an ancestral clan, and Ephron is one of the notables of the landed gentry, who speak in his name and depend on his consent.

[20] "People of the land" — *am ha-aretz*. Perhaps even "landed gentry." The scenario of Genesis 23 suggests that the reference is to the land-owning citizens assembled as a popular ruling body. (LL)

What status does Abraham seek in the city as head of an ancestral clan? The status of a "resident alien." He is not one of the "people of the land" nor a complete alien as he was in the land of the Philistines, but he has an intermediate status — a permanent resident who is not of the same nation. This is a carefully calculated legal-political definition. Abraham respects the law of the land and observes its provisions, but he nevertheless refuses to be a member of the people. In their first response, the Hittites make an enticing offer with a catch: "Hear us, our lord: You are a prince of God in our midst. Bury your dead in the choice of our graves! None of us will withhold his grave from you for the purpose of burying your dead." (23:6) Abraham is presented with the temptation to receive a grave gratis, and to enjoy the status of a "prince of God" in his city. The catch is in the attached condition: "in our midst," i.e. as one of us. Not as a resident alien, but as one of the "people of the land" in every respect.

It appears that the Hittites were interested in the assimilation of the rich and honored prince into their ranks, but Abraham stands firm: he belongs to another people. The ancestral home that he represents is not in Hebron but in Haran (to which he will afterwards send his servant to bring his son a wife), and as for his ethnic identity, Abraham wishes to preserve clear boundaries. He is a prince of God, not among the Hittites but in his own people, and as such he wishes to remain a permanent resident in the land that will someday be a possession for his seed. Abraham thus stands by his first offer to purchase the field-plot and cave at Machpelah for full value in cash. The rest of the recorded public discussion is for the purpose of emphasizing that the transfer of title was performed legally with the free will of both sides after the seller received the full payment that he requested. In order to dispel all doubts as to the free consent to the purchase, Abraham accepts Ephron's first offered price without haggling. The seller would have no grounds for complaining that he was forced to sell the field at a loss, and the whole assembly would be witness to the fact. The boundaries of the field are also spelled out for everyone's knowledge, as well as the purchase price. Everything is done in accordance with accepted Hittite law and in a manner acceptable to Abraham as well.

The result was a sale-and-acquisition agreement that was perpetually valid, about which no cavils could be raised. The burial-place of the patriarchs and matriarchs of the people would testify for generations to come that the dwelling of the people on its land was not on the basis of a divine promise that was given at the cost of injustice to other peoples dwelling on it, but was legal in the eyes of God and legally-knowledgeable people. We emphasize again: alongside the legal sanction of the perpetual divine promise — for God is Lord of the whole earth — stands the legal sanction of active possession of the land in accord with divine justice — for He is the righteous judge of all humankind and all peoples in equal manner. After valid acquisition of this kind, the field will be passed on from generation to generation as an ancestral possession, and a claim of acquisition will be formed that will never be revoked, unless the people become corrupt and forsake the ways of their God.

This legal enactment was held up as an example by the prophets and teachers of the Torah in Israel when they spoke of the conditions of implementation of the land to the people. It does not negate the forcible conquest of the land from the Canaanite peoples who dwelt on it, when their iniquity would reach its full measure and they would lose their right in God's eyes by straying from His commands, as was predicted in the "covenant between the pieces" (Genesis 15). However, the conquest itself was not regarded as consummating national possession of the land. Only settling on it by the universal rules of justice that the Torah imposes on the people of Israel in its land brings the promise from a state of potentiality to actuality in the right way. Only in this way will the land become an ancestral possession that cannot be revoked in any respect, as in the words of the prophet: "Zion shall be redeemed in justice, and its repentant ones in righteousness." (Isaiah 1:27)

Finally, we remark that the system of governance by the people, as described above, is a source for understanding the substance and mode of activity of the "assembly" as a framework of direct tribal democracy in the basic law of the Mosaic Torah, as we shall see later on. The "assembly," mentioned in the Torahitic law and afterwards in the historical books of the "early prophets" (Joshua, Judges, Samuel and Kings) is a gathering of the people led by the elders. This represents the people as a collective body with legal status and authority, such that no law, judicial institution, priestly or military directive, or taxation for the support of any of these, is regarded as binding without their consent. None of the institutions of leadership has the authority to abrogate the legal rights of possession of any of the families comprising it. These rights of possession, especially of land and other means of subsistence, are the basis of power of the assembly and of each clan individually. Therefore all the covenants that empower the legislative institutions, the judges and the leaders in times of war and peace, must be approved by the assembly on the basis of free choice. This applies also to the covenant that established the kingdom of God through the Torah that was given at Sinai. The sovereign authority of the Davidic dynasty was based both on God's choice of David as determined by the prophet Samuel, who anointed him and charged him with receiving God's commands in His Torah, but also on the consent of the Israelite assembly, who accepted him as their king. Indeed, as time went by, the assembly would meet and formally consent to the accession of every legal heir who ascended the Davidic throne. The story of the purchase that Abraham transacted for the field and cave of Machpelah is the fullest description that we have in the Bible of how such a democratic assembly operated. However, a parallel description, that confirms the parallel between the gathering of the "people of the land" in Hebron and the Israelite "assembly," is found in the Book of Ruth in the story of Boaz's "redemption" of Ruth and the land-holding of Elimelech's clan. (Ruth 4:1-13)

"True Kindness"

In preparation for the narrative of Abraham's last days, the narrator reveals several facts that he had no need of mentioning earlier, though they shed important light on his personality in a number of respects. (1) We have already mentioned that Abraham had several concubines, who bore him sons before Ishmael and Isaac were born. (2) Abraham and Sarah parted ways after Isaac's birth. Sarah died in Hebron, and Abraham came to mourn her from his dwelling in Beersheba in the land of the Philistines, where he had his fields. (Genesis 23:2) (3) After Sarah's death, Abraham took another wife, Keturah, who bore him no fewer than six sons. (25:1-2) All these attest to Abraham's sexual powers, that persisted after their renewal, whereas Sarah seems to have reverted to her withered state after weaning her only son Isaac. Sarah fulfilled her promise of royal progeny with a single child, whereas Abraham continued to fulfill his destiny from youth onward, to be a "father of a multitude of nations." Indeed, the evidence of his prodigious sexual powers explains also the depth of this "exalted father's" youthful sin. He could extricate himself from it only through awareness of his guilt and fear of God, which exalted him, harnessed his urge, and directed the fertility implicit in it to fulfillment of his destiny.

Toward the end of Abraham's life are revealed two additional facts that have bearing on his final project for assuring the future of his son Isaac — marrying him to a woman who will be appropriate for fulfilling his destiny in the land of Canaan. The first fact pertains to Abraham's family that remained in Haran:

> Some time later, Abraham was told, "Milcah too has borne children to your brother Nahor: Uz the first-born, and Buz his brother, and Kemuel the father of Aram; and Chesed, Hazo, Pildash, Jidlaph, and Bethuel" — Bethuel being the father of Rebekah. (Genesis 22:20–23)

It is clear that the mention of Rebekah's name provides the purpose of this report establishing her relation and elective affinity for Isaac. In addition, there is considerable significance in the mere mention of a second branch of the clan that Terah, father of Abraham and Nahor, established in Haran. In order to understand the future family history of Isaac and his sons, we should be reminded that the departure of Abram and Sarai from Haran to Canaan divided the clan that Terah had led toward the fulfillment of the destiny that was set for humanity in the covenant of Noah and his sons into two branches, each of them keeping faith with Terah's legacy but carving out its own particular path. The branch that remained in Haran no longer regarded Canaan as its promised land but remained in Aram of the Two Rivers, just as Lot settled in Sodom. It kept its identity but did not separate itself from the idolatrous culture of its environment in the rigorous manner that Abraham and Sarah separated themselves. From the narrative of Jacob in Laban's household we will learn later that assimilation was unavoidable. Still, the separation that Abraham and Sarah made from the idolatrous culture in Canaan required them to maintain the tie with their "homeland" — through the branch of the clan that remained in Haran. We will show later that in the continued historical narrative the tie with Haran also had important political implications, which influenced the decisions that were accepted at the crossroads between settling in Canaan or going into diaspora.

Given this background, the narrative of bringing Rebekah to be Isaac's wife (Genesis 24) takes on worldly, familial and political significance far more complex than the simple tale that ascribes the matchmaking and its revelation totally to divine providence. From the information that reached Abraham, we may deduce that he took pains and consideration over the matter, and may have hinted at his intentions. The servant who took the journey knew in advance who was the intended bride-to-be, and she and her family knew in advance that Abraham was going to send his servant in order to negotiate her coming. Abraham would not have sent his servant, had he not known in advance that the family would be ready to send their daughter to Canaan if the conditions were right. The servant set out in order to examine the young woman from up close to judge if she was right for Isaac; if his opinion of her was positive, he would then have to persuade her family of Abraham's wealth, generosity, and ability to guarantee their daughter's happiness.

All the details of the tale are consistent with this practical, realistic description. The resourceful servant knew where to meet the designated maiden in order to observe her before announcing his presence to her or to her parents. He stood before the well; the Hebrew *'ayin* suggests a double-entendre ("well / eye"), for it was the place where the maidens would come to draw water for their households, but also the place where the marriageable young men would come to observe the young women that were suitable matches for them. Rebekah, no less resourceful than the servant, understood immediately who was the man who came with a caravan of camels from afar to observe her, and it seems that the two did not disappoint each other. This does not contradict the faithful, smart servant's statement that God prospered his way, for it was the counsel of divine providence that guided this happy match. Rebekah indeed demonstrated that she was the woman in whom Isaac, the forty-year-old orphan, would find consolation for his mother's death.

But at this point we should mention the second important fact that we had not known until this last chapter in the story of Abram-Abraham's life: neither he nor Sarah were the principal parties who had achieved their high status and economic success in the land of Canaan, which was so great that the narrator could sum it up enthusiastically: "YHWH had blessed Abraham in everything." (Genesis 24:1) The principal actor was "his servant, the elder of his house, who managed all his affairs." (24:2) This simple sentence is laden with double and triple irony. To uncover it, we should pay attention to the relation between Abraham's being blessed in "all," and the servant's role in

managing "all"; to the contradiction between this man's being designated a "servant" and "elder of the household, managing all"; and to
the contradiction between this man's importance in Abraham's life —
he is the man who performed his assignments even in intimate family
matters — and his being anonymous, without a name. Who is this
man? What is his place in the story? What important truth, concealed
until now, is revealed at the point where the journey of the god-fearing
man's life approaches its end and there begins the journey of the second
couple, Isaac and Rebekah?

Before we examine what is the narrative truth that Abraham's servant
represents, let us go back and examine the manner of his presentation
in the story, which is surprising and cannot be without calculated
narrative intent. We recall that in the chapter that describes the
"covenant between the pieces" Abram bewailed his childlessness; he
had no heir. The only man who could inherit after him was "the son of
my household, Eliezer of Damascus." (Genesis 15:2) The commentators
deduced that the servant whom Abraham sent to Haran was Eliezer
of Damascus. The identification is so convincing that most readers
imagine it is written in the very text. Yet precisely because of the high
likelihood of this identification, the fact that the narrator prefers to
ignore it is striking. We saw before that the giving of a name is one of
the means by which the characteristics of Biblical heroes are conveyed.
The name Eliezer ("My God is a help") is appropriate to a man who
devoted himself to helping his God-fearing master. Yet the narrator
preferred to present the man who was accompanied by a divine angel
("He said to me: 'The Lord before whom I walk will send His angel with
you to prosper your way" — 24:40) — and who himself is like an angel
of God — by hiding his name. The paradox that is thus introduced
into the story is expressed in the fact that the anonymous man with
no name is the prime hero of the story, whereas all the supporting
characters are called by their names.

The narrator goes out of his way to emphasize this fact, and in place of
the name he mentions the descriptive characteristics that define his
roles in Abraham's household: he is Abraham's servant, the elder of
his house, the manager of his affairs. He is identified by his roles, but in
one place the narrator must call him "the man" which seems especially
nondescript — at the moment when he had to make by himself the
decision that was fateful for the success of his whole mission: did the
maiden whom he met by the well pass the test that he had set her? Was
she fitting to be wife to his master's son?

What does the title "man" indicate? From the context we learn that it is the intention to present him as the right man in the right place, the man who passes the test, stands firm with full confidence and does not back down at the moment of decision. He gives of himself one-hundred percent, invested fully in the action, knows how to see what he sees, knows how to judge correctly, knows how to draw the conclusion and act precisely at the right time.

Therefore it is possible to rely on him that he will succeed in his undertakings. It appears that it was for the same reason that Eve used the term "man" when she called her first son Cain — "I have gotten a man-child from the Lord" (Genesis 4:1) — for she meant that she had born a son in whom she could place her trust, a son in whom God could place His trust more than He could in her and her husband at the time of their test.

The meaning of concealing his name becomes clear, however, from the following: the emissary is a man who identifies with his mission to the point that he becomes unaware of his own ego. His attention is directed only at satisfying his master's will and bringing him the increased good that he hopes for. But let us not err in thinking that we are speaking of self-abnegation or self-sacrifice. When the "man" is devoted to his mission he fulfills the best that is in him. In all his words he sounds full of joy and thanks to God that his mission is successful: this is his privilege, to participate in the kindness that God performed for Abraham through his agency. This, then, is the hidden truth that the "servant" reveals through his mission: he himself is the embodiment of the divine kindness by which God prospered the God-fearing Abraham to be a leader who brought the reality of his human life and the life of his surrounding a bit closer to the divine vision of creation. In counterpoint to the congenital human urge to evil, the "man" embodies the divine gift planted in humanity to do the good for its own sake with the same power of longing as the evil urge seeks to do evil. This is the expression of love that overcomes fear in fulfilling humanity's destiny on earth.

The quality of kindness is expressed in this story in the prayers of the servant at the critical moments of his mission:

> He made the camels kneel down by the well outside the city, at evening time, the time when women come out to draw water. And he said, "O Lord, God of my master Abraham, grant me good fortune this day, and deal graciously with my master Abraham." (Genesis 24:11-12)

Later in the story when Rebekah acts as he had hoped:

> He said, "Blessed be the Lord, the God of my master Abraham, who has not withheld His steadfast faithfulness from my master. For I have been guided on my errand by the Lord, to the house of my master's kinsman." (Genesis 24:27)

And at the end in his words to Rebekah's relatives when he seeks to influence them to consent and allow him to bring Rebekah to Isaac in Canaan:

> "Then I bowed low in homage to the Lord and blessed the Lord, the God of my master Abraham, who led me on the right way to get the daughter of my master's brother for his son. And now, if you mean to treat my master with true kindness, tell me; and if not, tell me also, that I may turn right or left." (Genesis 24:48–49)

This is a calculated diplomatic speech that achieved its objective immediately and concluded the short negotiation without giving Laban — who, the servant notes, is unlike Rebekah not a model of generosity but whose heart is full of egoistic considerations — a chance to detain her in the hope of squeezing out more material benefits for himself in exchange for his consent for his sister to go to Canaan.

The manner of the agent's action thus realizes the "truth" in his kindness: he achieves the perfect good not when he merely satisfies the purpose for which he came, but when he realizes it in the best possible way, without causing secondary anguish, to teach us that only when the good is achieved in a good way is it truly good. It follows that by considering the servant's performance itself we can learn what is true kindness: fidelity out of love and not out of pursuit of reward or self-gratification, seeing the true reward for the deed in the deed itself when it achieves its objective, and a strategy focused on achieving the best result through the proper means, without detours dictated by ulterior selfish motives.

Does Rebekah in her conduct also embody the quality of true kindness? At first sight it appears that her passing the test that the servant has arranged testifies that she is a model of kindness as he is. Yet a deeper reflection will show that she was shrewd and knew how to satisfy the agent's expectations to the letter; first she served water to the man as he had asked; then she watered his camels too, though he had not asked this of her; later she expressed her preference for setting out with him at once, in order to be wife to Isaac who was waiting for her. Yet if we compare the way that she received the messenger with the way that Laban received him, we shall see that Rebekah did indeed know the meaning of kindness, but had not yet achieved the way of doing kindness for its own sake, i.e. for the other: like her brother Laban, who displayed his selfish considerations in a striking manner, Rebekah also weighed her advantage in view of the great wealth that the servant displayed before her in the caravan of camels that she watered and the gifts that he showered on her, and she was shrewd enough to understand that she would achieve more through her kindness than her brother would achieve through his open greediness to get as much as he could.

That Rebekah was quite different from her brother on the one hand, but also from the servant on the other hand, is confirmed by the narrator in that he does not let us hear in her words the same note of kindness that we hear in the messenger's words. Nor do we hear it in the parting blessing from her parents' household, but rather the whiff of victory: "O sister, may you become the thousands of myriads, and may your seed conquer the gate of their enemies!" (Genesis 24:60) Indeed, the additional confirmation is revealed in the continuation of the narrative of her family history with Isaac and her sons. At first she wrought kindness with Isaac, who loved her and was comforted by her for the death of his mother, but afterwards she transmitted the desire for aggrandizement, which is the root of howling injustice, to her husband Isaac and her son Esau, and in the last analysis also to Jacob with whom she identified, to teach us that kindness is not enough to achieve perfect good unless it is of the true variety.

From the Laughter of Happiness to Fear and Trembling

The period of Isaac's leadership after his marriage and his father's death is related as a period of trial of the permanence of Abraham's achievements in Canaan, from the internal aspect of the transmission of his spiritual legacy to his progeny and from the external aspect of his residency in the land. In both these aspects, Abraham prepared for Isaac as much as a father can ensure for his son for the sake of his happiness and fulfillment of his destiny, and it was Isaac's task to preserve his father's achievements, to extend them and fortify them, both in the political aspect of maintaining a foothold in Canaan and in the aspect of moral destiny. Without reinforcing the covenants and raising the bar of moral achievement, it would be impossible to maintain what was already achieved, because the conditions of survival as resident aliens in Canaan became more challenging. Did this successor couple understand how they had to cope with their mission? Did they possess the moral resources to fulfill it? From an overall survey of the history of Isaac, which is short in comparison with those of his father and his son Jacob, we can say that Isaac did not appreciate the magnitude of the obstacles, nor did he understand the significance of the change that occurred between his father's time and his own. Similarly, he did not understand how he should cope with the raising of his family so that his two sons could live together in Canaan. He imitated his father at every step, but the most striking difference between them was his short-sightedness. He was a man who does not see what is before his own eyes — in the spiritual sense, before he became physically blind with advancing age. He invested his energies in the political and economic aspects of his task, increasing his wealth through fair and just means, while leaving management of the spiritual destiny to Rebekah. He was a man of the field and devoted himself to agriculture — digging water-wells, increasing the crops, increasing the livestock. He succeeded in all these — "the man prospered, and increased substantially; he had livestock of the flocks and the herds and abundant crops, and the Philistines envied him." (Genesis 26:13–14)

The last phrase expresses the irony latent in Isaac's economic prosperity. We shall see that it was too much, and instead of strengthening his ties with his neighbors, it led to conflict with the covenantal partners among whom he dwelt as a resident alien. From the time that the covenant was established between them and Abraham, the Philistines multiplied and grew in wealth. Their government was still secure in the ways of justice, but their shepherds made use of the wells that Abraham had dug as well as those that Isaac added. The Philistines made a pact with Abraham because his success was to their benefit, but Isaac's prosperity aroused their envy. Perhaps it was possible to resolve the conflict by way of kindness through mutual assistance, but Isaac did not seek new economic-political solutions. He wanted to renew the same pact that his father had made and repeat his actions exactly, even to the point of his sojourn in Gerar with Rebekah and the unfortunate announcement that Rebekah was his sister (Genesis 26:6–12), an episode that certainly did not improve the tie between them! In the end, this was an absolute deception. And perhaps for this reason she did not hesitate to repay him with a deception of her own when the time was ripe.

Because of the envy of the shepherds of Gerar, Isaac had to remove himself to beyond their pasture-land, and this reawakened the interest of the king of Gerar and his army-chief to renew with him the pact that they had made with Abraham. Now there came a period of prosperity and wealth, but Isaac did not foresee that after several years the Philistines would desire the new wells that he had dug for himself. Indeed, in his old age he learned that he would not be able to provide an inheritance for both his sons in Canaan, as it says explicitly in the non-legendary, historical version of the narrative: Esau took his family and possessions that he had amassed in Canaan "and went to another land because of his brother Jacob, for their possessions were too great to dwell together, and the land where they resided was unable to support them both because of their livestock. So Esau settled in Mount Seir — Esau, who is Edom." (Genesis 36:6–8)

This is the practical background for the struggle of the brothers over the inheritance, and this is also the practical background for the fact that Isaac had only one blessing that he did not know how to divide between his two sons. Did he have to repeat the example of his father, who reserved the inheritance of Canaan for him, his special son, while arranging legacies outside Canaan for his many other sons? Was it impossible to find ways of kindness instead of competition between the brothers, so that they could dwell together in Canaan and strengthen their foothold in it as a united people? We shall see that this idea never occurred to Isaac, the man of the field, even though he did not have the contacts that Abraham must have had in the lands where he sent his other sons to find their legacies there. The blessing that Isaac imparted to his second son sent Esau out on the path that he carved for himself by making an alliance with his uncle Ishmael by marrying his daughter: he acquired a land-hold in proximity to his paternal uncle (Genesis 28:8–9) and dwelt in Mount Seir, as we saw. But until he went his way and discovered that even the one deprived of a blessing fared better in the interim than his brother, Jacob — the proud possessor of the blessing — was forced to flee with it to Haran to realize it after many years of hard labor. By his mother's advice he was supposed to dwell with his other uncle, on his mother's side in Haran, "a few days, until your brother's wrath subsides, until his anger to you subsides and he forgets what you did to him, then I will send for you and bring you back from there." (Genesis 27:44–45) Indeed, whether his mother sent for him after a few days or not (the narrator gives us no hint), Jacob was enticed to seek his fortune in Haran because greater opportunities opened up for him there. In other words, he discovered what Terah had discovered before him, and in fact he settled down there until he had to flee for the same reason that his brother Esau was forced to leave Canaan for Mount Seir: the land was insufficient to support his wealth along with that of his uncle and cousins, who regarded him as the one who had stolen their wealth.

Meanwhile, it appears that the inheritance in Canaan was neglected. Isaac, whose eyes grew dim from old age, could no longer maintain it properly, and there was no successor to Abraham's "servant." He had not the benefit of this kindness that his father had enjoyed. We may infer the state of the inheritance from Jacob's later story: when he returned from Haran he did not go back the way he had come to fulfill his vow at Bethel, but he first tried to get a foothold in the center of Mount Canaan, by Shechem, a place where his grandfather Abraham had turned aside when he first arrived from Haran to Canaan. Did he hope that he could establish there the place to worship the God who had prospered his way in order to fulfill the spiritual destiny that had been entrusted to him? We shall not know the answer because he did not succeed in accomplishing anything there. His plan was frustrated by his sons, and only then did he arrive where he had started out, as a fugitive, to the neglected territory where his aging parents still dwelt.

In summary, we see that the young Isaac's great prosperity, in which he enlarged his holdings in Canaan, ended in a sharp downturn, and the foothold that Abraham had succeeded in establishing for himself started to fall apart and decline. The gap between the vision of divine creation and the conditions required to fulfill it on earth — especially in the highlands, that depend on rainfall and not river-irrigation — this gap widened and was not closed. At this stage we can foresee the descent to the diaspora in the second river-land, Egypt, which indeed possessed the proper conditions for the development of this ancestral clan, that was splitting apart repeatedly because of the conditions in Canaan, into a great nation. But before that transition, there was given to Jacob and his twelve destined sons — who were his great achievement in Haran, anticipating the development of a people from his seed — a second opportunity to correct course and establish themselves in Canaan.

This continuation belongs to the story of the leadership of Jacob-Israel, but we must first go back and examine the historical narrative of Isaac from the viewpoint of Rebekah, because with respect to the unfolding of the family's destiny she was the dominant personality. We saw that Isaac imitated Abraham in every respect. Rebekah, for her part, imitated Sarah, whose place she took in the life of her husband and in the management of the household. The similarity between these two independent women is hinted in the story of her being brought to Sarah's tent — "and Isaac loved her, and he was comforted for his mother." (Genesis 24:67) Like Sarah, Rebekah was also barren at the start of her marriage, but there is signified here also the difference between Rebekah and Sarah, in respect of her sin and the division of duties between her and her husband.

At first it appears as if Isaac is regarded by the narrator as a hero, the destined one, because the fault that caused her barrenness is ascribed to Rebekah, not to him. Rebekah's barrenness is cured when Isaac intercedes "on behalf of his wife, for she was barren; and the Lord responded to his entreaty, and Rebekah his wife conceived." (Genesis 25:21) What, then, was her fault? The answer is alluded to in the tale of her conception: God's response to Isaac's plea was too generous, and not to her benefit. If barrenness was punishment, her pregnancy seemed like worse punishment: the twins with whom she was pregnant carried on a prodigious struggle within her belly, making her the victim of their exaggerated vitality: "The children struggled within her, and she said, 'If so, why do I live?' And she went to inquire of the Lord." (Genesis 24:22) The explanation that she heard contained comfort but also threat. The comfort was: "Two nations are in your belly, and two peoples shall be separated from your womb" — in this one may see the fulfillment of the first half of the blessing that Rebekah received when she left Haran — "our sister, be thousands of myriads!" The threat was: "One nation shall be stronger than the other, and the elder shall serve the younger." In this we may see the ironic fulfillment of the second half: "May your seed conquer his enemies' gates." The problem was that the enemy whose gates the one son was destined to conquer was the other son! From this it turns out that Rebekah's sin was on the moral plane, on which she struggled for fulfillment of the spiritual destiny: the practical selfishness, carefully calculated, that accompanied her quality of kindness and that served her when she overcame the obstacles that she encountered on her path. Each step that drew her nearer to the fulfillment of her destiny — to raise the life of her family to the rung of kindness — was bound up with the sin of inconsiderateness of the legitimate interests of those of her family who stood in her way. Therefore each step that advanced her toward the rung of kindness also pulled her back to below the rung of justice and equity. But the narrator, who sees the whole picture, turns our attention to the fact that in order to fulfill her destiny and bring the quality of kindness to her household, she must work hard on overcoming her own selfishness, for otherwise she will not be able to overcome the short-sightedness and limited vision of her husband and son.

And maybe the oracle that she heard concerning her sons' future can be interpreted as a warning, in the vein of "sin crouches by the door, its urge is to you, but you may have mastery over it"! Maybe it is possible to prevent family relations from deteriorating below the threshold of justice and firmness by exercising more kindness toward her husband and her son Esau, by means of a more equitable division of the mother-love that was in her? Yet precisely her mother-love embodied her egoism: she loved the son who was similar to her in his outward and inner being, and therefore she rejected the son who was more similar to her husband. To overcome this would require from her a measure of truthfulness that she had not yet achieved, whereas preferring the son who resembled her was in accordance with God's will, not only because such was said to her when she went to inquire of the Lord, but also because the son who resembled her was fitting for the spiritual leadership destined for him, whereas the son who resembled Isaac was not fitting for it in any respect, notwithstanding his earthy good-naturedness, simplicity and innocence. There was thus a measure of justice in the injustice that she perpetrated.

We return to the comparison of Rebekah and Sarah: in this limitation of her kindness she resembled Sarah, for like her mother-in-law she preferred her own son to her husband's favorite, out of the same mixture of justice and selfishness. But in light of this resemblance we see more clearly the major difference in respect of Rebekah's consciousness of divine destiny, and how this affected her relations with her husband. In the relationship between Abraham and Sarah, it was Abraham who filled the role of the man of spiritual destiny and moral action, whereas in the relationship of Isaac and Rebekah it was Rebekah who filled this role. She displayed the extra measure of spirit that was required of him. She was the woman who saw and knew, whereas Isaac was a decent enough man but without the extra measure of spirit and vision required of a leader of destiny.

This fact was evident to Rebekah on their first meeting. Isaac, the man of the field, went out on foot to anticipate his wife who was arriving seated high on the camel's back. He came alone, without escorts who might have arranged a welcoming ceremony similar to the parting ceremony she had just received from her own family:

> Raising her eyes, Rebekah saw Isaac. She alighted from the camel and said to the servant, "Who is that man walking in the field toward us?" And the servant said, "That is my master." So she took her veil and covered herself. (Genesis 24:64–65)

Nothing is explicitly said in this description, which is astonishing in its delicacy, yet Rebekah's gesture says it all. We should examine it in the light of the previous meeting between Rebekah and the servant, who had come to present to her the greatness and pedigree of his "lord." When she saw the man spying her from the well, riding high on his camel, she knew she was called to fulfill her destiny. But "this man," this peasant, who trod with measured steps on the clods of his field without majesty or exaltation of spirit, yearning for the woman in whom he will find comfort for the mother-love he is missing — this man was not the man she imagined in her heart as the son of Abraham whom the "servant" represented. Her dismounting from the camel, so that she should not be higher than her designated mate, who was standing on foot before her, and her veiling herself, could be interpreted as a gesture of modesty and courtesy, whereas internally it would be a gesture of deep disappointment and a decision to take on herself the management of her household on the way to her destiny. Isaac, who did not know how to see what he saw, took Rebekah to his mother's tent and was comforted by her for his mother's death, but Rebekah understood that the task that she had designated to Abraham's son would have to be done by herself. This is the key to understanding her sin and her righteousness.

Thus began the confrontation that matured against the background of the contradictory roles that Rebekah had to play — as mother-surrogate to her husband, and as mother to her children. This is the key to understanding her identification with Jacob, who resembled her, and her stinting relationship with Esau, who resembled his father Isaac. It was natural that her relationship transferred to her sons as well: Esau loved his father Isaac and was loyal to him, whereas Jacob loved his mother and was loyal to her. This is the remaining background of the family relations so remote from justice and equity, among people designated for the furtherance of kindness and truth. The depth of the contradiction comes out in the act of deception and terrible injustice that Rebekah perpetrated, with Jacob's help, against Isaac and Esau. The fearful trembling that Isaac trembled when he considered the deception, and the terrible outcry that burst from Esau's throat when he encountered the injustice (Genesis 27:30–40) reveal the depth of the moral sin in the egoism that accompanied Rebekah's kindness. But the narrator gives the reader an opening to understand Rebekah's actions from another higher vantage-point, that reveals — in her daring to do a deed that she knew was sinful, and for which she would be punished proportionately — a deeper kindness in her very being, through which Rebekah conquered her egoism. For how did Rebekah answer Jacob's question?

Jacob answered his mother Rebekah, "But my brother Esau is a hairy man and I am smooth-skinned. If my father touches me, I shall appear to him as a trickster and bring upon myself a curse, not a blessing." But his mother said to him, "Your curse, my son, be upon me! Just do as I say and go fetch them for me." (Genesis 27:11–13)

From where did Rebekah draw the readiness to take her son's curse on herself? Was it not from the moral certainty stemming from the consciousness of her destiny? — *this* was the deed that was incumbent on her to do. If she shirked it, a much greater injustice would be caused, a fateful mistake that could not be corrected. Through her deceptive act, she saved her short-sighted husband from that other major sin, thus doing him a kindness. Moreover, the injustice that she caused to her son Esau, and thus to her husband, though severe in its way, was a mistake that was correctible, and was itself the correction of a mistake, by means of which Rebekah was able to steer the relationships of the family back onto the right track.

In this connection, let us mention again the worldly significance of the inheritance struggle between Jacob and Esau: Jacob received the blessing as a promise for the remote future, but in the present he and his mother had to endure their punishment, for it was this punishment that directed him toward the fulfillment of their destiny on the roundabout way that he took. Rebekah, who loved Jacob, was forced to remain alone with her husband and her son Esau whom she had deceived, and Jacob was forced to flee empty-handed to his uncle's house. As we already learned from the story of Rebekah's betrothal, Uncle Laban was not a model of kindness or righteousness, and indeed he paid Jacob back measure for measure for his sin against his brother. The cheated Esau, on the other hand, remained home with his father and laid the basis of his short-term prosperity that did not involve any striving after far-off exalted spiritual destiny. He received a more modest blessing, but he did not have to wait long for it to materialize. He lived for the present, and he received his reward in the present. When he set out years later to welcome Jacob on the latter's return to Canaan (Genesis 32:4–33:20), he was able to avenge himself on him not by killing him, but by his prodigious generosity, as if to say, "Come, now, my brother, who deceived whom in that accursed hour? Who won the birthright and became lord, and who was forced to bow face-down before him? Who has now won the greater blessing, and who the smaller?" For Esau, the present is the main event.

It thus appears that also in their grappling with the mission of fulfilling the spiritual destiny in the life of their family and clan, on which their success in becoming permanently established in Canaan depended, Rebekah and Isaac were swept up into the same unsolved moral issues: in the effort to realize on earth the divine vision of creation, it became clear that the gap between the level of moral discipline required for that realization and the human being's ability to conquer his congenital evil urges was continually increasing, and was not small. Justice and right were no longer sufficient. A realization on the level of kindness and truth was required. But those who were designated to realize true kindness in their family and with their neighbors were human beings, not angels, and they were not able to free themselves at one blow either from the clutches of their own egoistic urges or from the short-sighted egoism of their relatives and neighbors. They therefore had to channel their own egos to contend with the egoisms of their opponents, and to achieve their higher goals through devious[21] and indirect methods. They must bear their punishment, and despite this, they will achieve, through that punishment, an attainment on whose basis it will be possible to mount a new effort, fraught with many struggles, full of ascents and declines, in order to progress further. The achievement that Rebekah managed

---

[21] "Devious" — *akubot,* calling attention to the etymology of the name Jacob ("crooked, heel-shaped, devious"), contrasting with Israel (related to *yashar,* "straight"). See Isaiah 40:4: "Let the rugged ground (*he-akov*) become level *(le-mishor)."*

was to gain the opportunity for Jacob-Israel to recapitulate the test of his grandfather Abraham, who came up from Haran in order to fulfill the promise that he received in Canaan, but this time not alone, but with twelve sons who became fathers not of diverse nations, but of the twelve tribes of the people that sprang from his seed.

The Perfect World of the Dream versus the Contradictions of Waking Reality

The story of Jacob is rooted in that of his mother Rebekah. It has its start, to be sure, in the purchase of the birthright from Esau by enticement and the theft of the blessing from him by deception, but these two stories are nevertheless embedded in the story of the central personality Rebekah, who took the initiative in directing her household. The story of Jacob the man, who acted on his own based on his own colloquy with God, starts with his fleeing, motivated by fear of his brother who hates him and the command of his parents, from Canaan that drinks the water of rainfall and wells, to Aram of the Two Rivers that drinks the water of rivers, rich in the promise that he has received. (Genesis 27:42–45) Poor and penniless in the present, but determined in his mind to fulfill the promises that he received through hard and grinding work, harder than the labors of his father Isaac and his brother Esau, though he was born to be a "dweller in tents."

The hour of his departure was the hour of failure, which was also the hour of beginning a new stage in the effort to bridge the gap between the vision of divine creation and its fulfillment on earth. A new literary development attests to this, for there now appears a narrative form that embodies a new layer of reality. In the course of our inquiry in the philosophy of Biblical narrative we have recognized so far three narrative forms that embody three planes of existence:

1. Myth — a narrative in which the sole personality acting in it is God, who created the heavens and earth and all that is on it, and similarly created man and commanded him to act for the fulfillment of his destiny. This is the plane of divine reality which myth perceives from the viewpoint of the capacity of human understanding.

2. Family history, or "generational narrative." This story continues the myth of Genesis through the family tree of Adam's descendants, who are the patriarchs of the nations that fill the earth to fulfill on

it their destiny as per their Creator's command. In the generational narrative are embedded brief historical episodes (*divrei ha-yamim*) — the major deeds innovated by individuals whose actions are regarded as significant by God, for bad or for good, but in short, topical summation.

3. History (*divrei ha-yamim* — "the events of the days") — historical narrative develops gradually and emerges as an essential form that pushes generational narrative to the margins. In historical narrative, events are depicted in poetic epic style, more elevated than generational narrative but without rising to the plane of existence of myth. On the plane of Biblical historical narrative, there is a reciprocal interaction between the deeds of human actors and the will of divine providence that guides them through divine command and through reward and punishment. In this way, the realistic historical story receives its religious significance — the significance of human actions in the eyes of God, who strives to close the gap between the vision of creation and historical reality through the mediation of the heroes of the narrative, caught between their understanding of their mission and their limited ability to stand up to it.

In Jacob's story appears a fourth narrative form: the dream. We note that the episodes of historical narrative in the Bible typically start at the morning of a "day" and conclude with its "evening," as in the narrative of creation. Thus, for instance, is the language of the story that tells about Abraham: in each event that brings about a substantive change in realizing his life's destiny, Abraham approaches it in the morning of the day: "Abraham arose early in the morning." By contrast, the time of the dream is the settling-in of night, as it says of Jacob: "He arrived at the place and lodged there because the sun had set. He took of the stones of the place and set them as his pillow, and lay down in that place, and dreamed..." (Genesis 28:11–12) It is the setting of the day, and the low-point of Jacob's life, but the dream reveals him the plane of divine revelation that prophesies the morning of the next day. Thus he can bridge the gap between the chronicles of the days and the myth of creation.

This narrative form did not emerge suddenly out of nothing, and we can discover its prototype in the prophetic visions of Abraham, which are mostly promises that consist of a divine utterance. Indeed, in the covenant "between the pieces" the utterance is preceded by an exalted symbolic vision that prophesies the future through a tangible gesture of its occurrence. If we compare Abraham's vision with Jacob's dreams, we will also discover a difference between them: in Jacob's dreams the action brings him to a plane of reality that is above that of the historical epic. In the covenant "between the pieces" Abraham experiences the darkness and dread that is going to come upon his descendants, but he is reassured that the darkness will come in the distant future and that his experience is not a present reality; but in Jacob's dream he ascends from the lowliness and failure of the present into a plane of divine presence that rules the earth from the heavens:

He had a dream; a stairway [or ladder] was set on the ground and its top reached to the sky, and angels of God were going up and down on it. And the Lord was standing over it and He said, "I am the Lord, the God of your father Abraham and the God of Isaac: the ground on which you are lying I will assign to you and to your offspring. Your descendants shall be as the dust of the earth; you shall spread out to the west and to the east, to the north and the south. All the families of the earth shall bless themselves by you and your descendants. Remember, I am with you: I will protect you wherever you go and will bring you back to this land. I will not leave you until I have done what I have promised you." (Genesis 28:12–15)

This promise is indeed similar to those that were given to Abraham along his whole journey. Indeed, not accidentally God addresses Jacob as Abraham's immediate son ("your father Abraham," while Isaac is mentioned without the title "father"). Jacob is continuing Abraham's way, following his footsteps on the same path: tarrying in Haran, going up to Canaan, trying to establish a foothold in Shechem, going south as far as Egypt, and in his death returned to the land of Canaan by his own directive and buried in the cave of Machpelah in Hebron. The difference between Jacob and Abraham is expressed in his taking the same journey as a head of a family that will lay the basis for the tribes of a single people. We shall see later that in this respect the biblical narrator alludes to the parallel between him and Moses. This is also the promise that was given him in his dream. But since it was given him on his way out of the land as an isolated individual fleeing for his life, this is not enough to reassure him. In his dream he ascends and sees God's kingship in its actuality. He senses on the ground on whose stones he has lain that this is the "house of God" opposite the "gate of heaven." He sees God "standing on it," the angels ascending and descending the ladder and performing their mission, and the promise is given to him as if he is one of them. In this encounter is given not just a promise, but also its present fulfillment: "behold, I am with you" — now, "and I will guard you wherever you go." From the certain knowledge that God is with him, Jacob draws the spiritual resources to go forward on his mission, to "wrestle" with God and with men, to maintain his position amid all the ascents and descents that are in store for him and to return as a man who wrestled with God and with men and prevailed. (Genesis 32:25–31)

The promise "here, I am with you" resembles the promise that was given to Moses when he went down to Egypt in order to go up from there with his people: "For I will be with you." (Exodus 3:12) Jacob goes forth to create the family that will go up to Canaan, and the promise accompanies him from his setting-out to his return. His experiences in Haran turned around two complementary axes: his struggles with Laban the Aramean, who exploited him as much as he could and afterwards pursued him as Pharaoh later pursued the Israelites on their departure from Egypt (Genesis 31:21–27), and the trials within his continually growing family with his two wives who were Laban's daughters. For the whole length of the way — a way of daily grinding labor, that did not seem to have any whiff of greatness about it — his dreams accompanied him, and he drew from them not only moral encouragement but also higher inspiration that helped him overcome all the obstacles in his path. This is attested by the third dream that he dreamed, which he reported to his two wives when he decided to flee from Laban's household and return to Canaan, in other words, at the crossroads where the two axes of his struggles — with God and with human beings — intersected directly.

This report is based on God's revelation to him after he himself felt that he was no longer welcome in Laban's household, and Laban himself and his sons were threatening him (31:1–2). This time God addresses him not in a dream but in a command that highlights both the parallel and the difference between him and Abraham. To Abraham God said, "Go forth from your land and your birthplace and your father's house"; to Jacob he said, "Return to the land of your fathers and your birthplace, and I will be with you." (31:3) He promises again to be with him, but this time in Canaan, for there are more adventures in store for him there — his encounter with his brother Esau, and the difficulties of establishing a foothold in the land among its peoples with his large family. Indeed, if Abraham was told to leave his land and birthplace, Jacob was told to return to Canaan as "the land of his fathers" and to return to his parents as his "birthplace." This also says something by way of negation: Aram of the Two Rivers will no longer be the land of Abraham's seed, and the house of Laban the Aramean will no longer be their birthplace. This is a fateful decision-point. (We are incidentally reminded of the parallel between Jacob, who tends the flock of Laban as well as his own family, and Moses, who tends the flock of Jethro and his people.) On the basis of this decision, Jacob and Laban later decided to part ways at the border between their lands. (Genesis 31:52)

In the face of this turning point and his decision to leave, there hung in the balance the question of the loyalty of Jacob's two wives — would they stand with him, or with their father? — and he had to elicit their agreement:

Jacob had Rachel and Leah called to the field, where his flock was, and said to them, "I see that your father's manner toward me is not as it has been in the past. But the God of my father has been with me. As you know, I have served your father with all my might; but your father has cheated me, changing my wages time and again. God, however, would not let him do me harm. If he said thus, 'The speckled shall be your wages,' then all the flocks would drop speckled young; and if he said thus, 'The streaked shall be your wages,' then all the flocks would drop streaked young. God has taken away your father's livestock and given it to me.

"Once, at the mating time of the flocks, I had a dream in which I saw that the he-goats mating with the flock were streaked, speckled, and mottled. And in the dream an angel of God said to me, 'Jacob!' 'Here,' I answered. And he said, 'Note well that all the he-goats which are mating with the flock are streaked, speckled, and mottled; for I have noted all that Laban has been doing to you. I am the God of Bethel, where you anointed a pillar and where you made a vow to Me. Now, arise and leave this land and return to your native land." (Genesis 31:4–13)

As we said, Jacob addressed his words to his wives to persuade them to go with him and cut their ties to their land and birthplace, but first he had to prove that he was in the right in his quarrel with their father over the property that would support them and their children for the future. There is an instructive difference between Jacob's account to his wives and the narrator's own account, for the latter is an objective witness to the events as they actually happened. (Genesis 30:31–42) In the original account, it is not told that Laban changed the terms of Jacob's compensation repeatedly. It was Jacob who suggested the conditions to Laban, and Laban agreed without haggling. This time Jacob kept his word, for he tended the flocks, and he set aside his wages without Laban being able to interfere or supervise. Thus one could argue that it was Jacob who changed the terms of agreement, though in a clever way that would have protected him from legal challenge: when Laban consented to the terms, he could not have known that Jacob, by breeding the flocks, would be able to increase his share far above what would have been expected in the natural way. As for the complaints of Laban's sons, that this time it was not Laban who exploited Jacob but the reverse — these hunches had a moral basis, though not a legal basis. However, Jacob had indeed paid back to Laban measure for measure, in the same manner that the Israelites repaid their Egyptian neighbors when they "despoiled" the Egyptians on leaving Egypt. Jacob could reply to Laban's moral complaint that Laban had exploited him all these years and benefited from his hard and grinding labors from the day that he came to Haran. (31:36–42) If we took into account all the credit due to Jacob from Laban in the intervening years, it would show that everything that Jacob had exacted from Laban's possessions was rightly his due.

Indeed, from this inclusive perspective we can see a broader consistency between the original objective account and Jacob's subjective account. If the accounting is made from the day of his arrival, Jacob did not wrong Laban through his shepherdly wiles, but collected what was rightly coming to him in the only way he could through his dealings with his exploiter. And now we come to the dream, to which Jacob resorts in order to attribute his success not just to himself but to God, who was with him and judged his case fairly. In the original story we are not told that it was his dreams that taught Jacob how to increase his streaked, spotted and mottled goats. By the account of his actions, it appears that this was a shepherds' device that Jacob learned from precise observation over his many years as shepherd of Laban's flocks. But what is the substantive difference between the statement that he saw this in his dream and the statement that he invented this from an inspiration? Every inspiration comes to a person from the divine spirit that rests on him, and the dream is one of those channels of inspiration with which Jacob was abundantly blessed.[22] Jacob

[22] Compare Maimonides' view of prophecy and providence in Schweid, *The Classic Jewish Philosophers (Ha-Filosofim ha-Gedolim Shelanu)*. (LL)

prefers to speak to his wives in a manner that stresses God's direct involvement in his prosperity, because he wishes to emphasize the rightness of his case as a divine judgment, and especially to prove to them that God is with him, so that they should feel no compunction against going with him — neither on account of their father nor on account of the future that they could anticipate when they arrived in Canaan. They could rely on the divine help that is manifest in all his resourceful deeds.

Indeed, we are talking about the cleverness of Jacob, who knew how persuade his wives, yet all this points to the cleverness of the narrator, who highlights the intentional difference between the original presentation of the facts and the calculated interpretation that Jacob placed on them in order to influence his undecided listeners. From the reader's standpoint, this is how the narrator interprets his own story: what was the meaning of the promise in his dreams that God would be with Jacob? What was the meaning of the promise that God would guard him? We learn the narrator's answer through the way that the promise is fulfilled: God's guarding and prospering presence is revealed through the inspiration and resourcefulness by whose aid Jacob succeeded in overturning all of Laban's efforts, wrapped in a hypocritical guise of legal fairness, to cheat and exploit him. By his great resourcefulness, Jacob knew how to convert the injustice-disguised-as-justice that was wrought on him into true justice, both for himself and for Laban's daughters, and thus indirectly for Laban himself. He redeemed Laban's daughters and Laban himself from blind selfishness. Laban put on the appearance of a devoted father concerned for his daughters' welfare, but in truth he treated them as he treated Jacob. He wanted to exploit them, too, as much as he could. Laban's daughters, who knew how to add up the score as well as their father did, were convinced at once:

Then Rachel and Leah answered him, saying, "Have we still a share in the inheritance of our father's house? Surely, he regards us as outsiders, now that he has sold us and has used up our purchase price. Truly, all the wealth that God has taken away from our father belongs to us and to our children. Now, then, do just as God has told you." (Genesis 31:14–16)

Here is further evidence that God was with Jacob through his cleverness and resourcefulness.

Punishment of False Justice, and Resourcefulness Converting Injustice to Kindness

The story of Jacob's wrangling with Laban is the story of his coming to terms with the punishment meted out for his sin, a punishment that flowed from the same source as the sin: seeking one's own right, without consideration of the right of one's opponent. In the end, Jacob's resourcefulness converts the punishment to kindness. We learned what happens to kindness without justice — kindness that proceeds from egotism without consideration of the rights of the opponent — from the example of Rebekah and Jacob. We learned what happens to justice without truth-in-kindness from the example of Isaac, who acted innocently but thoughtlessly. Laban, the brother of Rebekah (who is close to him in her calculating manner no less than in their familial relation) represents in this story the formal legal demand that cloaks transparent selfish motives: the desire to exploit his kinsman as much as possible, consistent with the law: this is false justice. He expresses the desire to preserve family relations, which are a necessary condition of his prosperity, but also the desire to get as much as possible out of his relative who is dependent on him, and to give him as little as possible in return. True justice is the reverse of false justice: it intends that the mutual relations be directed to the common good, and arrive at it from in-depth examination of the motives, intentions and effects over the long term, for sometimes an agreement that appears good for both sides in the present is likely to conceal a trap for the weaker party, who is more dependent on the other, and to cause him severe injustice in the future.

In the story of the relations of Jacob and Laban, this is no mere abstract theory but living experience. Laban received his nephew Jacob in a display of love: " 'You are my flesh and blood.' And he dwelt with him for a month." (Genesis 29:14) Though he arrived empty-handed, Jacob is the heir who after the passing of "a few days" should be called back home by his parents as Isaac's sole heir. Jacob came to take one of Laban's daughters in marriage, and Laban was interested in having him as a son-in-law. Meanwhile, Jacob started working in Laban's house in order not to be a freeloader, and he proved that his work was blessed. But the call to return home was a long time coming. Now Laban wanted him as a son-in-law for another reason: he wanted him as a hired hand of blessed productivity. Therefore he conveniently reminds himself that Jacob is only his nephew and not his brother: "Are you my brother, that you should work for me for nothing? Tell me, what shall your wages be?" (29:15) The difference between Laban's crafty pose and his true intention is transparently clear. When he turned his previous words that Jacob was his "flesh and blood" upside down, he was saying by implication that he had fulfilled his family obligation to him, and that he no longer wished to support him for nothing; when he said it was not right that Jacob work for him for nothing, he implied that if Jacob wished to dwell in his house and be his son-in-law, he must earn his bread through his labor.

Jacob agreed willingly not only because he had no other choice: this was the opportunity that opened up for him to provide for his future. He trusted in his own resources to enable him to prosper more than Laban wanted him to, for God was with him. The "accounting" was quite tangible: Jacob, who came in the first place to find a wife, chose Rachel, who greeted him on his arrival as Rebekah had greeted the "servant," but with a reversal of roles that stemmed from the reversal of their respective statuses: she was the master's daughter, while he was the penniless fugitive. (29:1–12) To even the balance with her, Jacob had to prove himself worthy of her love. Thus he single-handedly rolls the stone away from the well and waters her flock, and in order to water her as well, he kisses her amorously. Thus he proves that the blessing contained in him is far greater than the wealth that the "servant" carried on his camels. God was with him. Rachel accepted him, and he sought her hand from Laban as wage for his work. From his standpoint, this was the greatest compensation, greater than the benefit that Laban would derive from his work, even though in a monetary respect (which is how Laban would measure it) Jacob worked for Laban for nothing for seven years in order to get Rachel. The injustice in the contract with Laban thus turned out to be just: each side got what they wanted. This would of course be the case only if Laban honored the agreement to the letter.

Yet in Jacob's love for Rachel was bound a sin like the sin of Abraham and Sarah, that shines forth from the parallel between him and her — she was lovelier than her elder sister as he was finer than Esau, and like him she was the younger daughter: just as his mother preferred him to his older brother, so he preferred her to her older sister. Because she was like him, he bestowed the right of the first-born on her. But Laban brought Leah in place of Rachel to Jacob's tent, and afterwards extenuated himself by appealing to accepted mores: "It is not the practice in our place to marry off the younger before the older."

(29:26) Indeed he was right, but this was clearly cheating: they had an agreement "for Rachel, your younger daughter." What, then, decided this in Laban's favor? The fact that in wronging Jacob he repaid him in kind for Jacob's wronging his father and brother. One might say that God was with Laban. Yet this is so only in a legalistic appearance. Laban's deed did not stem from seeking justice either for his son-in-law Jacob or for his daughter Leah. It stemmed from his desire to exploit Jacob's love for Rachel as much as he could: by forcing him to marry both of his daughters — which would be a source of injustice to both of them — he secured Jacob's labor free for fourteen years.

But God was nevertheless with Jacob in all of this. The punishment that he rightly received harbored a kindness that Laban did not intend nor did Jacob expect: Leah was truly his predestined wife. It was she who wrought true kindness for him, inasmuch as she and her handmaid Zilpah bore him the majority of his sons and his sole daughter, thus building up the house of Israel in the true sense. Thus unknowingly and unintentionally Laban wrought kindness with Jacob by "punishing" him for his sin against his father and brother.

We now come to examine the period of Jacob's service after the completion of his fourteen years of exploitation as an unpaid laborer in order to build up his family. His position was now stronger. He could return now to his parents in Canaan. Thus Laban was at a disadvantage in negotiating Jacob's compensation for his blessed work. There was no substitute for Jacob, just as there was no substitute for Abraham's "servant." Jacob exploited his advantage and paid Laban back as he deserved, with the same clever dissembling; he requested a wage that seemed paltry to Laban in proportion to the blessing that he would gain. Laban swallowed the bait and fell into the trap. Jacob trusted likewise in the blessing that rested on his labor, but he knew its source better than Laban — God was with him in his striving "to provide for his house" so that he could return as an independent and prosperous man to his father's house. In the end, as we said, he took for himself, from the blessing that rested on his labor for Laban, the portion that was justly his, not just for the last years, but for the first fourteen years during which he had worked for Laban without monetary payment. If we judge the event narrowly based on the circumstances under which Laban accepted Jacob's proposal, there was indeed misrepresentation, for Laban did not know that Jacob could manipulate the numbers of streaked, spotted and speckled goats, and therefore he was doubly impacted: his profits from Jacob's blessing dwindled, and his reputation as a sharp dealer cost him. This brought about a change in his relation with Jacob: "Jacob saw that Laban's manner toward him was not as it had been in the past." (Genesis 31:12)

From his acquaintance with the moral character of Laban and his sons, Jacob drew the necessary conclusions: he fled from his house without giving notice, without taking leave or consent, as a thief and deceiver of Laban. That is the argument that Laban proffered in the name of justice when he pursued the fleeing Jacob and caught up with him, and again there was a legal basis for his complaints. However, this time God appeared in a night-vision not to Jacob but to Laban, to warn him against doing any harm to his son-in-law, husband of his daughters and father of his grandchildren. Did God indeed appear to Laban, or did he make up this story to salvage his reputation in the eyes of Jacob and his daughters? Laban was not a fool, and he knew that he could not bring back the fugitive who had already reached the border of Canaan. His daughters had gone with him willingly, and in the last analysis they were all his flesh and blood. If he harmed them, he would be harming himself and gaining nothing. Even Laban was not so blind in his egotism. The just and practical solution in all respects was to part in peace, once and for all. Thus the true justice was reestablished in the view of both parties, and a lasting covenant of peace was enacted between them. (Genesis 31: 29–30)

But this story had another ending, which we should consider to explore the Biblical view of justice from all angles. It provides a severe warning to all who seek to achieve justice in their human mortal lives: no one should trust in their absolute righteousness, even when it is shining bright, because in this kind of moral certainty there lies in wait for the righteous the sin whose punishment may be quite hard. In order to salvage something of his lost honor and explain his pursuit of the fleeing Jacob, Laban voiced one complaint that he could trust to be factual. His daughter Rachel had stolen the images of his gods when she set out on the journey. Laban's last complaint was thus: "Why have you stolen my gods?" (Genesis 31:30) In Jacob's view, this new claim of Laban against him exceeded all bounds. Was it conceivable to accuse a righteous man like him of stealing idols? The man who had God with him could not tolerate such an accusation, or maybe he could not suppress the temptation to prove that all his days with Laban he was the righteous victim without a black mark against him. It did not occur to him at all that maybe some other member of his household — even one of his wives, Laban's daughters — had stolen Laban's images and hidden the fact from him. The sin was indeed not his but Rachel's, but the words that came out of his mouth were untrue, for in his haste he declared not only his own innocence but the innocence of all his household members for whom he bore responsibility: "'Anyone with whom you find your gods shall not live! In the presence of our kinsmen, point out what I have of yours and take it.' Jacob, of course, did not know that Rachel had stolen them." (31:32) At that moment, Rachel was in her second pregnancy, and she took advantage of it to conceal her theft from her father, who went out to rummage in the possessions of all members of Jacob's household. Rachel's subterfuge saved Jacob, who seemed righteous in Laban's eyes and his own. But God, the judge of truth, carried out Jacob's hasty sentence: Rachel met her death on the road to Ephrat when she suffered complications in the birth of her second son Benjamin. As for why God was so severe in the judgment of Rachel and Jacob in this instance, we shall discuss this question later, for it is connected with the whole complicated matter of the relations between Jacob and Rachel, and between Rachel and Leah. As for the Biblical view of justice expressed here, we shall summarize by saying that the righteous are never perfect in their righteousness, and for them to pretend to perfect innocence is itself the sin that is liable to breed many more sins.

The Consciousness of Chosenness for Mission, and the Problem of Unity and Integration in the Family of Nations

The problem with which Jacob-Israel wrestled in his relations with his two wives, Leah and Rachel, is an open presentation of the hidden problem with which the narrative of the patriarchs has wrestled since its inception: we are speaking of a situation in which an individual's consciousness of chosenness, based on the abilities that identified him and made him a possible source of "blessing" for those around him, turns into a great stumbling-block that can destroy the "blessing" embodied in him. Being chosen by God in order to be His emissary for the good of humankind is a great privilege. It can also be a source of happiness and prosperity to the chosen individual himself. But when that individual regards his chosenness as his personal prerogative, and sees its purpose in his own self-gratification, this is the most dangerous egotism for himself and those around him. This is the great problem: the chosen one, despite his special talents, is just a human being and not an angel, and as such he is not different from other people. It is impossible that he not fall, at least at the start of his career, into the trap of consciousness of his chosenness. The more prominent the spiritual gifts that he displays, the greater is the sin bound up in his awareness of being chosen. If he does not overcome his sin and recognize that he is human like all other people, his chosenness is a failure.

We saw that in the stories of Abraham and Sarah, Isaac and Rebekah, the egotism in their consciousness of chosenness appeared as the "sin that crouches by the door" because of man's congenital evil urge, but from the standpoint of Jacob's story it appears that the sin is embodied in the consciousness of chosenness itself: it constitutes a special kind of egotism. This egotism consists in his preferring himself for his own sake and is expressed in a narcissistic self-love and in a consciousness of superiority that brings about separation and isolation from those around him, who are considered unworthy of him. It is as if he were a unique, pure-bred variety of humanity. The pitfall is obvious, for this constitutes a contradiction in the chosen one's consciousness of his destiny, which is directed toward achieving the good of all humanity and in that respect toward serving them, not raising oneself above them.

In the stories of Abraham and Isaac, the problem of the self-love of the chosen one and the feeling of superiority separating them from others was manifested in the phenomenon of the barrenness of the matriarchs Sarah and Rebekah. We saw that the barrenness had its source in the sin rooted in the lustful sexuality of the couple or the domineering egotism manifested in their relation to each other. However, the evidence that the stumbling-block is rooted in the consciousness of chosenness itself is the inability or unwillingness of the patriarchs to unify around them the clan at whose head they stood, in order to develop it and increase it into a single tribe and afterwards to a single people. The meager clan, together with its servant-workers, does not grow, but splits apart in every generation and remains as small as it was. Terah's clan split between Abram and Nahor; Abram's clan split first between him and his nephew Lot, and afterwards between Isaac, Ishmael and the other sons of Abraham who were born of various wives. All of Abraham's sons became patriarchs of various peoples, and through them Abraham became the father of a multitude of nations, but the people that would eventually be called by his name, the people destined to be numerous as the stars of heaven, remained a tiny clan.

In Isaac's family, two sons were born to Isaac's only wife. They were twins, but it was decreed that they separate and become the patriarchs of two rival peoples. The external explanation that was given for this fact was that the land of Abraham's and Isaac's sojournings was insufficient to support all the property and possessions of two clan-chiefs together, but it is a fact that other peoples that lived in Canaan did not divide but increased while preserving their unity. It follows from this that a solution could have been found if the patriarchs had only sought it. The fact that they did not want to find a solution had its source in them, not in external circumstances, and the story itself suggests this. However, after narrating the facts and presenting them as if they were natural and unavoidable, it does not define the internal problematic implicit in them.

On the contrary. It appears as if the narrator is not critical, either morally or legally: the principle by which the leadership of Abraham's and Sarah's clan must pass to the first-born, who alone enjoys chosen status, is accepted by him as a sanctified tradition. From the same standpoint he depicts the action of Jacob, the younger son who stole the birthright, as a sin. But he justifies the transfer of chosen status to the one son who is spiritually fit for it. Thus two conditions applicable to inheritance of the chosen status are revealed: it should properly pass to the first-born son of the chosen father and mother, but also to whoever displays the spiritual gifts that attest that God selects him. But even when the younger is chosen on account of his spiritual gifts, the special status of first-born still stands in effect: Jacob receives the blessing only after he purchases the birthright from his brother Esau and only after he stands before his father as if he were Esau his first-born. Thus all the other brothers are regarded as ordinary and not chosen, and they are required to yield their place to the single chosen one, who inherits everything. The ironic result, as it turns out from the story of Jacob and Esau, is that the unchosen sons succeed in growing a people from their seed quite quickly, while the chosen-quasi-firstborn sons remain aliens, exiles, full of the consciousness of their exalted mission and knowledge of the promise embodied in them together with their failure, that is their allotted portion in the present.

And the problem has another aspect: the consciousness of chosenness does not enable the chosen clan to integrate among the nations next to them, for whom they are intended to be a blessing. Even if the neighboring nations are accepting of them and their blessing, the special clan, distinguished in its special homeland, does not want to integrate. The highest degree of integration that it is prepared to settle for is that of "resident alien," even though according to the promise it will eventually give rise to a great nation that will integrate among the peoples and unite them around it. In other words, by clinging one-sidedly, exclusively to its first origin, the consciousness of its chosenness for the sake of humanity contradicts the destiny for which it was formed. This conclusion sheds light on the root of the sin of Abram and Sarai that caused their barrenness: their being brother and sister who became husband and wife in order to beget from their identical "flesh and bone" the only-child who will be born out of the pure blessed source, for only from him will issue the chosen ones. The same applies to Isaac: Abraham sends an emissary to acquire for him a wife from his "birthplace" because only it is graced by the blessing of chosenness. The same is the case with Jacob and Esau: Isaac and Rebekah considered it a bad thing that their sons, particularly Jacob, should take Canaanite wives, therefore Esau marries the daughter of Ishmael, which of course solves nothing, whereas Jacob is sent to Laban and chooses Rachel, who as the younger daughter vying for first-born status among Laban's daughters is like his predestined sister.

It seems that all this sheds light on the grave moral significance that the Mosaic Torah ascribes to those classes of incest that are manifested in the lives of the people's patriarchs and matriarchs: they are the embodiment of the infatuation with their own "flesh and bone" on the part of the first couple, who were destined to beget all humanity, as well as the second couple, who were destined to give birth to the chosen people. We are thus presented with the paradox of origin that bears in itself the contradiction between what is necessary with respect to the original creation and therefore commendable, as following from the fundamental principle, for the sake of the highest goal, and what is severely prohibited with respect to propriety of the process of physical reproduction, and afterwards with respect to the propriety of socialization of the members of the family, the clan, the tribe and the people, which is based on the coming together of people different from each other, out of their openness to each other, so that the advantages of the one may complement the deficiencies of their mate or the other members of their society.

The unity of the source is a guarantee of the purity of the chosen line and its legacy, a matter that will enable an original creative capacity that was only manifested in the first couple; but if the family should continue to remain enclosed in its origin, it will not be fertile, it will not increase and develop, but it will wither and collapse into its barren selfhood. The incestuous union between brother and sister, or between father and daughter (as in the story of Lot and his daughters) thus carries within it the contradiction embodied in the story of fundamental origins, and from here flow the two contradictory meanings of the word *ḥesed* (kindness, but also incest) in the Bible: in ethical contexts it expresses, as we saw, the most exalted ethical level, but in the context of physical sexuality it expresses the lowest abomination, the breaking of a sacred taboo. Thus we read:

> If a man marries his sister, the daughter of either his father or his mother, so that he sees her nakedness and she sees his nakedness, it is a disgrace (*ḥesed*); they shall be excommunicated in the sight of their kinsfolk. He has uncovered the nakedness of his sister, he shall bear his guilt. (Leviticus 20:17)

It thus turns out that the consciousness of chosenness can bring about the realization of its destiny — establishing a chosen people who shall be a blessing to all the nations and raise them as well to the level of chosenness — only if its carriers can free themselves of the fateful original sin of its origin. This is the destiny of Jacob, the man who struggled with the contradictions in his personality. His life apparently does not manifest any heroic dimension, despite its parallels with the lives of Abraham and Moses. Yet if precisely he is called "Israel" because he wrestled with God and with men and prevailed, this is because by following his "crooked"[23] path he succeeded in breaking the hereditary barrier of barrenness that blocked the way of his ancestors to realization of the vision that a people should issue forth from their seed.

This breakthrough is expressed already in his first sin — violating the principle that the infant that emerges first from his mother's womb is the designated first-born, for he maintains that the firstborn is the one who desires the first-born status together with the destined significance bound up with it. The first-born is the one whom God chose and gave the gifts of spirit required for realizing this destiny. The sin that was bound up in Jacob's breakthrough was compounded when he sought

---

[23] "Crooked" — *akov*, the play on Jacob's name. Note the connotation here is "curvey, indirect," not "immoral, criminal."

to turn his breakthrough into a principle and preferred the younger Rachel over Leah, but in his unseeing, devious way he broke through his own contrarian principle as well and freed himself of it. This is the meaning of the chapter of his convoluted relations with the two sisters who became his wives and competed for the status of the chosen wife, whose son should eventually be the chosen heir. Jacob wanted Rachel to occupy in his life the position of Rebekah in his father's life and Sarah in Abraham's life. But since his father-in-law Laban forced the elder Leah on him, he yielded and accepted the result. He accepted Leah as his wife and sired the majority of his sons from her and her maid Zilpah. Thus he stood firm against the efforts of his beloved, preferred wife Rachel to displace her sister from her deserved position as mother. The evidence that Rachel's efforts were rooted in sin is expressed in the quarrel that broke out between her and Jacob:

> When Rachel saw that she had borne Jacob no children, she became envious of her sister; and Rachel said to Jacob, "Give me children, or I shall die." Jacob was incensed at Rachel, and said, "Can I take the place of God, who has denied you fruit of the womb?" (Genesis 30:1–2)

The competition between the sisters continued, but Rachel's barrenness was broken only when she agreed to "hire" Jacob to her sister, "and he lay with her that night." (30:16) Thus she acknowledged her sister Leah's equal status. The fact that Jacob responded to the "hiring" and begat a fifth son of Leah (30:17–18) confirms that from his point of view the status of Leah as less-beloved mother of his children was preferable to that of the beloved Rachel whose sin had caused her infertility. Indeed, in the end Leah was buried in the Cave of Machpelah with Jacob, whereas Rachel was buried alone on the road to Ephrat.

Not less important than the way in which the respective status of Jacob's two wives in the common clan was determined — not by his personal preference but by their contribution to building the family — was the way that the status of the sons was determined. Did he not show preference among them? The continuation of the story shows that he did show preference, or more exactly, he tried to enforce his preference as he had tried in the case of Rachel. Moreover, his attempt to show preference to his son Joseph became the source of the conflict that generated the greatest fraternal enmity in the house of Israel. But the conflict that broke out shows that it was not Jacob's preferences that determined the statuses of the sons in the family in respect of their place as heirs whose views carried weight in governing the family. Just as Jacob responded to his wives' wishes perhaps more than they responded to his, so he responded to his sons' wishes perhaps more than they responded to his. In this respect their status was equal, and they operated independently against their father's decisions, as we shall see in the story of Dinah in Shechem and more emphatically in the story of Joseph. In the end Jacob submitted to the wishes of the majority of the brothers. He distanced himself from Joseph when he took a stand on his sin in his ambition to rule over his brothers and parents; and when he sent Joseph to serve his brothers and atone for his wronging them, he recognized their independent and equal status as leaders of the family.

The general picture of the status of the women and children in Jacob's family is depicted in the order of his camp when they set out to greet his brother Esau:

> Looking up, Jacob saw Esau coming, accompanied by four hundred men. He divided the children among Leah, Rachel, and the two maids, putting the maids and their children first, Leah and her children next, and Rachel and Joseph last. He himself went on ahead and bowed low to the ground seven times until he was near his brother. Esau ran to greet him. He embraced him and, falling on his neck, he kissed him, and they wept. Looking about, he saw the women and the children. "Who," he asked, "are these with you?" He answered, "The children with whom God has favored your servant." (Genesis 33:1–5)

The arrangement of the children, with their mothers at their head, attests to their relative status, but also to their being all equal as his children. He guards the welfare of all of them together as his most precious possession.

The same readiness to break with the rule of aristocratic chosenness comes to expression in Jacob's readiness to bow seven times before Esau, even though it was said of him in relation to his brother, "the elder shall serve the younger." The brothers' falling on each other's necks weeping is an expression of mutual remorse for their arrogance and enmity toward each other — when Jacob returns from his exile, the brothers recognize each other as equal in brotherhood. It is finally proper to point out that when Jacob arrived in Shechem he was willing to enter into a covenant of amalgamation into a single people with the inhabitants of the city, to give his daughter in marriage to Shechem, son of the local king, and to take wives for his sons from them. It would appear that it was he who initiated, in his "devious" way, his daughter Dinah's coming out "to visit [see, and be seen with] the daughters of the land" (Genesis 34:1) — evidently hoping to obtain an honorable match. The result was wildly successful in his view, but his sons took the leadership from his hands, and with cunning and deceit frustrated his whole plan (34:7–31). This was the beginning of the great confrontation between him and his sons, and it is against this background that we should try to understand Jacob's attempt to give preference to his son Joseph, who "brought bad reports" of his brothers to him. (37:2) Does this remark not show that in addition to expressing his love for the child of his old age, and aside from the feelings of guilt that he had on account of Rachel, who had been buried on the road to Ephrat, not in the Cave of Machpelah, Jacob was also attempting here to regain the full authority of leadership in his family, of which he had been deprived in the episode of Dinah, until it became clear that Joseph was endangering his leadership more than his other sons?

As for the unity of the family and conceiving the democratic leadership within it, we should emphasize two additional things that can be inferred from the story of Joseph: first, even at the height of the conflict, which was filled with hatred among the brothers, none of them considers splitting apart the family in the way it had been split by the conflict between Sarah and Hagar, between Isaac and Ishmael, or between Jacob and Esau. Jacob remained the recognized head of the united family, although they were obedient to him only when he succeeded in persuading his sons (or when they succeeded in persuading him). Second, it was not the issue of the status of first-born that determined their prominence as leaders of the family, but their initiative. Reuben, first-born of Leah, was disqualified by his sin when he slept with Bilhah, his father's concubine, "and Israel found out," (Genesis 35:22) and yet he was not thrown out of the fold. He also tried to recover his standing with his father in the Joseph episode (37:22), but failed (37:29–30). With the failure of Jacob's plans in Shechem, two of Leah's sons — Simeon and Levi — rose to prominence, but later in the story of the quarrel between the brothers, it was Joseph and Judah who became central. It was their assertive, commanding personalities and the paths that they mapped out that alone determined their standing. As for the substance of the dispute that was signified by the directions of their leadership, we will discuss that in the proper place.

Descent for the Sake of Ascent —
the Way to Exile and Slavery

The story of Abraham and Isaac continues after that of Noah and his sons according to the principle of the "second beginning." We recall that the achievement of Noah as the second Adam reached its climax in the enactment of the covenant for him and his sons — for all humanity — in which were laid down the ethical foundations that henceforth would unite all humanity, and in which God promised the human race that never again would He bring a flood to destroy them, along with all living beings, from the face of the earth. The moment when the covenant was enacted was also the moment when Noah and his descendants started on their moral decline, which reached its nadir in the story of the Tower of Babel: the story of the founding of a culture which strove to be a world power on the basis of the supreme authority of sinful humanity in Mesopotamia (the land between the Two Rivers). This incident amounted to a kind of renunciation of the Noahide covenant, but God still stood by His promise: He destroyed the sinful culture but not its people, rather he split them apart into many peoples who were then scattered over the face of the earth. The Biblical story portrays the settlement of the peoples, divided into different territories, as the realization of God's commandment to humanity, and in that respect it is possible to see in it the beginning of reformation. But the expectation that the people scattered around the world would live according to their obligations in the Noahide covenant was not realized. According to the continuation of the story we learn that the descendants of Ham and his son Canaan sank deep into the corruption of idolatry, whereas the peoples that issued from Shem and Japheth did better and did not deny their covenant, nevertheless they, too, were infected by idolatry. The "second beginning," that was intended to renew the covenant that had been betrayed, was the achievement of a single clan, a descendant of Noah's firstborn son Shem, namely Terah, the father of Abram and Sarai; it was he who founded this clan, and Abram and Sarai began the actual work of reformation.

We saw that just as Noah is presented in the genealogical narrative as a second Adam, Abram and Sarai are presented as a third Adam and Eve. They are chosen from sinful humanity (and they, too, embody that sin), and it is their destiny to advance the realization of God's vision — first of all by repairing themselves, so that it will be possible to develop in their seed another legacy. Abraham and Sarah arrived at the height of their achievement at the birth of their son Isaac and in making assurance for his future, but again, the height of achievement is the beginning of the slide back down the slope of sin. The next low-point is described in Jacob's flight from Canaan back to the same corrupted river-land from which Abraham and Sarah had begun their journey to Canaan. Yet precisely at this nadir was signified, as we saw above, the substantive turning-point that attests that the achievement of Abraham and Sarah was perpetuated through Isaac and Rebekah, though to a lesser extent and in an imperfect fashion, and was transmitted to their sons.

When we compare the decline of the human race to their low-point in the genealogical narratives of Adam and Noah, to the decline of the continuers of the legacy in the stories of Abraham and Sarah, Isaac and Rebekah, two differences stand out. First, the slide of Jacob, and later of his sons, down the slope of sin is indeed deep, but it does not hit that rock-bottom from which Adam and Noah started out. Something is still left of the prior achievement, from which it is possible to arrive eventually at a higher level than the patriarchs themselves achieved. Second, the punishment for the sins of Jacob and his sons not only strengthens the power of the will to reform and the understanding of the way to reform, as happened when Abram and Sarai descended to Egypt, but the punishment itself repairs what was damaged in the sin, and the causes of the sin are likewise repaired. In this way the sin itself — when it is examined within the context of the circumstances that led to it — is not just a sin. In the process of retribution for a sin that was sinned, the sinner experiences a restoration of justice to its proper state. When the sinner receives his punishment as outlining a way to make his own way straight, it turns from sin to kindness. This is the reason for which Jacob was elevated through the name Israel after his struggles with Laban. This is thus a substantive turning-point with respect to progress in the realization of the principles of the Noahide covenant by Abraham and Sarah: the "second beginning" is presented in the genealogical narrative of Jacob as a descent for the sake of ascent.

This idea was embodied in the difference that was manifested between the Covenant of the Pieces enacted with Abraham, and the Covenant of Bethel enacted with Jacob. The promise that was given to Jacob at the low-point of his life, that God would be with him in his exile, has something of a promise that the descent will not just be punishment for sin, but the first step required for his ascent and return to Canaan with the name of Israel, as one who will realize the mission of his grandfather Abraham on yet a higher level, and as one who prefigures the appearance of Moses — the founder of the people of Israel and the prophet who will lead them to receive Torah at Sinai and take possession of the land of Canaan. This principle is formulated explicitly just prior to the second, deeper descent of Jacob into Egypt:

God called to Israel in a vision by night: "Jacob! Jacob!" He answered, "Here." And He said, "I am God, the God of your father. Fear not to go down to Egypt, for I will make you there into a great nation. I Myself will go down with you to Egypt, and I Myself will also bring you back..." (Genesis 46:2–4)

The story of Joseph, in which Jacob and all his family are brought down to Egypt, is structured according to this principle: he is cast down into the pit and is sold in order to ascend to greatness in his master's house; he is cast down again into prison so that he can ascend to the position of Pharaoh's viceroy; he takes revenge on his brothers and his father — which is indeed a grave sin, even if it was deserved as a punishment for their sin against him — in order to ascend to the level of their rescuer and saver; and finally, his worst sin of all is turning all of Egypt into a house of slavery in which the Israelites themselves are enslaved, in order that they may be fertile and multiply and become a great people. Thus they arrive with the help of Moses — the leader whose career takes the opposite trajectory from Joseph's — to the assembly of the giving of the Torah. This will be a new creation, for the enactment of the second covenant — parallel to the Covenant of Noah — will have an aspect of ascent to a higher level, both in respect of the level of ethical requirements in it, and in respect of its being the law of a whole life-pattern for the life of a people that takes on itself the task of realizing on its land the vision of God in creation.

The Crossroads of Israel's History and the Descent into Egypt

His settlement in Shechem was the high-point in Jacob-Israel's leadership. In accordance with the vow that he had vowed at Bethel when he set out for Laban's house, he ought to have returned by the same route that he set out, by way of Bethel, but he preferred to arrive at the spot where Abram had gone first at the start of his journey through Canaan. "The parcel of land where he pitched his tent he purchased from the children of Hamor, Shechem's father, for a hundred *kesitahs*. He set up an altar there, and called it El-elohe-yisrael." (Genesis 33:19–20) This was all following Abraham's example: purchasing a field, just as Abraham had done in Hebron in his latter days; erecting an altar, just as Abraham had done in Shechem at the start of his journey through Canaan. The difference between them is expressed in Jacob's intention of settling permanently in the place, for Abraham had made no attempt to settle in Shechem, and not even in Hebron — he purchased the field of the Cave of Machpelah as a burial-place, not for settlement nor for building a sanctuary for worship of his God. And yet the comparison between Jacob's story and Abraham's requires that we mention one more important detail: Abraham was answered in Shechem with a general promise concerning his future inheritance of the land of Canaan, but Jacob is not answered at all. Is it the story's intention to suggest that Jacob erred or sinned when he did not fulfill his vow at Bethel? This surmise is confirmed by God's words to Jacob after his sons frustrate his initiative through their terrible sin. According to the words spoken to him, it appears that he also was unable to exonerate himself of responsibility for his sons' sin, for he had initiated a course whose time had not come, and in an improper manner:

God said to Jacob, Arise, go up to Bethel and remain there; and build an altar there to the God who appeared to you when you were fleeing from your brother Esau." So Jacob said to his household and to all who were with him, "Rid yourselves of the alien gods in your midst, purify yourselves, and change your clothes. Come, let us go up to Bethel, and I will build an altar there to the God who answered me when I was in distress and who has been with me wherever I have gone." They gave to Jacob all the alien gods that they had, and the rings that were in their ears, and Jacob buried them under the terebinth that was near Shechem....Thus Jacob came to Luz — that is, Bethel — in the land of Canaan, he and all the people who were with him. There he built an altar and named the site El-bethel, for it was there that God had revealed Himself to him when he was fleeing from his brother. (Genesis 35:1–7)

This is the description of the crossroads from which diverged three directions of leadership in the Israelite camp: (1) Simeon and Levi, (2) Joseph, and (3) Judah.

Simeon and Levi

Simeon and Levi were the first who forced their viewpoint on their father and on their whole family: they represented the way of the zealots, that appeared to them as a return from their father Jacob's policy of amalgamation with the peoples of Canaan to the way of his ancestors Abraham and Isaac — emphatic separation from the idolatrous peoples of Canaan. However, Simeon and Levi did not pursue this in the peaceful ways of their ancestors, but in the way of vengeance that sought to correct, as it were, what their father's attempt to join in a marital alliance with the Amorites of the central Canaanite hill-country had perverted. The great zeal of Simeon and Levi for their family honor attests to this: "Jacob's sons, having heard the news, came in from the field. The men were distressed and very angry, because [Shechem, son of Hamor] had committed an outrage in Israel by lying with Jacob's daughter — a thing not to be done." These words were still in their mouth, though in even a more extreme form, after the deed that brought down their father's stern admonition upon them: "Should our sister be treated like a whore?" (34:31)

Who was right in the controversy that broke out between Jacob and his two sons, in the narrator's view? From the factual circumstances as narrated we can tell that despite the righteous anger over the rape of their sister and the insult to the family honor, the vengeance that was directed not only at Shechem the son of Hamor, but on his entire innocent people, takes on the cast of a low and despicable deception; their taking spoil from the innocent murdered victims compounded one felony with another. The following was the judgment that Jacob formed and harbored in his heart until his dying day, to be uttered in his parting blessing to his sons:

Simeon and Levi are a pair;
Their weapons are tools of lawlessness.
Let not my person be included in their council,
Let not my being be counted in their assembly.
For when angry they slay men,
And when pleased they maim oxen.
Cursed be their anger so fierce,
And their wrath so relentless;
I will divide them in Jacob,
Scatter them in Israel. (Genesis 49:5-7)

Moreover, if Simeon and Levi believed that they could conquer Shechem by force of arms and settle in it without a covenant with its inhabitants, they surely did not take into account the true balance of power between them and the surrounding Canaanite population. Jacob judged correctly when after the base slaughter he said: "You have brought trouble on me, making me odious among the inhabitants of the land, the Canaanites and the Perizzites; my men are few in number, so that if they unite against me and attack me, I and my house will be destroyed." (34:30) We cannot disagree with this estimate. The house of Jacob had no other choice than to flee to Isaac's environs while their enemies were still nursing their wounds, disorganized and intimidated in their shock.

And yet Jacob did not go scot-free from divine judgment. After he had scolded his sons for their guilt, God visited him with a severe punishment that justifies his sons' objective in frustrating his plans, though it does not justify their methods. He ought first to have fulfilled his original vow and to have returned from Aram of the Two Rivers to the land of his fathers' sojourn by way of Bethel, not only because he had vowed thus, but also for a deeper ethical-spiritual reason. Before the attempt to gain a foothold in Canaan, he ought to have undergone purification and sanctification, to purify and sanctify his entire camp from the idolatry that clung to them from Aram-naharaim. Only after such a process would he and all his family be ready to settle in Canaan in a way that would not endanger their fidelity to their destiny through marrying with the idolatrous inhabitants of the land. It thus appears that in the narrator's view Jacob would have prevented the sin of his sons had he first engaged in sanctification for their destiny and purified his family from the idolatry that clung to them from Laban's household, as it is possible to learn from the episode of the teraphim (household gods) that Rachel had stolen. This is apparently the reason for the serious punishment suffered by Rachel, and by Jacob who had sealed her doom through his blindness. But this is also the reason for the idolatrous sin that Jacob's sons sinned through their perverted zealotry: they avenged themselves on an insult to the family honor by a base act that insulted the true honor of their family — its ethical destiny and spiritual mission.

The confirmation of this interpretation is to be found in the later genealogical narrative as it unfolded generations later. After their Pyrrhic victory, Simeon and Levi do not appear again as contenders for leadership of the family. However, during the exodus from Egypt, the tribe of Levi assumes the mantle of leadership of the entire people: Moses, Aaron and Miriam, the redeemers of Israel from Egypt, were of the tribe of Levi. The punishment that Jacob meted out to this tribe — scattering them in Israel — became a fateful blessing: the Levites were sanctified to the service of God in the Tent of Meeting and in the Temple, and they were appointed to be teachers of Torah, of law, equity, and the discipline of truth and justice among their people. The experience of slavery in Egypt purified them through suffering, and their zealotry was transformed from idolatrous, bloodthirsty defense of the family honor into absolute fidelity to God's commandments and teaching.

Joseph

The reasons why Jacob preferred Joseph were specified above, and they can be illustrated by specific incidents in his biographical narrative. But there was another reason not specified, that can be inferred from the narrative texture: Jacob and Joseph were close soul-mates, for they were similar in almost every respect that is of interest to the Biblical narrative. Unlike his brothers, who worked in the field, Joseph was a simple man dwelling in tents — handsome, noble, a man of spirit; he was a dreamer — striving for great things and seeing in them his destiny and his righteousness. Therefore he did not shrink from crafty means that might draw him closer to his goal; and in the last analysis he was a resourceful man for whom "God was with him," finding clever ways to turn his dreams into reality. In the last respect he surpassed his father, and his father distanced himself from him in the end: his ambitions exceeded the limits of his father's patience, who had still not abdicated his own authority.

To what did Joseph aspire? From the literary standpoint we can note that to the reader who is not influenced by later religious interpretation, the meaning of Joseph's dreams is as simple and clear as the interpretation of Pharaoh's dreams was to Joseph. The Egyptian magicians had difficulty interpreting Pharaoh's dreams because they feared to speak the truth; Joseph was not afraid because his resourcefulness enabled him to offer Pharaoh not only an interpretation but also a solution. Joseph's brothers had trouble understanding his dreams for another reason; his ambitions exceeded the bounds of their own ambitions, which were limited to the leadership of their family, and so they did not understand his aspirations, which went much farther.

The dream in which his brothers' sheaves bowed down to his sheaf (Genesis 37:7) pointed clearly to the wild grain in Egypt, that does not depend on rainfall but is nourished by river-water. The second dream about rulership, wherein he would hold sway over his brothers, even though he did not diminish their status in comparing them to the sun, moon and stars, was even clearer. This was a dream about a supra-regal, divine status like that of Pharaoh, a status that would hold sway over the high-ranking members of his family. In Canaan there was not yet a kingdom that could realize such superhuman greatness. But there was an idolatrous power close to the southern border of Isaac's and Jacob's surroundings. The young Joseph, whose horizons were broad, dreamed of arriving at greatness in that power where the honor of rule was considered a supreme value. His brothers were not able to conceive of such a thing, and felt that their brother was trying to lord it over them. It angered them because their father nurtured the dream of greatness in the heart of his gaudily-dressed favorite child, but it also aroused their scorn: how could this young upstart realize his unrealistic dreams? Jacob heard, scolded, but also "kept the matter in mind." (37:11) It sounds from this that he understood but also was afraid to understand completely. He rebuked Joseph with a scolding that expressed a whiff of sin and of the improbability of his holding sway even over his parents — "are we to come, I and your mother and your brothers, and bow low to you to the ground?" But even Judah, the smartest of the brothers, did not fully understand his intent: when he decided to sell him to the Ishmaelites who were going down to Egypt, he meant to block the way to fulfillment of his dreams, but in fact he facilitated the course of events. In the last analysis, unknowingly, he did Joseph a kindness and sent him on his way to rescue his family from the famine that only he could foresee.

Did Joseph dream of finding in Egypt a solution to the difficulties that his family encountered in its efforts to establish a foothold in Canaan and become a great nation there? Did he understand that in that small stomping-ground, populated by tiny kingdoms of Philistines and Canaanites, there was no chance of transforming the family that had already succeeded in overcoming its internal obstacles and started to grow and expand, into a people? Did he understand that the chance to be fertile, multiply, and become a people was to be found only in the broad, fertile, open expanses of Goshen, under the protection of a great, strong power that would have an interest in the good services both of Joseph himself and of his family, who were successful in raising those flocks that were an abomination to the Egyptians but also necessary to them? According to the story, Joseph understood all of this only when he was already governing all of Egypt in Pharaoh's name and his brothers came to buy grain:

> Now, do not be distressed or reproach yourselves because you sold me hither; it was to save life that God sent me ahead of you....God has sent me ahead of you to ensure your survival on earth, and to save your lives in an extraordinary deliverance. So, it was not you who sent me here, but God; and He has made me a father to Pharaoh, lord of all his household, and ruler over the whole land of Egypt. (Genesis 45:5–8)

Joseph was a political man and drew the practical conclusions: he advised his brothers and his father to beg Pharaoh to agree to their settlement in Goshen, and to suggest arrangements that would be acceptable to both sides. (46:31–47:7) But Jacob and his sons, who accepted the suggestion and implemented it, understood this only after the fact. They went down to Egypt with the intention of remaining there until the years of famine in Canaan would be over, just as Jacob had gone to Haran with the intention of finding a wife and returning after a few days. But just as Jacob delayed his return until he was forced to do so, so his family remained entrenched in Goshen until their latter-day descendants were forced to flee. They did not renege on their obligation to return to Canaan, but were only waiting until the time was ripe, whether because they were forced to escape from Egypt as from a trap, or because they were finally strong enough to conquer their promised land "with sword and bow."

However, Joseph's dreams did not express his regard for his people's future. His mind was only on his personal greatness and the ruling power that he craved, and so he completed the parallel between himself and his brothers: they sold him into slavery in Egypt, and he was their unwitting nemesis, embarking on a process that would eventually turn their children and grandchildren into slaves in Egypt. Here, too, he did not foresee the consequence to his own people, because he was interested only in his own personal success. After his brothers came to him and he rescued them, Joseph went back to his preoccupation with Pharaoh's fortunes, with which his own personal fortunes were intertwined; he bought all the land of Egypt for Pharaoh and turned all the Egyptians, except the magician-priests, into his slaves.

It is clear from this that the power structure that Joseph envisioned in his dream and afterwards carried out in his actions as Pharaoh's viceroy was not the power structure that was intended for the realization of Israel's destiny on its land, but the opposite. In counterpoint to the idolatrous Pharaonic model that Joseph established, the Mosaic law proposed the theocratic model: not the law of a Pharaonic house of bondage, but the law of a kingdom of God: a kingdom of freedom from the tyranny of moral man pretending to divinity. The people of Israel were indeed able to grow and consolidate in Egypt: they were able to train themselves for life in a commonwealth that they would one day establish for themselves, even under the conditions of Egyptian bondage. But in order to realize their destiny, it would be necessary to leave the house of bondage, to leave the wild-growing grain and the fleshpots, to draw the conclusions that follow from the experience of slavery, to receive a Torah that is the basic law of a freely-entered covenant into the sovereignty of God, and to go to Canaan in order to attempt its fulfillment. But the example of Joseph's leadership became a staple paradigm in Israelite history: it is the counter-paradigm whose origin was in the people's being attracted to the great centers of power that arose nearby in each generation. Joseph established the model of his people's adaptation in the lands of Diaspora after it failed to maintain its hold in its own land. The story of the Book of Esther, which is essentially a midrashic parody of the Joseph story, confirms this within the larger framework of the Biblical narrative.

Judah

We now come to examine the leadership style of Judah, the wisest and most loyal of all his brothers. His path toward shaping the leadership-model of the democratic covenantal law was already discussed above. In contrast to Joseph, Judah sought a way to strengthen the foothold of his family in the land of its sojournings. In contrast to Simeon and Levi, he sought a way of peaceful integration, out of a sense of beneficent mutuality based on justice and kindness, but without sacrificing the unique identity necessary for realizing the people's destiny. It appears as if Judah followed the path that Jacob had traced in Shechem, for he entered into a marital alliance with the local inhabitants. But there was a highly significant difference in this respect between him and his father: Jacob wanted to marry his daughter to the king of the idolatrous Amorite king of Shechem whose motives were selfish — his sexual desire for Jacob's lovely daughter, and the yearning to benefit from her father's family's great wealth. Judah, on the other hand, married a woman from the Canaanite populace who followed him loyally and joined his household. Afterwards he took a Canaanite wife for his eldest son, but his sons' sins made it necessary for him to be the father of her twins who continued his line. (Genesis Chapter 38)

The difference between the conduct of Judah's sons who sinned against YHWH and the conduct of Judah's wife / daughter-in-law who kept faith to the point of self-sacrificing devotion to perpetuating the family line, highlights the difference between Judah's way and his father's. By marrying women from the daughters of Canaan, Judah was forging ties of amity between his own family and the families of the Amorites of Canaan. But we should note that Judah did not become a part of the Amorite family that married with him, but he took his wife and daughter-in-law from them. It was these who left their families and joined his family of their own free will. Tamar acted in a marvelous fashion — she devoted herself to Judah's sons and afterwards, for want of an alternative, to Judah himself, not for her own sake but for his sake, for the sake of his destiny, in order to bear the son who should continue the line. This was a foundational action in which was repeated the paradox of idolatrous sin that is turned into kindness: the seduction by which Judah was enticed by his daughter-in-law was indeed incestuous, and it was carried out in a scenario that looked like sacred prostitution. But its higher intention turned into an act of kindness and sanctification to God's will. In these two respects, the value of the action that Tamar performed surpasses the actions of Rebekah and Leah: she came from an alien people and dedicated herself to her destiny after being born in an idolatrous milieu. One can see in this the realization of the vision that all peoples should accept God's sovereignty and honor Israel as God's chosen people. Confirmation of this interpretation of the Tamar story can be found in the later Book of Ruth. Ruth the Moabitess repeated the same act of kindness, giving herself to Boaz in a way that may also appear licentious, in order to make correction for the wrong path taken by Elimelech and his sons when they moved to Moab because of the famine (like Abram and Sarai in their time), and in order to bear to Boaz the son who would continue the family line that would eventually lead to establishing the Davidic dynasty.

Raising History to the Plane of Myth

The Book of Exodus opens with mention of two events that conclude the Book of Genesis — Jacob's death, and then the death of Joseph, together with the whole generation that came down from Canaan to Egypt. The narrative of Exodus thus takes its point of departure from that "day" in historical time. Yet the reader knows that the story of Exodus properly begins over four hundred years after Jacob and his sons settled in Egypt. This is known from the declaration to Abraham in the "Covenant of the Pieces," and calculation of the generations of Jacob's sons in Egypt as documented. Historically, the whole sweep of events from Joseph's death to Moses' birth is packed into one verse: "But the Israelites were fertile and prolific; they multiplied and increased very greatly, so that the land was filled with them." (Exodus 1:7) Stylistically, these events are proclaimed as a continuation of the epic historical narrative, but in the course of the narrative it becomes clear that this leap in time effects a shift in the plane of these events and elevation of the discourse depicting them. Just as the Genesis narrative starts in myth and unfolds into genealogy and history, so the narrative of Exodus, Leviticus and Numbers is rooted in myth, and only returns to prosaic history in Deuteronomy.

The explicit announcement of the transition from one plane to another comes in the description of God's revelation to Moses after his first failed appearance to Pharaoh and the Israelites' complaints that his intervention had worsened their plight and accomplished nothing: "God spoke to Moses and said to him, 'I am YHWH. I appeared to Abraham, Isaac and Jacob as El Shaddai (God Almighty), but I did not reveal Myself to them by My name YHWH.'"[24] (Exodus 6:2–3) Now according to Genesis, the name YHWH was indeed known to Abraham, Isaac and Jacob through divine revelation. However, His

[24] Of course, from a source-critical point of view, this verse can be taken as a signal that these verses are from the "E" or "P" documents that did not use the name YHWH until Exodus, and according to whose traditions the patriarchs did not know this name. But as Schweid points out in the Introduction, the work of the "redactor" of the final edition of the Torah combined all these documents into a new entity, which was the "Torah" for later generations of Judaism, and which demands to be read as a literary unity. It is from that viewpoint that this analysis is made — as was previously said, one of the innumerable possible readings of this richest of books. (LL)

providential care over them through direct involvement in prospering their affairs, was in the capacity of El Shaddai, i.e. through ordinary events that remain within the course of nature. YHWH appeared to the patriarchs only through promises and covenants that He enacted with them, and in their dreams. By contrast, the project of redemption from Egypt was achieved through the direct manifestation of God as YHWH, the name by which He acted directly as Creator. This name embodies God's absolute sovereignty over creation. Thus this speech heralds raising the plane of the epic narrative from the historical to the mythic plane, i.e. creating a new mythic genre — *the historical myth*.

God's direct intervention, through supernatural events that attest to His absolute sovereignty, is already recognized in the account of Moses' birth:

A certain man of the house of Levi went and married a Levite woman. The woman conceived and bore a son; and when she saw that he was good [JPS: "how beautiful he was"], she hid him for three months. When she could hide him no longer, she got a wicker basket for him and caulked it with bitumen and pitch. She put the child into it and placed it among the reeds by the bank of the Nile. And his sister stationed herself at a distance, to learn what would befall him.

The daughter of Pharaoh came down to bathe in the Nile, while her maidens walked along the Nile. She spied the basket among the reeds and sent her slave girl to fetch it....She made him her son. She named him Moses, explaining, "I drew him out of the water." (Exodus 2:1–10)

What is the sequence of narrative details that raise this story to the plane of myth, stylistically and existentially?

1. "A man went out from the house of Levi...and the woman conceived." From the genealogies of Simeon and Levi cited later (6:14–28) we learn the man's name — Amram, and the woman's — Jochebed. We also learn that Jochebed was Amram's aunt (reminiscent of Abram and Sarai) — again a kind of holy incest! However, in the conception-birth narrative the parents' names are not mentioned, only their Levitical origin, reminiscent of Jacob's zealous efforts to insure his clan's unity of origins. The verb "went" (*va-yelekh*, echoing *lekh lekha* of the Abraham saga) suggests a sense of destiny that would be fulfilled when the national redeemer was born as a result of his action.

2. The mystery implicit in the anonymity of the destiny-bound "man" and "woman" increases when the woman refrains from giving her

son a name, as is customary in the Bible. It is Pharaoh's daughter who names the child, and he thus becomes her son. From the name that she chooses we learn that from her viewpoint this "goodly" boy was born of the Nile, for the Nile-god rescued him from drowning for her sake.

3. Jochebed does not name the boy, but she sees "that he was good." This choice of words is not accidental, for they echo the creation narrative of Genesis. We recall that the first man was not called "good" at his creation, whereas of Moses, who was born intentionally for a special mission, his mother says the words that confirm the fulfillment of that mission: "that he was good." From this she deduces her special obligation to rescue the child, as well as her confidence when she entrusts the child to the ark floating on the Nile into which she ought to have cast the child at Pharaoh's command — thus rescuing the boy from the king's decree in outward conformity to the decree — while at the same time entrusting the child into God's hands, in the same way that Noah and his family were saved by the flood in an ark that they built by the divine command. From the mother's standpoint, the boy — whom she bore naturally as Sarah bore Isaac naturally — represented a divine intervention brought about by supernatural preparation. This was the substance of his being "good," and in this respect unique of all the children born to Hebrew mothers at that time. In the continuation of the saga of Adam, Noah and Abram, we may see Moses as a fourth "beginning of humanity," who this time was created as God intended that creation to take place, in God's image and likeness.

4. In addition to the comparison with the stories of Noah and his family, we should pay attention to the dramatic irony implicit in the rescue of Moses from the Nile, in which he should have been drowned by the daughter of that cruel, idolatrous Pharaoh who had commanded the drowning of all male infants in the Nile. The son who could not be hidden in his own mother's house was hidden in the house of Pharaoh who had commanded his drowning, surely out of fear that a redeemer would be born to his slaves' people! The Nile, where Pharaoh's daughter thought to immerse herself to purify herself for her gods, was considered a deity in Egypt. The rescue of Moses from its waters by Pharaoh's daughter, who saw him as a gift from her god, alludes to Moses' mission — to redeem his people and in effect to record the crushing victory that would be remembered for generations, of the God of Heaven, the King of all existence, over the mightiest of the idolatrous kingdoms.

Moses is a mortal human being. If he himself would vanquish Pharaoh to free his people, the victory would be depicted as the toppling of one Pharaonic demigod by a greater rival Pharaonic demigod. There is only one way to demonstrate the supremacy of God's kingdom in His world over the idolatrous power of mortal kings, which is all borrowed from the powers of nature that God created. For that purpose, the Creator must Himself come down to earth, with a name attesting to His creator-role, and to vanquish the idolatrous kingdom by Himself in a way that will negate it from its roots, by demonstrating to all who have eyes that it is not even master of those natural forces that it pretends to rule. In this way it will be known to all humanity that the ruling power of idolatrous regimes is based on smoke and mirrors inspiring fear, resting on fraudulent use of the powers of nature that God entrusted in man's hands to govern it in accord with God's commands for the good of all creation including humanity, not so that a human ruler should usurp God and rule in His place. Moreover, in this way it will be known to all humanity that the sin of obstinate power-grabbing idolatry undermines the true happiness and freedom of all mankind, including those who succeeded in taking the power into their own hands.

Moses' normal-human yet wondrous birth and his marvelous rescue — though not yet showing an openly supernatural dimension — nevertheless herald the full significance of his national-redemptive mission: he will not only bring his people out of Egypt, as he himself was rescued from drowning in the Nile, but he will establish it as a people that will receive Torah and thus raise itself to the rank of a people of whom all will say "that it was good," a people created in God's image and likeness. The story of Moses' birth is the story of the dawning of the "day" of the people's creation, that harks back to its origins in the creation-myth of Genesis. Confirmation of this understanding of the story, and of the level of reality it depicts, is found in the reiterated emphasis of the importance of the Sabbath, the day when creation reaches its perfection, as a sign of the covenant between YHWH the God of Creation and the people that God created for Himself when He brought them out of Egypt. The Sabbath, toward which all the days of the week strive, represents the vision toward which strives the history of the people that was set aside to be God's special treasure.

Moses' Preparation for His Destiny:
From Observer-Seer to Pastor-Overseer[25]

The unique historical myth of Exodus is reflected in the depiction of the "man" Moses in its narrative: a marvelously balanced conflation of his depiction as a representative literary-symbolic image of man in a state of nature — like the depiction of Adam and Eve and the visual depiction of the Garden of Eden, which also represents a natural life-environment, providing life's necessities, on an ideal plane — and his depiction as a *sui generis* personality in the biographical and historical mode, with human vulnerability like any other man, despite his unsurpassed greatness as leader to his people — God Himself could not come up with anyone better.

The image of Moses is painted fully from both these aspects together, both the symbolic representation of his being created in the divine image and likeness, i.e. as a "goodly" man, and the biographical-historical depiction of his being distinct and infinitely distant from divine perfection. Moses' human perfection is his humility. The Biblical narrative distinguishes him as the most humble of men (Numbers 12:3), not because he was unaware of his greatness in comparison with other men, but because he knew that he was on an equal plane with all other human beings vis-à-vis God. In his humility, Moses was more cognizant than other human beings of the boundary that is set against the human ambition to rise above one's natural abilities and to attempt to usurp God's place. Because Moses was supremely aware of man's imperfect condition, he was able to attain the highest possible human perfection.

Moses' symbolic-representative perfection as human being created in God's image is expressed in his fidelity to his mission, in his knowing God as his sender, in his knowledge of his people, and in his knowledge of his own abilities as emissary. (As we shall see in the sequel, it was in his striving to live according to this knowledge

---

[25] "From Observer-Seer to Pastor-Overseer": a play on the words האור (*ro'eh* with an *aleph*) and העור (*ro'eh* with an *ayin*). The latter word has the basic meaning of "feed, graze" and the extended meaning of "care for"; thus it applies to Moses' narrow role as shepherd of Jethro's flock and his larger role as "pastor" of the Israelite people (where the English word *pastor* has also evolved from the specific animal-shepherdly role to the larger role of tending a "flock" of people).

that there lurked for Moses the danger of his own human congenital evil impulse, in which he was tested as a leader and failed twice — at the beginning of his career and at its end.) On the plane of mythic symbolism, Moses is the embodiment of the mission that God laid on mankind at creation in order to draw them near to the perfection appointed for them in God's vision. The same applies to him as to Abraham's servant, but on the highest humanly possible level: he was "the man of God," the "prophet," identified with his task in everything that he did. As prophet, Moses "saw" the actuality of people's lives on this earth as seen by God, objectively without evasions. He relates to it by the yardstick of objective justice by which God judges the world. His authority as leader, legislator and judge is the projection of his devotion to truth and justice and is conditional on it: every deviation, however slight, from the standard of truth and justice undermines his authority in his own eyes and all the more in the eyes of others, for the root of his authority is the faith that God invests in him by trusting in him. He himself, as well as his auditors and followers, will sense immediately if his faith in himself, rooted in God's faith in him as God's representative, is tarnished (as we may learn especially from the tests of Moses' leadership toward the end of his career, as narrated in the Book of Numbers). In all these respects Moses reflects God, who created him in His image, without pretending to usurp His place.

Moses' perfection as a unique historical personage is seen in the fact that although identifying with his mission he is not just an anonymous figure like Abraham's servant. On the contrary, he has a name that places him squarely within his biographical narrative (Moses = the Drawer:[26] the man who was "drawn" out of the Nile is the one who will draw his people from the servitude of Egypt), and he has a unique personal biography that presents him against the backdrop of his age as a child of his age. From the standpoint of the literary analysis we should note that throughout the four books in which he

---

[26] "The Drawer." The Biblical account of the etymology of Moses' name has a slight anomaly (aside from ignoring — perhaps purposely — the Egyptian basis of the name — see the Pharaonic names Thutmose, etc.): the grammatical form of *Moshe* is active ("the one who draws") despite the circumstance that in his birth-narrative he is the passive recipient of the action of being drawn out of the water. Nevertheless, the active meaning also has application to his career, as demonstrated here. (LL)

plays a central role (Exodus, Leviticus, Numbers, Deuteronomy) the narrator takes care to give equal attention to Israel's history (from the Exodus through the initial settlement in Trans-Jordan) and to Moses' personal story. These two stories parallel and complement each other, but they are also separate, and there is a continual tension whose source is in the growing gap between Moses' personal experiences and development as this people's leader, and the development of his people as well as that of other leaders who work mostly with him but sometimes against him.

Moses' humanity is manifested first of all in the fact that he, too, displays the congenital evil urge. Sin crouches at his door, too. He controls it for the most part, thus surpassing all his predecessors from Noah through Levi, Joseph and Judah, but he does not escape scot-free. The very need to grapple with his urge in order to overcome his soul's tendency to sin partakes of the basic nature of sin, which forces one to guard constantly against sinning and to engage continually in self-reform (*teshuvah*, repentance). And yet even in this literary depiction of Moses as a man who, despite his self-control, succumbs to sin because he is human, there is a substantial difference between the mythological figure of Adam and the mythic-yet-historical biographical figure of Moses: in contrast to Adam, Moses is not the prisoner of the radical original sin that is a part of him from creation, but his impulse is manifested in specific sins, concrete acts in which he fails when it is incumbent on him as a leader to deal with ambiguous situations and events in which there are defensible grounds for choosing a given course of action and its opposite. In other words, it is God, not man, who decides if his actions were sinful.

But precisely from this complex standpoint, regarding a person's life from this double perspective — his own subjective view and God's objective view — Moses is conceived as a man who is born "good." Not as one complete and perfect from birth, but as a human being struggling with the evil in himself as well as in the people around him. For his whole life he strives to achieve perfection, and it eludes him. At the end of his career he confronts the tragedy of human existence: perfection seems within his grasp, but the moment when he imagines to have achieved it is the moment of his personal failure, as an individual striving for perfection. But with respect to his people, precisely by virtue of his imperfection that he sought unsuccessfully to repair, he arrived at perfection. In this respect, his continual struggle, the failure that precedes success and the process of learning from it is what brings him to success — the forced descent provides the leverage for a restorative choice. Thus is expressed the blend between the mythic and the historical: between being created in God's image and being created with the congenital evil impulse.

The meta-biographical essence of Moses' story arises from the early trials that prepare him for his role. Again, the narrative omits his growing-up years. Skipping over what happened to the man and his people in that period, the story of his being drawn from the Nile continues with:

> Some time after that, when Moses had grown up, he went out to his kinsfolk and witnessed their labors. He saw an Egyptian beating a Hebrew, one of his kinsmen. He turned this way and that and, seeing no one about, he struck down the Egyptian and hid him in the sand. (Exodus 2:11–12)

We have here a personal-biographical reworking of the myth of Cain and Abel in Genesis. Moses, who grew up in Pharaoh's house, is an observer-seer (*ro'eh* with an *aleph*), and the peculiar perfection for which he is destined is that of a pastor-overseer (*ro'eh* with an *ayin*). He sees his people's suffering. He is destined to oversee his people. What does it mean to oversee his people on the basis of his seeing? It is to be that fellow-person (*re'a*, "neighbor") who loves them as he loves himself (see Leviticus 19:18). But this is a very advanced level for which one must strive and be tested in order to arrive at it. The Moses who sets out from Pharaoh's house to see his people's suffering does not yet relate to them as pastor. He identifies with his brother's suffering, but he responds to it like Cain, with imperious anger.

Thus Moses becomes a manslayer. Nevertheless, even as a manslayer he is not quite the same as Cain, for he slays out of a striving for an objectively right act of judgment in response to an objectively unjust deed — blow for blow. Indeed, Moses sinned like Cain. He sinned when he took the divine prerogative of judgment into his own hands. But he learned quite quickly that his action hurt rather than helped his beaten kinsman:

> When he went out the next day, he found two Hebrews fighting; so he said to the offender, "Why do you strike your fellow?" He retorted, "Who made you chief and ruler over us? Do you mean to kill me as you killed the Egyptian?" Moses was frightened, and thought: Then the matter is known! (Exodus 2:13–14)

From this report we see that Moses learned something from the results of his previous action. Instead of punishing the perpetrator like a "princely judge" who takes justice into his own hands unjustly, he tries to assist the victim who is his Hebrew kinsman. But the unjust response that the aggressor throws at him nevertheless contains an element of justice, for it confronts Moses with the crux of his sin: after committing manslaughter, Moses is barred from aiding his suffering kinfolk, both because the exposure of his crime forces him to flee from the law, and because he has learned that before he can free his kinfolk from physical pain he must free them from their servile identification with the oppressing power. In his ignorance, he does not know how to do this.

This is a great moral lesson. As in Jacob's story, his first failure leads him to his first success:

> When Pharaoh learned of the matter, he sought to kill Moses; but Moses fled from Pharaoh. He arrived in the land of Midian, and sat down beside a well. Now the priest of Midian had seven daughters. They came to draw water, and filled the troughs to water their father's flock; but shepherds came and drove them off. Moses rose to their defense, and he watered their flock.... (Exodus 2:15–17)

This time, we have a revolutionary reworking of the narrative of the "servant" and Rebekah, of Jacob and Rachel. Moses rescues Jethro's daughters. He does not chastise the shepherds or drive them away. He assists the victims of injustice and waters their flock. His kindness to them is repaid by the kindness that the daughters and their father show him: he finds his home in the wilderness, marries Jethro's daughter Zipporah, even though she is not one of his people (is this possibly a reparation for Simeon and Levi's action, in the spirit of Judah?), and a son is born to him. Most important of all: the man who grew up in Pharaoh's house becomes in Jethro's house a tender of sheep. This grows naturally out of the kind deed that he performed by watering the daughters' sheep — "Now Moses, tending the flock of his father-in-law Jethro, the priest of Midian, drove the flock into the wilderness, and came to Horeb, the mountain of God." (Exodus 3:1) The personal narrative, which is a biographical narrative of one man in his humanity, thus arrives at its destination. Moses found in Jethro's house everything that was required for a normal man to be happy, and he is morally deserving of happiness. But when the narrative arrives at its human-biographical culmination, it stands before the crisis that is bound up with fulfillment of the human biography on the mythic plane.

The importance of Moses' occupation as the shepherd of Jethro's sheep is articulated in the fact that it is this function that brings the Egyptian fugitive to the heart of the wilderness, far from the governmental authorities who are liable to capture him and bring him to justice for his homicidal deed. But precisely in the depths of the wilderness — where there is no rule of law or human judgment and a man can do as he pleases, where it seems at first sight that no one sees a person in his sinful state — precisely in this place is revealed, over Moses and within him, the One who sees him, the One from whom no one can hide (as Adam attempted to hide amidst the trees of the garden): God appears in the burning-bush encounter and commands him to return to Egypt in order to fulfill the assignment from whose magnitude he fled.

Shepherding the flock can be interpreted along these lines as preparation for the unique brand of leadership that is the opposite of the murderous Pharaonic sort, and by means of which it will be possible to deliver the people who are suffering under Pharaoh's rule. This is the opposite route from the one that Moses trod when he went out as an "Egyptian man" (as Jethro's daughters called him [Exodus 2:19]). Moses' transformation into a shepherd completes the reworking of the Cain-Abel story in his life: Moses made reparation for the crime of manslaughter for which he was guilty, like Cain, when he became a shepherd, like Abel. But it was not in order to become a shepherd of sheep, as he may have wished; had he done so, his days would have passed by as a fleeting breath.[27] It was rather so that he might be prepared to become the pastor of his people. He was prepared not in respect of the art of leadership, which he started learning from the revelation of the burning bush, but in respect of changing his inner disposition from the dominating stance of the Pharaonic ruler to that of the shepherd tending his flock and looking out constantly for their welfare. But even after leaving God's presence after the burning-bush revelation, Moses did not make his peace with the fact that just as there is a difference between the ordinary shepherd and his flock of sheep, so there must be a difference in knowledge and responsibility between the human shepherd and his flock of people. In order to be shepherd to his people, Moses had to forsake the course of ordinary human happiness and devote himself to the exalted, solitary prophetic task of

---

[27]   "Fleeting breath" (*hevel*) — a play on Abel's name (*hevel*).

the leader acting in God's behalf. He would no longer be able to lead a private life but would have to stand between God and his people in order to serve them.

Fear and Lovingkindness in the Crisis of Dedication to Mission: The Idea of Sanctification

In the revelation of the burning bush, God promised Moses, "I will be with you" (Exodus 3:12), apparently the same as He had promised to Jacob. Nevertheless, in Moses' task as shepherd to his people the promise takes on another significance. Surely, God will prosper Moses' way in the superhuman task that has been laid on him, but the task is still superhuman, and in order to succeed in it he must rise to the highest level of spiritual and moral sanctity possible to mankind, so that he will be able to stand in the domain of God, who wills to act directly through him as redeemer of His people. We may emphasize: it is not Moses who will be the redeemer. It is God who will battle against Pharaoh and deliver His people from physical slavery. Precisely for that reason, Moses' task will become unbearably difficult, for he must be the go-between; and amid the power of deeds that no natural force can bring about, it will be his responsibility to make known and palpable to his people on the one hand and to Pharaoh on the other, who is indeed this invisible Presence!

The supreme dedication for the role of go-between in the great war that is going to take place between God and Pharaoh, representing the idolatrous power, is the supreme endangerment, endangerment from both sides, who will display all their destructive power in this engagement. This will be a supreme test of the emissary's faith in God and of his unqualified loyalty to Him and to His people. God tells him in advance that the task will be very difficult. Pharaoh will present stubborn opposition to God's will, and his opposition will bring the people — who in order to be ready to embrace freedom will have to learn through Moses to put their faith in God — to a state of complete desperation. The emissary will have to display rock-solid faith that God has not lost the battle, and that Pharaoh's opposition to Him is also a revelation of God's power — for Pharaoh has no true power of his own — in order to intensify the struggle to the point of absolute surrender.

Moses will thus have to stand the test of a paradoxical redemptive action whose miraculous success will proceed by way of successively more destructive stages of struggle, a struggle that will appear at each of its stages, until the very final act, as resulting in failure. This is the awesome responsibility that is laid on him. The success of redemption is contingent not only on God's physical victory over Pharaoh but also on the spiritual victory that will sprout from it. This victory requires that Pharaoh must know who is fighting against him, must acknowledge Him despite himself, and must know the consequences of his defeat. It also requires that the people must believe in Him who is fighting their cause, must know what they have to do to be redeemed from the servitude in which they are sunken, and must be ready to take on the responsibility bound up with a life of freedom.

The story of Moses' life when he sets out on his way to return to Egypt documents the complicated process of absorbing the fearful significance of his mission:

> Moses went back to his father-in-law Jether and said to him, "Let me go back to my kinsmen in Egypt and see how they are faring." And Jethro said to Moses, "Go in peace."
>
> The Lord said to Moses in Midian, "Go back to Egypt, for all the men who sought to kill you are dead." So Moses took his wife and sons, mounted them on an ass, and went back to the land of Egypt; and Moses took the rod of God with him.
>
> And the Lord said to Moses, "When you return to Egypt, see that you perform before Pharaoh all the marvels that I have put within your power. I, however, will stiffen his heart so that he will not let the people go. Then you shall say to Pharaoh, 'Thus says the Lord: Israel is my first-born son. I have said to you, "Let My son go, that he may worship Me," yet you refuse to let him go. Now I will slay your first-born son.' "
>
> At a night encampment on the way, the Lord encountered him and sought to kill him. So Zipporah took a flint and cut off her son's foreskin, and touched his legs with it, saying, "You are truly a bridegroom of blood to me!" And when He let him alone, she added, "A bridegroom of blood because of the circumcision."
>
> The Lord said to Aaron, "Go to meet Moses in the wilderness." He went and met him at the mountain of God, and he kissed him. (Exodus 4:18–27)

The first verses of this narrative passage, that touchingly conveys the paradox of the tragic vulnerability of Moses' mission in all its fearsome sanctity, attest that Moses sets out on his way without realizing the full significance of his mission and the danger fraught with it, even though he did take the divine rod in his hand. He has learned from God that his persecutors have died, and he wishes to know how his kinsmen are faring. He takes his wife and sons and proceeds as if his happy life as a private person in the circle of his family will continue into the future. The meaning of this event — totally unanticipated both by Moses and by the innocent reader of the story (Moses obeys God's command, yet God attacks him lethally, as if to sabotage the realization of His plan) must be explained from the context of God's words to Moses when he is about to set out — it is God's purpose to remind Moses that he is not going to pay his kinsfolk a social call, he is going to lead them into freedom. God's speech emphasizes two points: (1) Israel is regarded as God's first-born, and so Pharaoh will let the people go only after God slays his first-born as revenge for Pharaoh's refusal to allow God's first-born to serve their God, for by this refusal Pharaoh had the effrontery to stand in place of God. (2) Pharaoh will refuse to let the people go because God will harden his heart. It is God who will cause Pharaoh to sin that sin whose punishment is the slaying of the first-born.

All the fearsomeness of the paradox embodied in these words (that God will cause Pharaoh to sin and will then punish him for his sin, as if it was done without any alternative) is made tangible for Moses when he comes to the lodging on the way: God attacks him, just as He had promised to attack Pharaoh, even though Moses set out to do God's bidding. Why? Zipporah's saving action shows that Moses' sin is connected with the fact that Moses failed to infer, from God's words about Israel being His first-born and threatening Pharaoh with the slaying of his first-born, that he ought to sanctify himself scrupulously before setting out on such a mission. How? By dedicating his first-born son to God through circumcision. This is a severe warning as to the level of absolute sanctity — overcoming all interest of private happiness — required of whoever is designated to live in the domain of the holy God and to convey His word that requires absolute obedience from everyone. In this context let us recall those words that Moses himself said after Aaron's two sons died in the Tent of Meeting because they offered "strange fire" on the altar: "This is what the Lord meant when He said: 'Through those near to Me I show Myself holy, and gain glory before all the people.' " (Leviticus 10:33)

It thus appears that this moment, which looks like a reversal of the Binding of Isaac — here Moses is bound by God — is the moment in which Moses is required to realize the fearful significance of his mission:

he must forsake the happiness of his ordinary family life, to dedicate himself without a trace of concession to personal interest and to devote himself to fulfilling God's will as He shall command, even if it involves mortal danger. On this point, it is right to emphasize that this story and the story of Aaron's sons restore the proper dimension to the story of the binding of Isaac. This dimension consists in the fearful significance that is liable to result from consecration to God's service, in the devotion that is not compromised by the pursuit of personal happiness. Whoever truly serves God must overcome his selfishness and act as commanded. This is the deeper aspect of the idea of holiness that is enunciated in the Mosaic Torah: "You shall be holy, for I am holy." (Leviticus 19:2)

Indeed, in order to understand the full significance of the paradoxical event that occurred in the lodging on the way to Egypt, we should pay attention also to the part played by Zipporah, who rescued Moses from God's hands and thus consecrated him to a mission that would take him away from her and from her children. We already saw above that for the whole path that Moses traversed up to the lodging on the way to Egypt, his way was graced by the kindness of the God-fearing women who were close to him — his mother, his sister, Pharaoh's daughter — they, who were immersed neither in slavery nor in the arrogance of Pharaoh's court, but were dedicated to their destiny. Their merit, along with the merit of the midwives and the women who bore and rescued their children despite Pharaoh's decree, was what enabled this people, enslaved in body and spirit, to go out into freedom. Moses' wife Zipporah continued that line of kindness that strengthened him for the fulfillment of the superhuman mission that had been imposed on him. She was married to him, she served him and helped him assume his mission, and she stood by him later by remaining faithful to him and raising their children in her father's house, even when he himself had to withdraw from family life and live just for the sake of his mission.

The line of kindness supporting Moses can be seen also in the second positive incident that introduces him into the core of his mission: God sends his brother Aaron out to him to give Moses the opportunity to play the role of "god" to him (Exodus 4:27–28). Thus Aaron becomes a partner to Moses' mission, and they act in concert and present themselves before the people and Pharaoh. To be sure, after the sin of the Golden Calf, Aaron accepted the role of priest and gave up the leadership role in which he had failed. The task of leadership became steadily heavier because of the people's sin and God's anger, but Moses alone remained to face God and became so sanctified as a result that the people were afraid to approach him as well, and when he went out to address the people he had to cover his face with a veil. This was the climax of his tragic solitude, and is what eventually led to the rebellion of the communal elders against Moses, and to the sin on whose account he was sentenced to die on Mount Nebo without entering the land to which he led his people. From this standpoint, Moses' personal life is interlaced with the tragic motif, taking the place of the comic motif that was manifested in the lives of the patriarchs.

The Justice Implanted in Creation Returns to Its Foundation

The elevation of the historical narrative to the plane of the creation myth proceeds from the particulars of Moses' personal narrative to the recounting of historical events in the scene where Moses and Aaron stand before Pharaoh and his magicians demanding that they let Israel go and worship their God in the wilderness (Exodus 5:1–5). This demand is the declaration of war between God and Pharaoh's court, who pretend to rule as gods or as the embodiment of the divine force emanated upon them in their land — now they are asked to let their slaves go out from their rule and to permit them to leave the domain of their authority so that they can serve their God whom they recognize as their true King, the King of all existence, and thus also the true King of Egypt. This is thus a wholesale protest against the idolatrous regime, a denial of its legitimacy. It follows from this that the question that was posed at the outset in the confrontation by Moses and Aaron against Pharaoh and his magicians was: Who is the true sovereign over Egypt? To give the slaves permission to leave Egypt to worship their God, even just for three days, would thus constitute acknowledgement that the God who so urgently demands this is the true sovereign.

Therefore Pharaoh cannot accede to this demand as long as he feels that he has the power to oppose it, and so even when he is forced to compromise or surrender for a limited time on account of the severe plagues that come upon him, while they are in full force, he reverses himself as soon as the plague recedes and he feels in power again. We can understand from this the profound meaning of God's word to Moses that He Himself will harden Pharaoh's heart and cause him to be stubborn and not send the people to worship Him in the wilderness until the coming of the last plague, the slaying of the first-born. The demand on Pharaoh to acknowledge that he is not sovereign, that his position as Pharaoh is only a deception and an illusion, really leaves him no choice but to harden his heart, to be obstinate and refuse, until the slaying of the first-born. Why does the slaying of the first-born force him to surrender? Because it is the very annihilation of the tyrannical idolatrous regime. A tyrannical regime bases sovereign authority on the rulers themselves. In their own mind they do not receive the authority of government or its laws from God above them or from the people below them, but they themselves hold the power of rule and give themselves its authority. That is what makes them sovereign.

It is clear that by this concept of authority, the transfer of power and legitimacy from one Pharaoh to his heir is only possible by inheritance from father to son in a way that perpetuates the dynasty without relying on any outside factor, and in order to avoid a war of succession, the first-born son is recognized as the sole heir of the regime. Slaying the first-born is thus the most striking internal shattering of the regime itself, of its proper structure of authority. Thus broken, Pharaoh is forced to acknowledge the sovereignty of whoever slew his first-born. And yet even then his stubbornness is not entirely broken, as long as he holds in his hand the external instrument of imposing his authority — his army. When Pharaoh perceives that the Israelites are escaping never to return, and that they have lost their way, he goes out to pursue them in order to take vengeance on them and destroy them. The war against the tyrannical idolatrous regime concludes with the drowning of the whole Egyptian army and their king in the Sea of Reeds.

This comprehensive analysis of the meaning of the myth of the Ten Plagues suggests that this is a reprise of the story of the reversion of the world to primal chaos by drowning in the floodwaters of Noah's time, with due adjustment for the later historical conditions. The drowning of Pharaoh's army in the Sea of Reeds and the rescue of the Israelites walking dry-shod through the sea confirm this parallel, though restricted to the land of Egypt. What distinguishes the story of the plagues is its understanding and elaboration as an execution of cosmic justice: God sits in judgment over Egypt and its rulers. All the forces of creation, over which the Egyptians pretended to rule, participate in the execution of justice as witnesses who uncover the deception and injustice in the idolatrous regime, and who carry out the divine sentence, because they are determined to enforce justice — to attack the guilty and to rescue their victims. In the gradual, calculated execution of the sentence, the kingdom of Egypt collapses by stages as vengeance is exacted by all the forces of nature that it had exploited in order to extract their sustenance and power unjustly: the plagues come from the waters of the Nile, from the dust of the earth, from the beasts of the wilderness, from the wind, from the spaces of heavens, and finally also from the lights of heaven, who withhold their light from her until she sinks to the verge of the slaying of the first-born in that primal darkness that prevailed over the abyss of creation. The final judgment is realized when Egypt no longer sees itself — "the darkness covered the land from sight and the land was dark." (Exodus 10:15) It is no longer visible to its Egyptian masters and it it does not exist for them. It exists only for those whose light shines for them in righteousness beside the darkness that descended on the wicked.

The philosophical idea at the root of the narrative of the plagues as a narrative of execution of the Creator's judgment, with the help of His creation, upon the idolatrous kingdom, is the idea of the justice that was implanted in the order of existence for the sake of humankind who are appointed to rule it for their own good and the world's with them. According to this idea, which recapitulates and elaborates the creation narrative from a historical standpoint, the whole world arises from chaos as an orderly arrangement of forces that operate through the creatures that exist separately yet perpetuate themselves together in harmony. It is this harmony that enables them to achieve their happiness inasmuch as they were created for themselves but also for each other, as their Creator intended them. This is the just order whose observance is a condition for the perpetuation of the world and its cyclical renewal. Humanity was created in order to fit in with this order and to perpetuate it through the just ordering of their society, both in respect of the distribution of the resources of the world that were created for them and in respect of their relation to all the creatures of nature which they are charged to govern for the benefit of the governed.

The idolatrous regime violates both these requirements. Therefore it contradicts not only God's command to humanity created in His image, but also the just order that preserves the created world by the divine law implanted within it. Therefore even the mightiest of the idolatrous kingdoms, which rules by exploiting the forces of nature and exploiting the labor of its citizens, must eventually collapse under the obstinacy of its perverse sovereign. The idolatrous regime destroys itself. The more obstinate and tyrannical it becomes, the more it hastens its doom. It is able to survive as long as people fear it, internalizing its perverted principles and participating in their own oppression, and as long as the natural habitat from which the kingdom sustains itself is not destroyed. Yet no matter how mighty and fearful it may be, it is a false regime, therefore it is temporary and transient, and it must eventually totter and collapse. When its exploited natural infrastructure is exhausted, it will take vengeance on its masters (all the plagues and afflictions of Egypt come upon it from its Nile, from its earth, from its air and from the heavens), and the fear inspired by the government — which is helpless in the face of Nature's plagues — evaporates. The exploited slaves return to their original nature and stop cooperating with the regime in their own oppression and exploitation. On the contrary, they take back for themselves everything of which the regime robbed them. Thus the regime falls apart and crumbles even without the intervention of an external foe. This is the meaning of the just divine sentence that took vengeance on the tyrannical regime by the stern and exact principle of "measure for measure": every injustice that was done by them will come back and exact retribution from them until the balance that was disturbed is restored and the process of natural life is renewed.

The idea of ecological justice that is exemplified in the myth of the ten plagues and the Exodus from Egypt is the philosophical-moral basis for the basic divine law that was given through Moses at Sinai: the constitution of freedom standing in opposition to the tyrannical idolatrous regime, in which is embodied the moral-legal meaning of the idea of the kingdom of God on earth, the rule of justice and truth. This is the purpose of the myth of the Exodus from Egypt. It finds its climax in the giving of the Torah. The people that goes out from the house of bondage will testify to the kingdom of the God of heaven on earth by observing the law of its God in its land.

Index

Printed in the United States
101697LV00005B/81-150/A